ISBN 978-1-330-28486-5
PIBN 10013295

English
Français
Deutsche
Italiano
Español
Português

www.forgottenbooks.com

Mythology Photography **Fiction**
Fishing Christianity **Art** Cooking
Essays Buddhism Freemasonry
Medicine **Biology** Music **Ancient
Egypt** Evolution Carpentry Physics
Dance Geology **Mathematics** Fitness
Shakespeare **Folklore** Yoga Marketing
Confidence Immortality Biographies
Poetry **Psychology** Witchcraft
Electronics Chemistry History **Law**
Accounting **Philosophy** Anthropology
Alchemy Drama Quantum Mechanics
Atheism Sexual Health **Ancient History**
Entrepreneurship Languages Sport
Paleontology Needlework Islam
Metaphysics Investment Archaeology
Parenting Statistics Criminology
Motivational

he

History and Romance of Northern Europe

A Library of Supreme Classics Printed in Complete Form

MCMVI

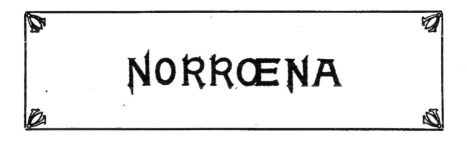

NORRŒNA

ythology

Gods and Goddesses
of the Northland

IN THREE VOLUMES

By VIKTOR RYDBERG, Ph.D.,

MEMBER OF THE SWEDISH ACADEMY; AUTHOR OF "THE LAST ATHENIAN"
AND OTHER WORKS.

AUTHORISED TRANSLATION FROM THE SWEDISH

BY

RASMUS B. ANDERSON, LL.D.,

LATE UNITED STATES MINISTER TO DENMARK; AUTHOR OF "NORSE
MYTHOLOGY," "VIKING TALES," ETC.

HON. RASMUS B. ANDERSON, LL.D., Ph.D.,
EDITOR IN CHIEF.

J. W. BUEL, Ph.D.,
MANAGING EDITOR.

VOL. III.

PUBLISHED BY THE
NORRŒNA SOCIETY,
LONDON COPENHAGEN STOCKHOLM BERLIN NEW YORK

Teutonic Mythology

Gods and Goddesses
of the Northland

IN

THREE VOLUMES

By VIKTOR RYDBERG, Ph.D.,

MEMBER OF THE SWEDISH ACADEMY; AUTHOR OF "THE LAST ATHENIAN"
AND OTHER WORKS.

AUTHORISED TRANSLATION FROM THE SWEDISH

BY

RASMUS B. ANDERSON, LL.D.,

EX-UNITED STATES MINISTER TO DENMARK; AUTHOR OF "NORSE
MYTHOLOGY," "VIKING TALES," ETC.

———

HON. RASMUS B. ANDERSON, LL.D., Ph.D.
EDITOR IN CHIEF.

J. W. BUEL, Ph.D.,
MANAGING EDITOR.

———

VOL. III.

———

PUBLISHED BY THE
NORRŒNA SOCIETY,
LONDON COPENHAGEN STOCKHOLM BERLIN NEW YORK
1906

TEUTONIC MYTHOLOGY.

TABLE OF CONTENTS.

VOLUME THREE

LIST OF PHOTOGRAVURES.

VOL. III.

THE MYTH IN REGARD TO THE LOWER WORLD.

(Part IV. Continued from Volume II.)

94.

THE SEVEN SLEEPERS.

Völuspa gives an account of the events which forebode and lead up to Ragnarok. Among these we also find that *leika Mims synir,* that is, that the sons of Mimer "spring up," "fly up," "get into lively motion." But the meaning of this has hitherto been an unsolved problem.

In the strophe immediately preceding (the 44th) Völuspa describes how it looks on the surface of Midgard when the end of the world is at hand. Brothers and near kinsmen slay each other. The sacred bonds of morality are broken. It is the storm-age and the wolf-age. Men no longer spare or pity one another. Knives and axes rage. Volund's world-destroying sword of revenge has already been fetched by Fjalar in the guise of the red cock (str. 41), and from the Ironwood, where it hitherto had been concealed by Angerboda and guarded by Egther; the wolf-giant Hate with his companions have invaded the world, which it was the duty of the gods

707

to protect. The storms are attended by eclipses of the sun (str. 40).

Then suddenly the Hjallar-horn sounds, announcing that the destruction of the world is now to be fulfilled, and just as the first notes of this trumpet penetrate the world, Mimer's sons spring up. "The old tree," the world-tree, groans and trembles. When Mimer's sons "spring up" Odin is engaged in conversation with the head of their father, his faithful adviser, in regard to the impending conflict, which is the last one in which the gods are to take a hand.

I shall here give reasons for the assumption that the blast from the Hjallar-horn wakes Mimer's sons from a sleep that has lasted through centuries, and that the Christian legend concerning the seven sleepers has its chief, if not its only, root in a Teutonic myth which in the second half of the fifth or in the first half of the sixth century was changed into a legend. At that time large portions of the Teutonic race had already been converted to Christianity: the Goths, Vandals, Gepidians, Rugians, Burgundians, and Swabians were Christians. Considerable parts of the Roman empire were settled by the Teutons or governed by their swords. The Franks were on the point of entering the Christian Church, and behind them the Alamannians and Longobardians. Their myths and sagas were reconstructed so far as they could be adapted to the new forms and ideas, and if they, more or less transformed, assumed the garb of a Christian legend, then this guise enabled them to travel to the utmost limits of Christendom; and if they also contained, as in the case here in question, ideas that were not entirely foreign to the Greek-Roman world, then they might the more easily acquire the right of Roman nativity.

In its oldest form the legend of "the seven sleepers" has the following outlines (*Miraculorum Liber*, vii., i. 92):

"Seven brothers"* have their place of rest near the city of Ephesus, and the story of them is as follows: In the time of the Emperor Decius, while the persecution of the Christians took place, seven men were captured and brought before the ruler. Their names were Maximianus, Malchus, Martinianus, Constantius, Dionysius, Joannes, and Serapion. All sorts of persuasion was attempted, but they would not yield. The emperor, who was pleased with their courteous manners, gave them time for reflection, so that they should not at once fall under the sentence of death. But they concealed themselves in a cave and remained there many days. Still, one of them went out to get provisions and attend to other necessary matters. But when the emperor returned to the same city, these men prayed to God, asking Him in His mercy to save them out of this danger, and when, lying on the ground, they had finished their prayers, they fell asleep. When the emperor learned that they were in the above-mentioned cave, he, under divine influence, commanded that the entrance of the cave should be closed with large stones, "for," said he, "as they are unwilling to offer sacrifices to our gods, they must perish there."

---

*For "brothers" the text, perhaps purposely, used the ambiguous word *germani*. This would, then, not be the only instance where the word is used in both senses at the same time. Cp. Quintil, 8, 3, 29.

While this transpired a Christian man had engraved the names of the seven men on a leaden tablet, and also their testimony in regard to their belief, and he had secretly laid the tablet in the entrance of the cave before the latter was closed. After many years, the congregations having secured peace and the Christian Theodosius having gained the imperial dignity, the false doctrine of the Sadducees, who denied resurrection, was spread among the people. At this time it happens that a citizen of Ephesus is about to make an enclosure for his sheep on the mountain in question, and for this purpose he loosens the stones at the entrance of the cave, so that the cave was opened, but without his becoming aware of what was concealed within. But the Lord sent a breath of life into the seven men and they arose. Thinking they had slept only one night, they sent one of their number, a youth, to buy food. When he came to the city gate he was astonished, for he saw the glorious sign of the Cross, and he heard people aver by the name of Christ. But when he produced his money, which was from the time of Decius, he was seized by the vendor, who insisted that he must have found secreted treasures from former times, and who, as the youth made a stout denial, brought him before the bishop and the judge. Pressed by them, he was forced to reveal his secret, and he conducted them to the cave where the men were. At the entrance the bishop then finds the leaden tablet, on which all that concerned their case was noted down, and when he had talked with the men a messenger was despatched to the Emperor Theodosius. He came and kneeled on the ground and worshipped them, and they said to the ruler:: "Most august Augustus! there has sprung up a false doctrine which tries to turn the Christian people from the promises of God, claiming that there is no resurrection of the dead. In order that you may know that we are all to appear before the judgment-seat of Christ according to the words of the Apostle Paul, the Lord God has raised us from the dead and commanded us to make this statement to you. See to it that you are not deceived and excluded from the kingdom of God." When the Emperor Theodosius heard this he praised the Lord for not permitting His people to perish. But the men again lay down on the ground and fell asleep. The Emperor Theodosius wanted to make graves of gold for them, but in a vision he was prohibited from doing this. And until this very day these men rest in the same place, wrapped in fine linen mantles.

At the first glance there is nothing which betrays the Teutonic origin of this legend. It may seemingly have had an independent origin anywhere in the Christian world, and particularly in the vicinity of Ephesus.

Meanwhile the historian of the Franks, Bishop Gregorius of Tours (born 538 or 539), is the first one who presented in writing the legend regarding the seven sleepers. In the form given above it appears through him for the first time within the borders of the christianised western Europe (see Gregorius' *Miraculorum Liber,* i., ch. 92). After him it reappears in Greek records, and thence it travels on and finally gets to Arabia and Abyssinia. His account is not written before the year

571 or 572. As the legend itself claims in its preserved form not to be older than the first years of the reign of Theodosius, it must have originated between the years 379-572.

The next time we learn anything about the seven sleepers in occidental literature is in the Longobardian historian, Paulus Diaconus (born about 723). What he relates has greatly surprised investigators; for although he certainly was acquainted with the Christian version in regard to the seven men who sleep for generations in a cave, and although he entertained no doubt as to its truth, he nevertheless relates another—and that a Teutonic—seven sleepers' legend, the scene of which is the remotest part of Teutondom. He narrates (i. 4):

"As my pen is still occupied with Germany, I deem it proper, in connection with some other miracles, to mention one which *there is on the lips of everybody.* In the remotest western boundaries of Germany is to be seen near the sea-strand under a high rock a cave where seven men have been sleeping no one knows how long. They are in the deepest sleep and uninfluenced by time, not only as to their bodies but also as to their garments, so that they are held in great honour by the savage and ignorant people, since time for so many years has left no trace either on their bodies or on their clothes. To judge from their dress they must be Romans. When a man from curiosity tried to undress one of them, it is said that his arm at once withered, and this punishment spread such a terror that nobody has since then dared to touch them. Doubtless it will some day be apparent why Divine Providence has so long preserved them. Perhaps by their preaching—for they are believed to be none other than Christians—this people shall once more be called to salvation. In the vicinity of this place dwell the race of the Skritobinians ('the Skridfinns')."

In chapter 6 Paulus makes the following additions, which will be found to be of importance to our theme: "Not far from that sea-strand which I mentioned as lying far to the west (in the most remote Germany), where the boundless ocean extends, is found the unfathomably deep eddy which we traditionally call the navel of the sea. Twice a-day it swallows the waves, and twice it vomits them forth again. Often, we are assured, ships are drawn into this eddy so violently that they look like arrows flying through the air, and frequently they perish in this abyss. But sometimes, when they are on the point of being swallowed up, they are driven back with the same terrible swiftness."

From what Paulus Diaconus here relates we learn that in the eighth century the common belief prevailed among the heathen Teutons that in the neighbourhood of that ocean-maelstrom, caused by Hvergelmer ("the roaring kettle"), seven men slept from time immemorial under a rock. How far the heathen Teutons believed that these men were Romans and Christians, or whether this feature is to be attributed to a conjecture by Christian Teutons, and came through influence from the Christian version of the legend of the seven sleepers, is a question which it is not necessary to discuss at present. That they are some day to awake to preach Christianity to "the stubborn," still heathen Teutonic tribes is manifestly a supposition on the part of Paulus himself, and he does not present it as anything else. It has nothing to do with the saga in its heathen form.

The first question now is: Has the heathen tradition in regard to the seven sleepers, which, according to the testimony of the Longobardian historian, was common among the heathen Teutons of the eighth century, since then disappeared without leaving any traces in our mythic records?

The answer is: Traces of it reappear in Saxo, in Adam of Bremen, in Norse and German popular belief, and in Völuspa. When compared with one another these traces are sufficient to determine the character and original place of the tradition in the epic of the Teutonic mythology.

I have already given above (No. 46) the main features of Saxo's account of King Gorm's and Thorkil's journey to and in the lower world. With their companions they are permitted to visit the abodes of torture of the damned and the fields of bliss, together with the gold-clad world-fountains, and to see the treasures preserved in their vicinity. In the same realm where these fountains are found there is, says Saxo, a *tabernaculum* within which still more precious treasures are preserved. It is an *uberioris thesauri secretarium.* The Danish adventurers also entered here. The treasury was also an armoury, and contained weapons suited to be borne by warriors of superhuman size. The owners and makers of these arms were also there, but they were perfectly quiet and as immovable as lifeless figures. Still they were not dead, but made the impression of being half-dead (*semineces*). By the enticing beauty and value of the treasures, and partly, too, by the dormant condition of the owners, the Danes were betrayed into an attempt to secure some of these precious things. Even the usually cautious Thorkil set a bad example and put his hand on a garment (*amiculo manum inserens*). We are not told by Saxo whether the garment covered anyone of those sleeping in the treasury, nor is it directly stated that the touching with the hand produced any disagreeable consequences for Thorkil. But further on Saxo relates that Thorkil became unrecognisable, because a withering or emaciation (*marcor*) had changed his body and the features of his face. With this account in Saxo we must compare what we read in Adam of Bremen about the Frisian adventurers who tried to plunder treasures belonging to giants who in the middle of the day lay concealed in subterranean caves (*meridiano tempore latitantes antris subterraneis*). This account must also have conceived the owners of the treasures as sleeping while the plundering took place, for not before they were on their way back were the Frisians pursued by the plundered party or by other lower-world beings. Still, all but one succeeded in getting back to their ships. Adam asserts that they were such beings *quos nostri cyclopes appellant* ("which among us are called cyclops"), that they, in other words, were gigantic smiths, who, accordingly, themselves had made the untold amount of golden treasures which the Frisians there saw. These northern cyclops, he says, dwelt within solid walls, surrounded by a water, to which, according to Adam of Bremen, one first comes after traversing the land of frost (*provincia frigoris*), and after passing that *Euripus,* "in which the water of the ocean flows back to its mysterious fountain" (*ad initia quædam fontis sui arcani recurrens*), "this deep subterranean abyss wherein the ebbing streams of the sea, according to report, were swallowed up to return," and which "with most violent force drew the unfortunate seamen down into the lower world" (*infelices nautos vehementissimo impetu traxit ad Chaos*).

It is evident that what Paulus Diaconus, Adam of Bremen, and Saxo here relate must be referred to the same tradition. All three refer the scene of these strange things and events to the "most remote part of Germany" (cp. Nos. 45, 46, 48, 49). According to all three reports the boundless ocean washes the shores of this sagaland which has to be traversed in order to get to "the sleepers," to "the men half-dead and resembling lifeless images," to "those concealed in the middle of the day in subterranean caves." Paulus assures us that they are in a cave under a rock in the neighbourhood of the famous maelstrom which sucks the billows of the sea into itself and spews them out again. Adam makes his Frisian adventurers come near being swallowed up by this maelstrom before they reach the caves of treasures where the cyclops in question dwell; and Saxo locates their tabernacle, filled with weapons and treasures, to a region which we have already recognised (see Nos. 45-51) as belonging to Mimer's lower-world realm, and situated in the neighbourhood of the sacred subterranean fountains.

In the northern part of Mimer's domain, consequently in the vicinity of the Hvergelmer fountain (see Nos. 59, 93), from and to which all waters find their way, and which is the source of the famous maelstrom (see Nos. 79, 80, 81), there stands, according to Völuspa, a golden hall in which Sindre's kinsmen have their home. Sindre is, as we know, like his brother Brok and others of his kinsmen, an artist of antiquity, a cyclops, to use the language of Adam of Bremen. The Northern records and the Latin chronicles thus correspond in the statement that in the neighbourhood of the maelstrom or of its subterranean fountain, beneath a rock and in a golden hall, or in subterranean caves filled with gold, certain men who are subterranean artisans dwell. Paulus Diaconus makes a "curious" person who had penetrated into this abode disrobe one of the sleepers clad in "Roman" clothes, and for this he is punished with a withered arm. Saxo makes Thorkil put his hand on a splendid garment which he sees there, and Thorkil returns from his journey with an emaciated body, and is so lean and lank as not to be recognised.

There are reasons for assuming that the ancient artisan *Sindre* is identical with *Dvalinn,* the ancient artisan created by Mimer. I base this assumption on the following circumstances:

Dvalinn is mentioned by the side of *Dáinn* both in Havamál (43) and in Grimnersmal (33); also in the sagas, where they make treasures in company. Both

2   717

the names are clearly epithets which point to the mythic destiny of the ancient artists in question. *Dáinn* means "the dead one," and in analogy herewith we must interpret *Dvalinn* as "the dormant one," "the one slumbering." (cp. the Old Swedish *dvale,* sleep, unconscious condition). Their fates have made them the representatives of death and sleep, a sort of equivalents of Thanatos and Hypnos. As such they appear in the allegorical strophes incorporated in Grimnersmal, which, describing how the world-tree suffers and grows old, make *Dáinn* and *Dvalinn,* "death" and "slumber," get their food from its branches, while Nidhog and other serpents wound its roots.

In Hyndluljod (6) the artists who made Frey's golden boar are called *Dáinn* and *Nabbi.* In the Younger Edda (i. 340-342) they are called *Brokkr* and *Sindri.* Strange to say, on account of mythological circumstances not known to us, the skalds have been able to use *Dáinn* as a paraphrase for a rooting four-footed animal, and *Brokkr* too has a similar signification (cp. the Younger Edda, ii. 490, and Vigfusson, Dict., under *Brokkr*). This points to an original identity of these epithets. Thus we arrive at the following parallels:

Dáinn (-Brokkr) and Dvalinn made treasures together;
(Dáinn-) Brokkr and Sindri made Frey's golden boar;
Dáinn and Nabbi made Frey's golden boar;

and the conclusion we draw herefrom is that in our mythology, in which there is such a plurality of names, *Dvalinn, Sindri,* and *Nabbi* are the same person, and that *Dáinn* and *Brokkr* are identical. I may have an opportunity later to present further evidence of this identity.

The primeval artist Sindre, who with his kinsmen inhabits a golden hall in Mimer's realm under the Hvergelmer mountains, near the subterranean fountain of the maelstrom, has therefore borne the epithet *Dvalinn,* "the one wrapped in slumber." "The slumberer" thus rests with his kinsmen, where Paulus Diaconus has heard that seven men sleep from time out of mind, and where Adam of Bremen makes smithying giants, rich in treasures, keep themselves concealed in lower-world caves within walls surrounded by water.

It has already been demonstrated that *Dvalinn* is a son of Mimer (see No. 53). Sindre-Dvalin and his kinsmen are therefore Mimer's offspring (*Mims synir*). The golden citadel situated near the fountain of the maelstrom is therefore inhabited by the sons of Mimer.

It has also been shown that, according to Solarljod, the sons of *Mimer-Nidi* come from this region (from the north in Mimer's domain), and that they are in all seven:

> Nordan sá ek rida
> Nidja sonu
> ok váru sjau saman;

that is to say, that they are the same number as the "economical months," or the changes of the year (see No. 87).

In the same region Mimer's daughter Nat has her hall, where she takes her rest after her journey across the heavens is accomplished (see No. 93). The "chateau dormant" of Teutonic mythology is therefore situated in Nat's udal territory, and Dvalin, "the slumberer," is Nat's brother. Perhaps her citadel is identical with the one in which Dvalin and his brothers sleep. According to Saxo, voices of women are heard in the *tabernaculum* belonging to the sleeping men, and glittering with weapons and treasures, when Thorkil and his men come to plunder the treasures there. Nat has her court and her attendant sisters in the Teutonic mythology, as in Rigveda (*Ushas*). *Simmara* (see Nos. 97, 98) is one of the dises of the night. According to the middle-age sagas, these dises and daughters of Mimer are said to be twelve in number (see Nos. 45, 46).

Mimer, as we know, was the ward of the middle root of the world-tree. His seven sons, representing the changes experienced by the world-tree and nature annually, have with him guarded and tended the holy tree and watered its root with *aurgom forsi* from the subterranean horn, "Valfather's pledge." When the god-clans became foes, and the Vans seized weapons against the Asas, Mimer was slain, and the world-tree, losing its wise guardian, became subject to the influence of time. It suffers in crown and root (Grimnersmal), and as it is ideally identical with creation itself, both the natural and the moral, so toward the close of the period of this world it will betray the same dilapidated condition as nature and the moral world then are to reveal.

Logic demanded that when the world-tree lost its chief ward, the lord of the well of wisdom, it should also lose that care which under his direction was bestowed upon it by his seven sons. These, voluntarily or involuntarily, retired, and the story of the seven men who sleep in the citadel full of treasures informs us how they thenceforth spend their time until Ragnarok. The details of the myth telling how they entered into this condition cannot now be found; but it may be in order to point out, as a possible connection with this matter, that one of the older Vanagods, Njord's father, and possibly the same as Mundilfore, had the epithet *Svafr, Svafrthorinn* (Fjölsvinnsmal). *Svafr* means *sopitor,* the sleeper, and *Svafrthorinn* seems to refer to *svefnthorn,* "sleep-thorn." According to the traditions, a person could be put to sleep by laying a "sleep-thorn" in his ear, and he then slept until it was taken out or fell out.

Popular traditions scattered over Sweden, Denmark, and Germany have to this very day been preserved, on the lips of the common people, of the men sleeping among weapons and treasures in underground chambers or in rocky halls. A Swedish tradition makes them equipped not only with weapons, but also with horses which in their stalls abide the day when their masters are to awake and sally forth. Common to the most of these traditions, both the Northern and the German, is the feature that this is to happen when the greatest distress is at hand, or when the end of the world approaches and the day of judgment comes. With regard to the German sagas on this point I refer to Jacob Grimm's *Mythology.* I simply wish to point out here certain features which are of special importance to the subject under discussion, and which the popular memory in certain parts of Germany has preserved from the heathen myths. When the heroes who have slept through centuries sally forth, the trumpets of the last day sound, a great battle with the powers of evil (Antichrist) is to be fought, *an immensely old tree, which has withered, is to grow green again,* and a happier age is to begin.

This immensely old tree, which is withered at the close of the present period of the world, and which is to become green again in a happier age after a decisive conflict between the good and evil, can be no other than the world-tree of Teutonic mythology, the Ygdrasil of our Eddas. The angel trumpets, at whose blasts the men who sleep within the mountains sally forth, have their prototype in Heimdal's horn, which proclaims the destruction of the world; and the battle to be fought with Antichrist is the Ragnarok conflict, clad in Christian robes, between the gods and the destroyers of the world. Here Mimer's seven sons also have their task to perform. The last great struggle also concerns the lower world, whose regions of bliss demand protection against the thurs-clans of Nifelhel, the more so since these very regions of bliss constitute the new earth, which after Ragnarok rises from the sea to become the abode of a better race of men (see No. 55). The "wall rock" of the Hvergelmer mountain and its "stone gates" (Völuspa; cp. Nos. 46, 75) require defenders able to wield those immensely large swords which are kept in the sleeping castle on Nat's udal fields, and Sindre-Dvalin is remembered not only as the artist of antiquity, spreader of Mimer's runic wisdom, enemy of Loke, and father of the man-loving dises (see No. 53), but also as a hero. The name of the horse he rode, and probably is to ride in the Ragnarok conflict, is according to a strophe cited in the Younger Edda, *Modinn;* the middle-age sagas have connected his name to a certain viking, *Sindri,* and to Sintram of the German heroic poetry.

I now come back to the Völuspa strophe, which was the starting-point in the investigation contained in this chapter:

> Leika Mims synir
> en mjotudr kyndisk
> at hinu gamla
> gjallarhorni;
> hátt blæss Heimdallr,
> horn er á lothi.

"Mimer's sons spring up, for the fate of the world is proclaimed by the old gjallar-horn. Loud blows Heimdal—the horn is raised."

In regard to *leika,* it is to be remembered that its old meaning, "to jump," "to leap," "to fly up," reappears not only in Ulfilas, who translates *skirtan* of the New Testament with *laikan* (Luke i. 41, 44, and vi. 23; in the former passage in reference to the child slumbering in Elizabeth's womb; the child "leaps" at her meeting with Mary), but also in another passage in Völuspa, where it is said in regard to Ragnarok, *leikr hár hiti vid himin sjalfan*—"high leaps" (plays) "the fire against heaven itself." Further, we must point out the preterit form *kyndisk* (from *kynna,* to make known) by the side of the present form *leika.* This juxtaposition indicates that the sons of Mimer "rush up," while the fate of the world, the final destiny of creation *in advance* and immediately beforehand, was proclaimed "by the old gjallar-horn." The bounding up of Mimer's sons is the effect of the first powerful blast. One or more of these follow: "Loud blows Heimdal—the horn is raised; and Odin speaks with Mimer's head." Thus we have found the meaning of *leika Mims synir.* Their waking and appearance is one of the signs best remembered in the chronicles in popular traditions of Ragnarok's approach and the return of the dead, and in this strophe Völuspa has preserved the memory of the "chateau dormant" of Teutonic mythology.

Thus a comparison of the mythic fragments extant with the popular traditions gives us the following outline of the Teutonic myth concerning the seven sleepers:

The world-tree—the representative of the physical and moral laws of the world—grew in time's morning gloriously out of the fields of the three world-fountains, and during the first epochs of the mythological events (*ár alda*) it stood fresh and green, cared for by the subterranean guardians of these fountains. But the times became worse. The feminine counterpart of Loke, Gulveig-Heid, spreads evil runes in Asgard and Midgard, and he and she cause disputes and war between those god-clans whose task it is to watch over and sustain the order of the world in harmony. In the feud between the Asas and Vans, the middle and most important world-fountain—the fountain of wisdom, the one from which the good runes were fetched—became robbed of its watchman. Mimer was slain, and his seven sons, the superintendents, of the seven seasons, who saw to it that these season-changes followed each other within the limits prescribed by the world-laws, were put to sleep, and fell into a stupor, which continues throughout the historical time until Ragnarok. Consequently the world-tree cannot help withering and growing old during the historical age. Still it is not to perish. Neither fire nor sword can harm it; and when evil has reached its climax, and when the present world is ended in the Ragnarok conflict and in Surt's flames, then it is to regain that freshness and splendour which it had in time's morning.

Until that time Sindre-Dvalin and Mimer's six other sons slumber in that golden hall which stands toward the north in the lower world, on Mimer's fields. Nat, their sister, dwells in the same region, and shrouds the chambers of those slumbering in darkness. Standing toward the north beneath the Nida mountains, the hall is near Hvergelmer's fountain, which causes the famous maelstrom. As sons of Mimer, the great smith of antiquity, the seven brothers were themselves great smiths of antiquity, who, during the first happy epoch, gave to the gods and to nature the most beautiful treasures (Mjolner, Brisingamen, Slidrugtanne, Draupner). The hall where they now rest is also a treasure-chamber, which preserves a number of splendid products of their skill as smiths, and among these are weapons, too large to be wielded by human hands, but intended to be employed by the brothers themselves when Ragnarok is at hand and the great decisive conflict comes between the powers of good and of evil. The seven sleepers are there clad in splendid mantles of another cut than those common among men. Certain mortals have had the privilege of seeing the realms of the lower world and of inspecting the hall where the seven brothers have their abode. But whoever ventured to touch their treasures, or was allured by the splendour of their mantles to attempt to secure any of them, was punished by the drooping and withering of his limbs.

When Ragnarok is at hand, the aged and abused world-tree trembles, and Heimdal's trumpet, until then kept in the deepest shade of the tree, is once more in the hand of the god, and at a world-piercing blast from this trumpet Mimer's seven sons start up from their sleep and arm themselves to take part in the last conflict. This is to end with the victory of the good; the world-tree will grow green again and flourish under the care of its former keepers; "all evil shall then cease, and Balder shall come back." The Teutonic myth in regard to the seven sleepers is thus most intimately connected with the myth concerning the return of the dead Balder and of the other dead men from the lower world, with the idea of resurrection and the regeneration of the world. It forms an integral part of the great epic of Teutonic mythology, and could not be spared. If the world-tree is to age during the historical epoch, and if the present period of time is to progress toward ruin, then this must have its epic cause in the fact that the keepers of the chief root of the tree were severed by the course of events from their important occupation. Therefore Mimer dies;

therefore his sons sink into the sleep of ages. But it is necessary that they should wake and resume their occupation, for there is to be a regeneration, and the world-tree is to bloom with new freshness.

Both in Germany and in Sweden there still prevails a popular belief which puts "the seven sleepers" in connection with the weather. If it rains on the day of the seven sleepers, then, according to this popular belief, it is to rain for seven weeks thereafter. People have wondered how a weather prophecy could be connected with the sleeping saints, and the matter would also, in reality, be utterly incomprehensible if the legend were of Christian origin; but it is satisfactorily explained by the heathen-Teutonic mythology, where the seven sleepers represent those very seven so-called economic months—the seven changes of the weather—which gave rise to the division of the year into the months—*gormánudr, frerm., hrútm., einm., sólm., selm.,* and *kornskurdarmánudr.* Navigation was also believed to be under the protection of the seven sleepers, and this we can understand when we remember that the hall of Mimer's sons was thought to stand near the Hvergelmer fountain and the Grotte of the skerry, "dangerous to seamen," and that they, like their father, were lovers of men. Thorkil, the great navigator of the saga, therefore praises Gudmund-Mimer as a protector in dangers.

The legend has preserved the connection found in the myth between the above meaning and the idea of a resurrection of the dead. But in the myth concerning Mimer's seven sons this idea is most intimately connected with the myth itself, and is, with epic logic, united with the whole mythological system. In the legend, on the other hand, the resurrection idea is put on as a trade-mark. The seven men in Ephesus are lulled into their long sleep, and are waked again to appear before Theodosius, the emperor, to preach a sermon illustrated by their own fate against the false doctrine which tries to deny the resurrection of the dead.

Gregorius says that he is the first who recorded in the Latin language this miracle, not before known to the Church of Western Europe. As his authority he quotes "a certain Syrian" who had interpreted the story for him. There was also need of a man from the Orient as an authority when a hitherto unknown miracle was to be presented—a miracle that had transpired in a cave near Ephesus. But there is no absolute reason for assuming that Gregorius presents a story of his own invention. The reference of the legend to Ephesus is explained by the antique saga-variation concerning Endymion, according to which the latter was sentenced to confinement and eternal sleep in a cave in the mountain Latmos. Latmos is south of Ephesus, and not very far from there. This saga is the antique root-thread of the legend, out of which rose its localisation, but not its contents and its details. The contents are borrowed from the Teutonic mythology. That Syria or Asia Minor was the scene of its transformation into a Christian legend is possible, and is not surprising. During and immediately after the time to which the legend itself refers the resurrection of the seven sleepers, the time of Theodosius, the Roman

Orient, Asia Minor, Syria, and Egypt were full of Teutonic warriors who had permanent quarters there. A *Notitia dignitatum* from this age speaks of hosts of Goths, Alamannians, Franks, Chamavians, and Vandals, who there had fixed military quarters. There then stood an *ala Francorum,* a *cohors Alamannorum,* a *cohors Chamavorum,* an *ala Vandilorum,* a *cohors Gothorum,* and no doubt there, as elsewhere in the Roman Empire, great provinces were colonised by Teutonic veterans and other immigrants. Nor must we neglect to remark that the legend refers the falling asleep of the seven men to the time of Decius. Decius fell in battle against the Goths, who, a few years later, invaded Asia Minor and captured among other places also Ephesus.

95.

ON THE ANTHROPOLOGY OF THE MYTHOLOGY.

The account now given of the myths concerning the lower world shows that the hierologists and skalds of our heathendom had developed the doctrine in a perspicuous manner even down to the minutest details. The lower world and its kingdom of death were the chief subjects with which their fancy was occupied. The many sagas and traditions which flowed from heathen sources and which described Svipdag's, Hadding's, Gorm's, Thorkil's, and other journeys down there are proof of this, and the complete agreement of statements from totally different sources in regard to the topography of the lower world and the life there below shows that the ideas were

reduced to a systematised and perspicuous whole. Svipdag's and Hadding's journeys in the lower world have
been incorporated as episodes in the great epic concerning the Teutonic patriarchs, the chief outlines of which
I have presented in the preceding pages. This is done
in the same manner as the visits of Ulysses and Æneas
in the lower world have become a part of the great Greek
and Roman epic poems.

Under such circumstances it may seem surprising that
Icelandic records from the middle ages concerning the
heathen belief in regard to the abodes after death should
give us statements which seems utterly irreconcilable
with one another. For there are many proofs that the
dead were believed to live in hills and rocks, or in grave-
mounds where their bodies were buried. How can this
be reconciled with the doctrine that the dead descended
to the lower world, and were there judged either to receive abodes in Asgard or in the realms of bliss in Hades,
or in the world of torture?

The question has been answered too hastily to the
effect that the statements cannot be harmonised, and that
consequently the heathen-Teutonic views in regard to
the day of judgment were in this most important part
of the religious doctrine unsupported.

The reason for the obscurity is not, however, in the
matter itself, which has never been thoroughly studied,
but in the false premises from which the conclusions have
been drawn. Mythologists have simply assumed that
the popular view of the Christian Church in regard to
terrestrial man, conceiving him to consist of two fac-

tors, the perishable body and the imperishable soul, was the necessary condition for every belief in a life hereafter, and that the heathen Teutons accordingly also cherished this idea.

But this duality did not enter into the belief of our heathen fathers. Nor is it of such a kind that a man, having conceived a life hereafter, in this connection necessarily must conceive the soul as the simple, indissoluble spiritual factor of human nature. The division into two parts, *lif ok sála, líkamr ok sála,* body and soul, came with Christianity, and there is every reason for assuming, so far as the Scandinavian peoples are concerned, that the very word soul, *sála, sál,* is, like the idea it represents, an imported word. In Old Norse literature the word occurs for the first time in Olaf Trygveson's contemporary Halfred, after he had been converted to Christianity. Still the word is of Teutonic root. Ulfilas translates the New Testament *psyche* with *saiwala,* but this he does with his mind on the Platonic New Testament view of man as consisting of *three* factors: spirit (*pneuma*), soul (*psyche*), and body (*soma*). Spirit (*pneuma*) Ulfilas translates with *ahma.*

Another assumption, likewise incorrect in estimating the anthropological-eschatological belief of the Teutons, is that they are supposed to have distinguished between matter and mind, which is a result reached by the philosophers of the Occident in their abstract studies. It is, on the contrary, certain that such a distinction never entered the system of heathen Teutonic views. In it all things were *material,* an *efni* of course or fine grain, tangible or intangible, visible or invisible. The imperishable factors of man were, like the perishable, *material,* and a force could not be conceived which was not bound to matter, or expressed itself in matter, or *was* matter.

The heathen Teutonic conception of human nature, and of the factors composing it, is most like the Aryan-Asiatic as we find the latter preserved in the traditions of Buddhism, which assume more than three factors in a human being, and deny the existence of a soul, if this is to mean that all that is not corporal in man consists of a single simple, and therefore indissoluble, element, the soul.

The anthropological conception presented in Völuspa is as follows: Man consists of six elements, namely, to begin with the lower and coarser and to end with the highest and noblest:

(1)   The earthly matter of which the body is formed.
(2)   A formative vegetative force.
(3)   and (4) Loder's gifts.
(5)   Honer's gifts.
(6)   Odin's gifts.

Völuspa's words are these: The gods

fundu á landi	found on the land
litt megandi	with little power,
Ask ok Embla	Ask and Embla
orlauglausa.	without destiny.
Aund thau ne átto,	Spirit they had not,
óth thau ne baufdo,	"ódr" they had not,
la ne læti,	neither "lá" nor "læti,"
ne lito goda.	nor the form of the gods.

Aund gaf Odin,	Spirit gave Odin,
oth gaf Henir,	"ódr" gave Honer,
la gaf Lodur	"lá" gave Loder
ok lito goda.	and the form of the gods.

The two lowest factors, the earthly material and the vegetative force, were already united in Ask and Embla when the three gods found them "growing as trees." These elements were able to unite themselves simply by the course of nature without any divine interference. When the sun for the first time shone from the south on "the stones of the hall," the vegetative force united with the matter of the primeval giant Ymer, who was filled with the seed of life from Audhumbla's milk, and then the "ground was overgrown with green herbs."

Thus man was not created directly from the crude earthly matter, but had already been organised and formed when the gods came and from the trees made persons with blood, motion, and spirtual qualities. The vegetative force must not be conceived in accordance with modern ideas, as an activity separated from the matter by abstraction and at the same time inseparably joined with it, but as an *active matter* joined with the earthly matter.

Loder's first gift *lá* with *læti* makes Ask and Embla animal beings. Egilsson's view that *lá* means blood is confirmed by the connection in which we find the word used. The *læti* united with *lá* (compare the related Swedish word "*later*," manners) means the way in which a conscious being moves and acts. The blood and the power of a motion which is voluntary were to the Teutons, as to all other people, the marks distinguishing animal

3 · 733

from vegetable life. And thus we are already within the domain of psychical elements. The inherited features, growth, gait, and pose, which were observed as forming race- and family-types, were regarded as having the blood as *efni* and as being concealed therein. The blood which produced the family-type also produced the family-tie, even though it was not acquired by the natural process of generation. A person not at all related to the family of another man could become his *blódi,* his blood-kinsman, if they resolved *at blanda blódi saman.* They thereby entered into the same relations to each other as if they had the same mother and father.

Loder also gave at the same time another gift, *litr goda.* To understand this expression (hitherto translated with "good complexion"), we must bear in mind that the Teutons, like the Hellenes and Romans, conceived the gods in human form, and that the image which characterises man was borne by the gods alone before man's creation, and originally belonged to the gods. To the hierologists and the skalds of the Teutons, as to those of the Greeks and Romans, man was created *in effigiem deorum* and had in his nature a divine image in the real sense of this word, a *litr goda.* Nor was this *litr goda* a mere abstraction to the Teutons, or an empty form, but a created *efni* dwelling in man and giving shape and character to the earthly body which is visible to the eye. The common meaning of the word *litr* is something presenting itself to the eye without being actually tangible to the hands. The Gothic form of the word is *wlits,* which Ulfilas uses in translating the Greek *prosopon*—look, appearance, expression. Certain persons were regarded as able to separate their *litr* from its union with the other factors of their being, and to lend it, at least for a short time, to some other person in exchange for his. This was called to *skipta litum, vixla litum.* It was done by Sigurd and Gunnar in the song of Sigurd Fafnersbane (i. 37-42). That factor in Gunnar's being which causes his earthly body to present itself in a peculiar individual manner to the eyes of others is transmitted to Sigurd, whose exterior, affected by Gunnar's *litr,* accommodates itself to the latter, while the spiritual kernel in Sigurd's personality suffers no change.

> Lit hefir thu Gunnars
> oc læti hans,
> mælsco thina
> oc meginhyggior (Sig., i. 39).

Thus man has within him an inner body made in the image of the gods and consisting of a finer material, a body which is his *litr,* by virtue of which his coarser tabernacle, formed from the earth, receives that form by which it impresses itself on the minds of others. The recollection of the belief in this inner body has been preserved in a more or less distorted form in traditions handed down even to our days (see for example, Hyltén-Cavallius, *Värend och Virdarne,* i. 343-360; Rääf in Småland, *Beskr. öfver Ydre,* p. 84).

The appearance of the outer body therefore depends on the condition of the *litr,* that is, of the inner being. Beautiful women have a "joyous fair *litr*" (Havamál, 93). An emotion has influence upon the *litr,* and through it on the blood and the appearance of the outward body. A sudden blushing, a sudden paleness, are among the results thereof, and can give rise to the question, *Hefir thu lit brugdit?*—Have you changed your *litr?* (Fornald., i. 426). To translate this with, Have you changed colour? is absurd. The questioner sees the change of colour, and does not need to ask the other one who cannot see it.

On account of its mythological signification and application, it is very natural that the word *litr* should in every-day life acquire on the one hand the meaning of complexion in general, and on the other hand the signification of *hamr,* guise, an earthly garb which persons skilled in magic could put on and off. *Skipta litum, vixla litum,* have in Christian times been used as synonymous with *skipta hömum, vixla hömum.*

In physical death the coarser elements of an earthly person's nature are separated from the other constituent parts. The tabernacle formed of earth and the vegetative material united therewith are eliminated like the animal element and remain on earth. But this does not imply that the deceased descend without form to Hades. The form in which they travel in "deep dales," traverse the thornfields, wade across the subterranean rivers, or ride over the gold-clad Gjallar-bridge, is not a new creation, but was worn by them in their earthly career. It can be none other than their *litr,* their *umbra et imago.* It also shows distinctly what the dead man has been in his earthly life, and what care has been bestowed on his dust. The washing, combing, dressing, ornamenting, and supplying with Hel-shoes of the dead body has influence upon one's looks in Hades, on one's looks when he is to appear before his judge.

Separated from the earthly element, from the vegetative material, and from the blood, the *lit* is almost imponderable, and does not possess the qualities for an intensive life, either in bliss or in torture.   Five fylkes of dead men who rode over the Gjallar-bridge produced no greater din than Hermod alone riding on Sleipner; and the woman watching the bridge saw that Hermod's exterior was not that of one separated from the earthly element. It was not *litr daudra manna* (Gylfaginning).   But the *litr* of the dead is compensated for what it has lost. Those who in the judgment on *daudan hvern* are pronounced worthy of bliss are permitted to drink from the horn decorated with the serpent-symbol of eternity, the liquids of the three world-fountains which give life to all the world, and thereby their *litr* gets a higher grade of body and nobler blood (see Nos. 72, 73).   Those sentenced to torture must also drink, but it is a drink *eitri blandinn miok,* "much mixed with venom," and it is *illu heilli,* that is, a warning of evil.   This drink also restores their bodies, but only to make them feel the burden of torture.   The liquid of life which they imbibe in this drink is the same as that which was thought to flow in the veins of the demons of torture.   When Hadding with his sword wounds the demon-hand which grasps after Hardgrep and tears her into pieces (see No. 41), there flows from the wound "more venom than blood" (*plus tabi quam cruoris*—Saxo, *Hist.,* 40).

When Loder had given Ask and Embla *litr goda,* an inner body formed in the image of the gods, a body which gives to their earthly tabernacle a human-divine type, they received from Honer the gift which is called *ódr.* In signification this word corresponds most closely to the Latin *mens,* the Greek *nous* (cp. Vigfusson's Lexicon), and means that material which forms the kernel of a human personality, its ego, and whose manifestations are understanding, memory, fancy, and will.

Vig·fusson has called attention to the fact that the epithet *langifótr* and *aurkonungr,* "Longleg" and "Mireking," applied to Honer, is applicable to the stork, and that this cannot be an accident, as the very name *Hœnir* suggests a bird, and is related to the Greek *kuknos,* and the Sanscrit *sakunas (Corpus Poet. Bor.,* i. p. cii.).* It should be borne in mind in this connection that the stork even to this day is regarded as a sacred and protected bird, and that among Scandinavians and Germans there still exists a nursery tale telling how the stork takes from some saga-pond the little fruits of man and brings them to their mothers. The tale which now belongs to the nursery has its root in the myth, where Honer gives our

---

*There is a story of the creation of man by three wandering gods, who become in mediæval stories Jesus and SS. Peter and Paul walking among men, as in Champfleury's pretty apologue of the *bonhomme misére,* so beautifully illustrated by Legros. In the eddic legend one of these gods is called *Hœne;* he is *the speech-giver* of Wolospa, and is described in praises taken from lost poems as "the long-legged one" [*langifotr*], "the lord of the ooze" [*aurkonungr*]. Strange epithets, but easily explainable when one gets at the etymology of Hæne = *hohni* = Sansc. *sakunas* = Gr. *kuknos* = the white bird, swan, or stork, that stalks along in the mud, lord of the marsh; and it is now easy to see that this bird is the Creator walking in chaos, brooding over the primitive mish-mash or tohu-bohu, and finally hatching the egg of the world. Hohni is also, one would fancy, to be identified with Heimdal, *the walker,* who is also a creator-god, who sleeps *more lightly than a bird,* who is also the "*fair Anse,*" and *the* "*whitest of the Anses,*" the "waker" of the gods, a celestial chanticleer as it were (Vigfusson, *Corpus Poeticum Boreale,* vol. i., Introduction, p. cii., quoted by the translator).

first parents that very gift which in a spiritual sense makes them human beings and contains the personal ego. It is both possible and probable that the conditions essential to the existence of every person were conceived as being analogous with the conditions attending the creation of the first human pair, and that the gifts which were then given by the gods to Ask and Embla were thought to be repeated in the case of each one of their descendants—that Honer consequently was believed to be continually active in the same manner as when the first human pair was created, giving to the mother-fruit the ego that is to be. The fruit itself out of which the child is developed was conceived as grown on the world-tree, which therefore is called *manna mjötudr* (Fjölsvinnsmal, 22). Every fruit of this kind (*aldin*) that matured (and fell from the branches of the world-tree into the mythic pond [?]) is fetched by the winged servants of the gods, and is born *á eld* into the maternal lap, after being mentally fructified by Honer.

> Ut af hans (Mimameids) aldni
> skal á eld bera
> fyr kelisjúkar konur;
> utar hverfa
> thaz thær innar skyli,
> sá er hann med mönnum mjötudr.

Above, in No. 83, it has been shown that *Lodurr* is identical with *Mundilföri*, the one producing fire by friction, and that *Hœnir* and *Lodurr* are Odin's brothers, also called *Vei* and *Vili*. With regard to the last name it should be remarked that its meaning of "will" developed out of the meaning "desire," "longing," and that the word preserved this older meaning also in the secondary sense of *cupido, libido,* sexual desire. This epithet of *Lodurr* corresponds both with the nature of the gifts he bestows on the human child which is to be—that is, the blood and the human, originally divine, form—and also with his quality of fire-producer, if, as is probable, the friction-fire had the same symbolic meaning in the Teutonic mythology as in the Rigveda. Like Honer, Loder causes the knitting together of the human generations. While the former fructifies the embryo developing on the world-tree with *ódr,* it receives from Loder the warmth of the blood and human organism. The expression *Vilja byrdr,* "*Vili's* burden," "that which *Vili* has produced," is from this point of view a well-chosen and at the same time an ambiguous paraphrase for a human body. The paraphrase occurs in Ynglingatal (Ynglingasaga, 17). When Visbur loses his life in the flames it is there said of him that the fire consumed his *Vilja byrdi,* his corporal life.

To Loder's and Honer's gifts the highest Asa-god adds the best element in human nature, *önd,* spirit, that by which a human being becomes participator in the divine also in an inner sense, and not only as to form. The divine must here, of course, be understood in the sense (far different from the ecclesiastical) in which it was used by our heathen ancestors, to whom the divine, as it can reveal itself in men, chiefly consisted in power of thought, courage, honesty, veracity, and mercy, but who knew no other humility than that of patiently bearing such misfortunes as cannot be averted by human ingenuity.

These six elements, united into one in human nature, were of course constantly in reciprocal activity. The personal kernel *óðr* is on the one hand influenced by *önd*, the spirit, and on the other hand by the animal, vegetative, and corporal elements, and the personality being endowed with will, it is responsible for the result of this reciprocal activity. If the spirit becomes superior to the other elements then it penetrates and sanctifies not only the personal kernel, but also the animal, vegetative, and corporal elements. Then human nature becomes a being that may be called divine, and deserves divine honour. When such a person dies the lower elements which are abandoned and consigned to the grave have been permeated by, and have become participators in, the personality which they have served, and may thereafter in a wonderful manner diffuse happiness and blessings around them. When Halfdan the Black died different places competed for the keeping of his remains, and the dispute was settled by dividing the corpse between Hadaland, Ringerike, and Vestfold (Fagerskinna, Heimskringla). The vegetative force in the remains of certain persons might also manifest itself in a strange manner. Thorgrim's grave-mound in Gisle's saga was always green on one side, and Laugarbrekku-Einar's grave-mound was entirely green both winter and summer (Landn., ii. 7).

The elements of the dead buried in the grave continued for more or less time their reciprocal activity, and formed a sort of unity which, if permeated by his *óðr* and *önd*,

741

preserved some of his personality and qualities. The grave-mound might in this manner contain an *alter ego* of him who had descended to the realm of death. This *alter ego*, called after his dwelling *haugbúi*, hill-dweller, was characterised by his nature as a *draugr*, a branch which, though cut off from its life-root, still maintains its consistency, but gradually, though slowly, pays tribute to corruption and progresses toward its dissolution. In Christian times the word *draugr* acquired a bad, demoniacal meaning, which did not belong to it exclusively in heathen times, to judge from the compounds in which it is found: *eldraugr, herdraugr, hirdidraugr,* which were used in paraphrases for "warriors;" *ódaldraugr,* "rightful owner," &c. The *alter ego* of the deceased, his representative dwelling in the grave, retained his character: was good and kind if the deceased had been so in life; in the opposite case, evil and dangerous. As a rule he was believed to sleep in his grave, especially in the daytime, but might wake up in the night, or could be waked by the influence of prayer or the powers of conjuration. Ghosts of the good kind were *hollar vættir,* of the evil kind *úvættir.* Respect for the fathers and the idea that the men of the past were more pious and more noble than those of the present time caused the *alter egos* of the fathers to be regarded as beneficent and working for the good of the race, and for this reason family grave-mounds where the bones of the ancestors rested were generally near the home. If there was no grave-mound in the vicinity, but a rock or hill, the *alter egos* in question were believed to congregate there when something of importance to the family was impending. It might also happen that the lower elements, when abandoned by *óðr* and *önd,* became an *alter ego* in whom the vegetative and animal elements exclusively asserted themselves. Such an one was always tormented by animal desire of food, and did not seem to have any feeling for or memory of bonds tied in life. Saxo (*Hist.,* 244) gives a horrible account of one of this sort. Two foster-brothers, Asmund and Asvid, had agreed that if the one died before the other the survivor should confine himself in the foster-brother's grave-chamber and remain there. Asvid died and was buried with horse and dog. Asmund kept his agreement, and ordered himself to be confined in the large, roomy grave, but discovered to his horror that his foster-brother had become a *haugbúi* of the last-named kind, who, after eating horse and dog, attacked Asmund to make him a victim of his hunger. Asmund conquered the *haugbúi,* cut off his head, and pierced his heart with a pole to prevent his coming to life again. Swedish adventurers who opened the grave to plunder it freed Asmund from his prison. In such instances as this it must have been assumed that the lower elements of the deceased consigned to the grave were never in his lifetime sufficiently permeated by his *óðr* and *önd* to enable these qualities to give the corpse an impression of the rational personality and human character of the deceased. The same idea is the basis of belief of the Slavic people in the vampire. In one of this sort the vegetative element united with his dust still asserts itself, so that hair and nails continue to grow as on a living being, and the animal element, which likewise continues to operate in the one buried, visits him with hunger and drives him in the night out of the grave to suck the blood of surviving kinsmen.

The real personality of the dead, the one endowed with *litr, ódr,* and *önd,* was and remained in the death kingdom, although circumstances might take place that would call him back for a short time. The drink which the happy dead person received in Hades was intended not only to strengthen his *litr,* but also to soothe that longing which the earthly life and its memories might cause him to feel. If a dearly-beloved kinsman or friend mourned the deceased too violently, this sorrow disturbed his happiness in the death kingdom, and was able to bring him back to earth. Then he would visit his grave-mound, and he and his *alter ego,* the *haugbúi,* would become one. This was the case with Helge Hundingsbane (Helge Hund., ii. 40, &c.). The sorrow of Sigrun, his beloved, caused him to return from Valhal to earth and to ride to his grave, where Sigrun came to him and wanted to rest in his arms during the night. But when Helge had told her that her tears pierced his breast with pain, and had assured her that she was exceedingly dear to him, and had predicted that they together should drink the sorrow-allaying liquids of the lower world, he rode his way again, in order that, before the crowing of the cock, he might be back among the departed heroes. Prayer was another means of calling the dead back. At the entrance of his deceased mother's grave-chamber Svipdag beseeches her to awake. Her ashes kept in the grave-chamber (*er til moldar er komin*) and her real personality from the realm

744

of death (*er ór ljodheimum er lidin*) then unite, and Groa speaks out of the grave to her son (Grogaldr., i. 2). A third means of revoking the dead to earth lay in conjuration. But such a use of conjuration was a great sin, which relegated the sinner to the demons. (Cp. Saxo's account of Hardgrep.)

Thus we understand why the dead descended to Hades and still inhabited the grave-mounds. One died "to Hel" and "to the grave" at the same time. That of which earthly man consisted, in addition to his corporal garb, was not the simple being, "the soul," which cannot be divided, but there was a combination of factors, which in death could be separated, and of which those remaining on earth, while they had long been the covering of a personal kernel (*ódr*), could themselves in a new combination form another ego of the person who had descended to Hades.

But that too consisted of several factors, *litr, ódr,* and *önd,* and they were not inseparably united. We have already seen that the sinner, sentenced to torture, dies a second death in the lower world before he passes through the Na-gates, the death from Hel to Nifelhel, so that he becomes a *nár*, a corpse in a still deeper sense than that which *nár* has in a physical sense. The second death, like the first (physical), must consist in the separation of one or more of the factors from the being that dies. And in the second death, that which separates itself from the damned one and changes his remains into a lower-world *nár*, must be those factors that have no blame in connection with his sins, and consequently should not suffer his punishment, and which in their origin are too noble to become the objects of the practice of demons in the art of torturing. The venom drink which the damned person has to empty deprives him of that image of the gods in which he was made, and of the spirit which was the noble gift of the Asa-father. Changed into a *monster*, he goes to his destinty fraught with misfortunes.

The idea of a regeneration was not foreign to the faith of the Teutonic heathens. To judge from the very few statements we have on this point, it would seem that it was only the very best and the very worst who were thought to be born anew in the present world. Gulveig was born again several times by the force of her own evil will. But it is only ideal persons of whom it is said that they are born again—*e.g.,* Helge Hjorvardson, Helge Hundingsbane, and Olaf Geirstadaralf, of whom the last was believed to have risen again in Saint Olaf. With the exception of Gulveig, the statements in regard to the others from Christian times are an echo from the heathen Teutonic doctrine which it would be most interesting to become better acquainted with—also from the standpoint of comparative Aryan mythology, since this same doctrine appears in a highly-developed form in the Asiatic-Aryan group of myths.

V.

THE IVALDE RACE.

96.

SVIPDAG AND GROA.

GROA's son Svipdag is mentioned by this name in two Old Norse songs, Grogalder and Fjölsvinnsmal, which as Bugge has shown, are mutually connected, and describe episodes from the same chain of events.

The contents of Grogalder are as follows:

Groa is dead when the event described in the song takes place. Svipdag is still quite young. Before her death she has told him that he is to go to her grave and call her if he needs her help. The grave is a grave-chamber made of large flat stones raised over a stone floor, and forming when seen from the outside a mound which is furnished with a door (str. 1, 15).

Svipdag's father has married a second time. The stepmother commands her stepson to go abroad and find *Menglödum*, "those fond of ornaments." From Fjölsvinnsmal we learn that one of those called by this name is a young maid who becomes Svipdag's wife. Her real name is not given: she is continually designated as *Menglöd*, Menglad, one of "those fond of ornaments," whom Svipdag has been commanded to find.

This task seems to Svipdag to exceed his powers. It must have been one of great adventures and great dangers, for he now considers it the proper time to ask his deceased mother for help. He has become suspicious of his step-mother's intentions; he considers her *lævis* (cunning), and her proposition is "a cruel play which she has put before him" (str. 3).

He goes to Groa's grave-chamber, probably in the night (*verda auflgari allir a nottum dauthir*—Helge Hund., ii. 51), bids her wake, and reminds her of her promise. That of Groa which had become dust (*er til moldar er komin*), and that of her which had left this world of man and gone to the lower world (*er ór ljódheimum lidin*), become again united under the influence of maternal love and of the son's prayer, and Svipdag hears out of the grave-chamber his mother's voice asking him why he has come. He speaks of the errand on which he has been sent by his stepmother (str. 3, 4).

The voice from the grave declares that long journeys lie before Svipdag if he is to reach the goal indicated. It does not, however, advise him to disobey the command of his stepmother, but assures him that if he will but patiently look for a good outcome of the matter, then the norn will guide the events into their right course (str. 4).

The son then requests his mother to sing protecting incantations over him. She is celebrated in mythology as one mighty in incantations of the good kind. It was Groa that sang healing incantations over Thor when with a wounded forehead he returned from the conflict with the giant Hrungner (Gylfag.).

Groa hears his prayer, and sings from the grave an incantation of protection against the dangers which her prophetic vision has discovered on those journeys that now lie before Svipdag: first, the incantation that can inspire the despondent youth who lacks confidence in himself with courage and reliance in his own powers.   It is, Groa says, the same incantation as another mother before her sang over a son whose strength had not yet been developed, and who had a similar perilous task to perform.   It is an incantation, says Groa, which Rind, Vale's mother, sang over *Ránr*.   This synonym of Vale is of saga-historical interest.   Saxo calls Vale *Bous*, the Latinised form for Beowulf, and Beowulf's grave-mound, according to the Old English poem which bears his name, is situated on *Hrones næss, Ránr's* ness.   Here too a connection between Vale and the name *Ránr* is indicated.

Groa's second incantation contains a prayer that when her son, joyless, travels his paths and sees scorn and evil before his eyes, he may always be protected by Urd's *lokur* (an ambiguous expression, which may on the one hand refer to the bonds and locks of the goddess of fate, on the other hand to Groa's own phrophetic magic song: *lokur* means both songs of a certain kind and locks and prisons).

On his journey Svipdag is to cross rivers, which with swelling floods threaten his life; but Groa's third incantation commands these rivers to flow down to Hel and to fall for her son. The rivers which have their course to Hel (*falla til Heljar hedan*—Grimnersmal, 28) are subterranean rivers rising on the Hvergelmer mountain (59, 93).

749

Groa's fourth and fifth incantations indicate that Svipdag is to encounter enemies and be put in chains. Her
songs are then to operate in such a manner that the hearts
of the foes are softened into reconciliation, and that the
chains fall from the limbs of her son. For this purpose
she gives him that power which is called *"Leifnir's* fires"
(see No. 38), which loosens fetters from enchanted limbs
(str. 9, 10).

Groa's sixth incantation is to save Svipdag from perish-
ing in a gale on the sea. In the great world-mill (*ludr*)
which produces the maelstrom, ocean currents, ebb and
flood tide (see Nos. 79-82), calm and war are to "gang
thegither" in harmony, be at Svipdag's service and prepare him a safe voyage.

The seventh incantation that comes from the grave-
chamber speaks of a journey which Svipdag is to make
over a mountain where terrible cold reigns. The song
is to save him from becoming a victim of the frost there.

The last two incantations, the eighth and the ninth,
show what was already suggested by the third, namely,
that Svipdag's adventurous journeys are to be crowned
with a visit in the lower world. He is to meet Nat *á
Niflvegi,* "on the Nifel-way," "in Nifel-land." The word
nifl does not occur in the Old Norse literature except in
reference to the northern part of the Teutonic Hades, the
forecourt to the worlds of torture there. *Niflhel* and
Niflheim are, as we know, the names of that forecourt.
Niflfarinn is the designation, as heretofore mentioned, of
a deceased whose soul has descended to Nifelhel; *Nifl-
gódr* is a nithing, one deserving to be damned to the

tortures of the lower world. Groa's eighth incantation is to protect her son against the perilous consequences of encountering a "dead woman" (*daud kona*) on his journey through Nifelhel. The ninth incantation shows that Svipdag, on having traversed the way to the northern part of the lower world, crosses the Hvergelmer mountain and comes to the realm of Mimer; for he is to meet and talk with "the weapon-honoured giant," Mimer himself, under circumstances which demand "tongue and brains" on the part of Groa's son:

> ef thú vid inn náddgöfga
> ordum skiptir jötun:
> máls ok mannvits
> sé ther á Mimis bjarta
> gnóga of getit.

In the poem Fjölsvinnsmal, which I am now to discuss, we read with regard to Svipdag's adventures in the lower world that on his journey in Mimer's domain he had occasion to see the *ásmegir's* citadel and the splendid things within its walls (str. 33; cp. No. 53).

97.

SVIPDAG OUTSIDE OF THE GATES OF ASGARD.   MENGLAD'S IDENTITY WITH FREYJA.

In the first stanzas of Fjölsvinnsmal we see Svipdag making his way to a citadel which is furnished with *forgördum*—that is to say, ramparts in front of the gate in the wall which surrounds the place. On one of these ramparts stands a watchman who calls himself *Fjölsvinnr*, which is an epithet of Odin (Grimnersmal, 47).

The first strophe of the poem calls Svipdag *thursa thjódar sjólr* (*sjóli*), "the leader of the Thurs people." The reason why he could be designated thus has already been given (see Nos. 24, 33): During the conflicts between the powers of winter and the sons of Ivalde, and the race connected with them, on the one side, and the Teutonic patriarch Halfdan, favoured by the Asa-gods, on the other side, Svipdag opposed the latter and finally defeated him (see No. 93).

From the manner in which Fjölsvin receives the traveller it appears that a "leader of the Thurs people" need not look for a welcome outside of such a citadel as this. Fjölsvin calls him a *flagd*, a *vargr*, and advises him to go back by "moist ways," for within this wall such a being can never come. Meanwhile these severe words do not on this occasion appear to be spoken in absolute earnest, for the watchman at the same time encourages conversation, by asking Svipdag what his errand is. The latter corrects the watchman for his rough manner of receiving him, and explains that he is not able to return, for the burgh he sees is a beautiful sight, and there he would be able to pass a happy life.

When the watchman now asks him about his parents and family he answers in riddles. Himself "the leader of the Thurs people," the former ally of the powers of frost, he calls Windcold, his father he calls Springcold, and his grandfather Verycold (*Fjölkaldr*). This answer gives the key to the character of the whole following conversation, in which Svipdag is the questioner, whose interrogations the watchman answers in such a manner that he gives persons and things names which seldom are their usual ones, but which refer to their qualities.

What castle is this, then, before which Svipdag stopped, and within whose walls he is soon to find Menglad, whom he seeks?

A correct answer to this question is of the greatest importance to a proper understanding of the events of mythology and their connection. Strange to say, it has hitherto been assumed that the castle is the citadel of a giant, a resort of thurses, and that Menglad is a giantess.

Svipdag has before him a scene that enchants his gaze and fills him with a longing to remain there for ever. It is a pleasure to the eyes, he says, which no one willingly renounces who once has seen a thing so charming. Several "halls," that is to say, large residences or palaces, with their "open courts," are situated on these grounds. The halls glitter with gold, which casts a reflection over the plains in front of them (*gardar gloa mer thykkja af gullna sali*—str. 5). One of the palaces, a most magnificent one (an *audrann*), is surrounded by "wise Vaferflame," and Fjölsvin says of it that from time immemorial there has been a report among men in regard to this dwelling. He calls it *Hýrr*, "the gladdening one," "the laughing one," "the soul-stirring one." Within the castle wall there rises a hill or rock, which the author of the song conceived as decorated with flowers or in some other ravishing way, for he calls it *a joyous rock*. There the fair Menglad is seen sitting like an image (*thruma*), surrounded by lovely dises. Svipdag here sees the world-tree, invisible on earth, spreading its branchs loaded with fruits (*aldin*) over all lands. In the tree sits the cock *Vidofnir,* whose whole plumage glitters like gold (str. 19, 22, 23, 31, 32, 35, 49).

The whole place is surrounded by a wall, "so solid that it shall stand as long as the world" (str. 12). It is built of Lerbrimer's (Ymer's) limbs, and is called *Gastrofnir,* "the same one as refuses admittance to uninvited guests." In the wall is inserted the gate skilfully made by Sol-blinde's sons, the one which I have already mentioned in No. 36. Svipdag, who had been in the lower world and had there seen the halls of the gods and the well-fortified castle of the *ásmegir* (see No. 53), admires the wall and the gate, and remarks that no more dangerous contriv-anecs (for uninvited guests) than these were seen among the gods (str. 9-12).

The gate is guarded by two "garms," wolf-dogs. Fjölsvin explains that their names are *Gifr* and *Geri,* that they are to live and perform their duty as watch-dogs to the end of the world (*unz rjúfask regin*), and that they are the watchers of watchers, whose number is eleven (*vardir ellifu, er their varda*—str. 14).

Just as the mythic personality that Svipdag met outside of the castle is named by the Odin-epithet *Fjölsvidr,* so we here find one of the watching dogs called after one of Odin's wolf-dogs, *Geri* (Grimnersmal, 19). Their duty of watching, which does not cease before Ragnarok, they perform in connection with eleven mythic persons dwell-ing within the citadel, who are themselves called *vardir,* an epithet for world-protecting divinities. Heimdal is *vördr goda,* Balder is *vördr Hálfdanar jarda.* The number of the Asas is eleven after Balder descended to the lower world. Hyndluljod says: *Voru ellifu æsir taldir, Balldr er hne vid banathufu.*

These wolf-dogs are foes of giants and trolls. If a *vættr* came there he would not be able to get past them (str. 16—*ok kemt thá vættr, ef thá kom*). The troll-beings that are called *gifr* and *kveldridur* (Völuspa, 50; Helge Hjorv., 15), and that fly about in the air with *lim* (bundles of sticks) in their hands, have been made to fall by these dogs. They have made *gifr-lim* into a "land-wreck" (*er gjordu gífrlim reka fyrir löndin*—str. 13). As one of the dogs is himself called *Gifr,* his ability, like that of those chased by him, to fly in the air seems to be indicated. The old tradition about Odin, who with his dogs flies through the air above the earth, has its root in the myth concerning the duty devolving upon the Asa-father, in his capacity of lord of the heavens, to keep space free from *gifr, kveddridur, tunridur,* who "*leika á lopti,*" do their mischief in the air (cp. Havamál, 155).

The hall in which Menglad lives, and that part of the wall-surrounded domain which belongs to her, seems to be situated directly in front of the gate, for Svipdag, standing before it, asks who is the ruler of the domain which he sees before him, and Fjölsvin answers that it is Menglad who there holds sway, owns the land, and is mistress of the treasure-chambers.

The poem tells us in the most unmistakable manner that Menglad is an asynje, and that one of the very noblest ones. "What are the names," asks Svipdag, "of the young women who sit so pleasantly together at Menglad's feet?" Fjölsvin answers by naming nine, among whom are the goddess of healing, *Eir* (Prose Edda, i. 114), and the dises *Hlif*, "the protectress," *Björt*, "the shining," *Blid*, "the blithe," and *Frid*, "the fair." Their place at Menglad's feet indicates that they are subordinate to her and belong to her attendants. Nevertheless they are, Fjölsvin assures us, higher beings, who have sanctuaries and altars (str. 40), and have both power and inclination quickly to help men who offer sacrifices to them. Nay, "no so severe evil can happen to the sons of men that these maids are not able to help them out of their distress." It follows with certainty that their mistress Menglad, "the one fond of ornaments," must be one of the highest and most worshipped goddesses in the mythology. And to none of the asynjes is the epithet "fond of ornaments" (Menglad) more applicable than to the fair owner of the first among female ornaments, Brisingamen—to Freyja, whose daughters *Hnoss* and *Gersami* are called by names that mean "ornaments," and of whose fondness for beautiful jewels even Christian saga authors speak. To the court of no other goddess are such dises as *Björt, Blid,* and *Frid* so well suited as to hers. And all that Fjölsvinnsmal tells about Menglad is in harmony with this.

· Freyja was the goddess of love, of matrimony, and of fertility, and for this reason she was regarded as the divine ruler and helper, to whom loving maids, wives who are to bear children, and sick women were to address themselves with prayers and offerings. Figuratively this is expressed in Fjölsvinnsmal with the words that every sick woman who walks up the mountain on which Menglad sits regains her health. "That mountain has long been the joy of the sick and wounded" (str. **3**6). The great tree whose foliage spreads over Menglad's palace bears the fruits that help *kélisjúkar konur,* so that *utar hverva that thær innar skyli* (str. 22). In the midst of the fair dises who attend Menglad the poem also mentions *Aurboda,* the giantess, who afterwards becomes the mother-in-law of Freyja's brother, and whose appearance in Asgard as a maid-servant of Freyja, and as one of those that bring fruits from the world-tree to *kélisjúkar konur,* has already been mentioned in No. 35. If we now add that Menglad, though a mighty goddess, is married to Svipdag, who is not one of the gods, and that Freyja, despite her high rank among the goddesses, does not have a god for her husband, but, as Gylfaginning expresses it, *giptist theim manni er Ódr heitir,* and, finally that Menglad's father is characterised by a name which refers to Freyja's father, Njord,* then these circumstances alone, without the additional and decisive proofs which are to be presented as this investigation progresses, are sufficient to from a solid basis for the identity of Men-

---

*In strophe 8 Fjolsvin says of Menglad:

Menglòd of heitir,
en hana módir of gat
vid Svafrthorins syni.

Svafr alone, or as a part of a compound, indicates a Vana-god. According to an account narrated as history in Fornaldersaga (i. 415), a daughter of Thjasse was married to "king" *Svafrlami.* In the mythology it is Freyja's father, the Vana-god Njord, who gets Thjasse's daughter for his wife. The Sun-song (str. 79, 80) mentions Njord's daughters together with *Svafr* and *Svafrlogi.* The daughters are nine, like Menglad and her dises.

glad and Freyja, and as a necessary consequence for the identity of Svipdag and *Ódr*, also called *Óttarr*.

The glorious castle to which Svipdag travelled "up" is therefore Asgard, as is plain from its very description —with its gold-glittering palace, with its wall standing until Ragnarok, with its artistic gate, with its eleven watchers, with its Fjölsvin-Odin, with its asynje *Eir*, with its benevolent and lovely dises worshipped by men, with its two wolf-dogs who are to keep watch so long as the world stands, and which clear the air of *tunridur*, with its shady arbour formed by the overhanging branches of the world-tree, and with its gold-feathered cock *Vidofnir* (Völuspa's *Gullinkambi*).

Svipdag comes as a stranger to Asgard's gate, and what he there sees he has never before seen. His conversation with Fjölsvin is a series of curious questions in regard to the strange things that he now witnesses for the first time. His designation as *thursa thjodar sjólr* indicates not only that he is a stranger in Asgard, but also that he has been the foe of the Asgards. That he under such circumstances was able to secure admittance to the only way that leads to Asgard, the bridge Bifrost; that he was allowed unhindered to travel up this bridge and approach the gate unpunished, and without encountering any other annoyances than a few repelling words from Fjölsvin, who soon changes his tone and gives him such information as he desires—all this presupposes that the mythology must have had strong and satisfactory reasons for permitting a thing so unusual to take place. In several passages in Grogalder and in Fjölsvinnsmal it is hinted that the powers of fate had selected Svipdag to perform extraordinary things and gain an end the attaining of which seemed impossible. That the norns have some special purpose with him, and that Urd is to protect him and direct his course with invisible bonds, however erratic it may seem, all this gleams forth from the words of his mother Groa in the grave-chamber. And when Svipdag finally sees Menglad hasten to throw herself into his arms, he says himself that it is Urd's irresistible decree that has shaped things thus: *Urdar ordi kvedr engi madr.* But Urd's resolve alone cannot be a sufficient reason in the epic for Svipdag's adoption in Asgard, and for his gaining, though he is not of Asabirth, the extraordinary honour and good luck of becoming the husband of the fairest of the asynjes and of one of the foremost of the goddesses. Urd must have arranged the chain of events in such a manner that Menglad *desires* to possess him, that Svipdag has deserved her love, and that the Asa-gods deem it best for themselves to secure this opponent of theirs by bonds of kinship.

98.

SVIPDAG BRINGS TO ASGARD THE SWORD OF REVENGE FORGED BY VOLUND.

The most important question put to Fjölsvin by Svipdag is, of course, the one whether a stranger can enter. Fjölsvin's answer is to the effect that this is, and remains, impossible, unless the stranger brings with him a certain sword. The wall repels an uninvited comer; the gate holds him fast if he ventures to lay hands on it; of the two wolf-dogs one is always watching while the other sleeps, and no one can pass them without permission.

To this assurance on the part of Fjölsvin are added a series of questions and answers, which the author of the poem has planned with uncommon acumen. Svipdag asks if it is not, after all, possible to get past the watching dogs. There must be something in the world delicate enough to satisfy their appetite and thus turn away their attention. Fjölsvin admits that there are two delicacies that might produce this effect, but they are pieces of flesh that lie in the limbs of the cock Vidofner (str. 17, 18). He who can procure these can steal past the dogs. But the cock Vidofner sits high in the top of the world-tree and seems to be inaccessible. Is there, then, asks Svipdag, any weapon that can bring him down dead? Yes, says Fjölsvin, there is such a weapon. It was made outside of Na-gate (*nagrindr*). The smith was one *Loptr*. He was robbed (*rúinn*) of this weapon so dangerous to the gold-glittering cock, and now it is in the possession of *Sinmara,* who has laid it in a chest of tough iron beneath nine *njard*-locks (str. 25, 26).

It must have been most difficult and dangerous to go to the place where *Sinmara* has her abode and try to secure the weapon so well kept. Svipdag asks if anyone who is willing to attempt it has any hope of returning. Fjölsvin answers that in Vidofner's ankle-bones (*völum*) lies a bright, hook-shaped bone. If one can secure this, bring it to *Ludr* (the place of the lower-world mill), and give it to *Sinmara,* then she can be induced to part with the weapon in question (str. 27-30).

It appears from this that the condition on which Svipdag can get into the castle where Menglad dwells is that he shall be in possession of a weapon which was smithied by an enemy of the gods, here called *Loptr,* and thus to be compared with Loke, who actually bears this epithet. If he does not possess this weapon, which doubtless is fraught with danger to the gods, and is the only one that can kill the gold-glittering cock of the world-tree, then the gate of the citadel is not opened to him, and the watching wolf-dogs will not let him pass through it.

But Fjölsvin also indicates that under ordinary circumstances, and for one who is not particularly chosen for this purpose by Fate, it is utterly impossible to secure possession of the sword in question. Before Sinmara can be induced to lend it, it is necessary to bring Vidofner dead down from the branches of the world-tree. But to kill the cock that very weapon is needed which Sinmara cannot otherwise be induced to part with.

Meanwhile the continuation of the poem shows that what was impossible for everybody else has already been accomplished by Svipdag. When he stands at the gate of the castle in conversation with Fjölsvin he has the sword by his side, and knows perfectly well that the gate is to be opened so soon as it pleases him to put an end to the talk with Fjölsvin and pronounce his own name. The very moment he does this the gate swings on its hinges, the mighty wolf-dogs welcome (*fagna*) him, and Menglad, informed by Fjölsvin of his arrival,

hastens eagerly to meet him (str. 42, &c.). Fjölsvinnsmal, so far as acumen in plot and in execution is concerned, is the finest old poem that has been handed down
to our time, but it would be reduced to the most absurd
nonsense if the sword were not in Svipdag's possession, as
the gate is never to be opened to anyone else than to him
who brings to Menglad's castle the sword in question.

So far as the sword is concerned we have now learned:

That it was made by an artist who must have been
a foe of the gods, for Fjölsvin designates him by the
Loke-epithet *Loptr;*

That the place where the artist dwelt when he made
the weapon was situated *fyr nágrindr nedan;*

That while he dwelt there, and after he had finished
the sword, he was robbed of it (*Loptr rúinn fyr nágrindr
nedan*) ;

That he or they who robbed him of it must have been
closely related to Nat and the night discs, for the sword
was thereafter in the keeping of the night-being *Sinmara;*

That she regarded it as exceedingly precious, and also
dangerous if it came into improper hands, since she keeps
it in a "tough iron chest" beneath nine magical locks;

That the eleven guards that dwell in the same castle
with Menglad regard it as of the greatest importance to
get the sword within their castle wall;

That it has qualities like no other weapon in the world:
this sword, and it alone, can kill the golden cock on the
world-trec—a quality which seems to indicate that it
threatens the existence of the world and the gods.

It is evident that the artist who made this incomparable and terrible weapon was one of the most celebrated smiths in mythology. The question now is, whether the information given us by Fjölsvinnsmal in regard to him is sufficient to enable us to determine with certainty who he is.

The poem does not name him by any of his names, but calls him by the Loke-epithet *Loptr*, "the airy." Among the ancient smiths mentioned in our mythic fragments there is one who refers to himself with the epithet *Byrr*, "Wind," suggesting to us the same person—this one is Volund. After he in his sleep had been made prisoner by Mimer-*Nidadr* and his Njarians (see No. 87), he says when he awakes:

> Hverir 'ro iofrar
> their er a laugdo
> besti Byr sima
> oc mic bundo?

"Who are the mighty, who with bonds (*besti*, dative of *böstr*) bound the wind (*laugdo sima a Byr*) and fettered me? The expression implies that it is as easy to bind the wind as Volund. He was also able to secure his liberty again in spite of all precautions.

According to the Norse version of the Volund saga, one of the precautions resorted to is to sever the sinews of his knees (str. 17 and the prose). It is *Nidadr's* queen who causes this cruel treatment. In Fjölsvinnsmal the nameless mythic personality who deprived the "airy one" of his weapon has left it to be kept by a feminine person, *Sinmara*. The name is composed of *sin*, which means "sinew," and *mara,* which means "the one that maims." (*Mara* is related to the verb *merja,* "to maim" —see Vigfusson's Dict.) Thus *Sinmara* means "the one who maims by doing violence to the sinews." The one designated by this epithet in Fjölsvinnsmal has therefore acted the same part as Mimer-*Nidadr's* queen in the Volundarkvida.

Mimer-*Nidadr,* who imprisons Volund and robs him of his sword and the incomparable arm-ring, is the father of Nat and her sisters (see No. 85). He who robs "the airy one" of his treasures must also have been intimately related to the dises of night, else he would not have selected as keeper of the weapon Sinmara, whose quality as a being of night is manifested by the meaning *incubus nocturnes* which is the name *Mara* acquired. In Fjölsvinnsmal (str. 29) Sinmara is called *hin fölva gygr,* "the ashes-coloured giantess"—a designation pointing in the same direction.

She is also called *Eir aurglasis* (str. 28), an expression which, as I believe, has been correctly interpreted as "the dis of the shining arm-ring" (cp. Bugge Edda, p. 348). In Volundarkvida the daughter of Mimer-*Nidadr* receives Volund's incomparable arm-ring to wear.

According to Fjölsvinnsmal "the airy one" makes his weapon *fyr nágrindr nedan.* The meaning of this expression has already been discussed in No. 60. The smith has his abode in the frost-cold and foggy Nifelheim, while he is at work on the sword. Nifelheim, the land *fyr nágrindr nedan,* as we already know, is the northern subterranean border-land of Mimer's domain. The two realms are separated by Mount Hvergelmer, on which the Na-gates are set, and where the world-mill, called *Eylúdr* and *Lúdr* have their foundation-structure (see Nos. 59, 60, 79, 80). In its vicinity below the southern slope of the Hvergelmer mountain Nat has her hall (Nos. 84, 93). According to Fjölsvinnsmal Sinmara also dwells here. For Fjölsvin says that if Svipdag is to borrow the sword which she keeps, he must carry the above-mentioned hooked bone "to *Ludr* and give it to Sinmara" (*ljósan ljá skaltu i Lúdr bera Sinmöra at selja*—str. 30). *Lúdr,* the subterranean world-mill, which stands on the Nida mountain above Nat's hall, has given its name to the region where it stands. In Volundarkvida Mimer-*Nidadr* suddenly appears with his wife and daughter and armed Njarians in the remote cold Wolfdales, where Volund thinks himself secure, and no one knows whence these foes of his come. The explanation is that the "Wolfdales" of the heroic saga were in the mythology situated in Nifelheim, the border-land of Mimer's realm. Like "the airy one," Volund made his sword *fyr nágrindr nedan;* the latter, like the former, was robbed of the weapon as soon as it was finished by a lower-world ruler, whose kinswomen are discs of the night; and in the saga of the one, as of the other, one of these night dises has caused a maiming by injuring the sinews.

Thus we can also understand why Svipdag must traverse Nifelheim, "meet Nat on Nifelway," visit the world-mill, wade across Hel-rivers, and encounter Mimer himself, "the weapon-honoured." If Svipdag wants the sword made by *Loptr,* he must risk these adventures, since the sword is kept in the lower world by a kinswoman of Mimer.

The heroic saga about Volund is therefore identical with the myth concerning the maker of the sword which opens Asgard for Svipdag. The former, produced in Christian times, is only a new version of the latter. Volund is a foe of the gods, an elf-prince who was deeply insulted by beings more powerful than himself (No. 87). "The airy one" must likewise be a foe of the gods, since the weapon he has made is dangerous to the golden cock of the world-tree, and is bought by "the eleven wards" with the opening of Asgard's gate and the giving of Menglad as wife to Svipdag. Its danger to Asgard must also be suggested by Fjölsvin's statement, that the splendid hall, called *Hýrr*, "the gladdener," "the soul-stirring," that hall which is situated within the castle wall, which is encircled by vaferflames, and which from time out of mind has been celebrated among men—that this hall has already long trembled *á brodds oddi*, "on the point of the sword" (str. 32). No other weapon can here be meant than one which was fraught with the greatest danger to the safety of the gods, and which filled them with anxiety; and unless we wish to deny that there is sense and connection in the poem, this sword can be no other than that which Svipdag now has with him, and which, having been brought to Asgard, relieves the gods of their anxiety. And to repeat the points of similarity, Volund, like "Loptr," makes his weapon in the northern borderland of Mimer's domain; and when the sword is finished he is surprised by subterranean powers. In Loptr's saga, as in Volund's, a magnificent arm-ring is mentioned, and in both a dis of night received this ring to wear. In Loptr's saga, as in Volund's, a night-dis is mentioned who injures sinews. And Volund himself calls himself *Byrr*, "the wind," which is a synonym of *Loptr*.

Thus Svipdag has made a journey to the lower world to get possession of the sword of Volund, and he has been successful.

99.

SVIPDAG'S FATHER ORVANDEL, THE STAR-HERO. EXPLA-
NATION OF HIS EPITHET SÓLBJARTR.

The conversation between Fjölsvin and Svipdag ends when the latter gives his name, and requests the former to ask Menglad if she wishes to possess his love. Menglad then hastens to meet him, but before she shows what she feels for him, he must confirm with his own name and that of his father's that he really is the one he pretends to be—the one she has long been longing for. The young hero then says: *Svipdagr ek heitir, Sólbjartr hét minn fadir* (str. 47).

When Fjölsvin asked Svipdag what the name of his father was, he answered: Springcold, *Várkaldr* (str. 6); and I have already stated the reason why he was so called. Now he gives another name of his father—*Sólbjartr*— which also is a mere epithet, but still, as Svipdag must here speak plainly, it has to be such a name as can refer to his father in a distinct and definite manner.

Svipdag's mother, Groa, was married to *Örvandill hinn*

frækni (Younger Edda, 276-278). The epithet *Sólbjartr*, "he who has a brightness like that of the sun," if it really refers to Orvandel, must be justified and explained by something that the mythology had to report of him. Of Orvandel, we know from the Younger Edda that he and Groa had at least for a time been good friends of Thor; that on one of his expeditions in Jotunheim, north of the Elivagar rivers, the latter had met Orvandel and had carried him in his provision-basket across the water to his home; that Orvandel there froze his toe; that Thor broke this off, and, in honour of Orvandel, threw it up into the heavens, where it became that star which is called *Orvandel's toe*. Of ancient Teutonic star-names but very few have been handed down to our time, and it is natural that those now extant must be those of constellations or separate stars, which attracted attention on account of their appearance, or particularly on account of the strength of their light. One of them was "Orvandel's toe." By the name Orvandel (*Earendel*) a star was also known among the Teutons in Great Britain. After being converted to Christianity they regarded the *Earendel* star as a symbol of Christ. The Church had already sanctified such a view by applying to Christ the second epistle of Peter i. 19: "We have also a more sure word of prophecy; whereunto ye do well that ye take heed, as unto a light that shineth in a dark place, until the day dawn, and the day-star arise in your hearts." The morning star became, as we read in a Latin hymn, "typus Christi."

But it would be a too hasty conclusion to assume that Orvandel's star and the morning star were identical in heathen times. All that we can assert with certainty is that the former must have been one of the brightest, for the very name *Earendel* gradually became in the Old English an abstract word meaning "splendour."

Codex Exoniensis has preserved a hymn to Christ, the introductory stanzas of which appear to be borrowed from the memory of the heathen hymn to Orvandel, and to have been adapted to Christ with a slight change:

Eala Earendel	O Orvandel,
engla beorhtast,	brightest shining of angels,
ofer Middangeard	thou who over Midgard
monnum sended	art sent to men,
and sodiästa	thou true
sunnan leoma,	beam of the sun
tohrt ofer tunglas	shining above
thu tida gehvane	the lights of heaven,
of sylfum the	thou who always
symle inlihtes.	of thyself
	givest light.

From this Old English song it appears as if the Orvandel epithet *Sólbjartr* was in vogue among the Saxon tribes in England. We there find an apparent interpretation of the epithet in the phrases adapted to Earendel, "brightest (*beorhtast*) of angels" and "true beam of the sun." That Svipdag's name was well known in England, and that a Saxon royal dynasty counted him among their mythical forefathers, can be demonstrated by the genealogy of the Anglo-Saxon Chronicle. That Svipdag with sufficient distinctness might characterise his father as *Sólbjartr* is accordingly explained by the fact that Orvandel is a star-hero, and that the star bearing his name was one of the "brightest" in the heavens, and in brilliancy was like "a beam from the sun."

100.

SVIPDAG RESCUED FREYJA FROM THE HANDS OF THE GIANTS. SAXO ON OTHARUS AND SYRITHA. SVIPDAG IDENTICAL WITH OTHARUS.

When Menglad requests Svipdag to name his race and his name, she does so because she wants *jartegn* (legal evidence; compare the expression *med vitnum ok jartegnum*) that he is the one as whose wife she had been designated by the norns (*ef ek var ther kván of kvedin*—str. 46), and that her eyes had not deceived her. She also wishes to know something about his past life that may confirm that he is Svipdag. When Svipdag had given as a *jartegn* his own name and an epithet of his father, he makes only a brief statement in regard to his past life, but to Menglad it is an entirely sufficient proof of his identity with her intended husband. He says that the winds drove him on cold paths from his father's house to frosty regions of the world (str. 47). That word used by him, "drove" (*reka*), implies that he did not spontaneously leave his home, a fact which we also learn in Grogalder. On the command of his stepmother, and contrary to his own will, he departs to find Menglads, "the women fond of ornaments." His answer further shows that after he had left his father's house he had made journeys in frost-cold regions of the world. Such regions are Jotunheim and

Nifelheim, which was in fact regarded as a subterranean part of Jotunheim (see Nos. 59, 63).

Menglad has eagerly longed for the day when Svipdag should come. Her mood, when Svipdag sees her within the castle wall sitting on "the joyous mount" surrounded by asynjes and dises, is described in the poem by the verb *thruma,* "to be sunk into a lethargic, dreamy condition." When Fjölsvin approaches her and bids her "look at a stranger who may be Svipdag" (str. 43), she awakes in great agony, and for a moment she can scarcely control herself. When she is persuaded that she has not been deceived either by Fjölsvin's words or by her own eyes, she at once seals the arrival of the youth with a kiss. The words which the poem makes her lips utter testify, like her conduct, that it is not the first time she and Svipdag have met, but that it is a "meeting again," and that she long ere this knew that she possessed Svipdag's love. She speaks not only of her own longing for him, but also of his longing and love for her (str. 48-50), and is happy that "he has come again to her halls" (*at thu est aptr komin, mögr, til minna sala*—str. 49). This "again" (back), which indicates a previous meeting between Menglad and Svipdag, is found in all the manuscripts of Fjölsvinnsmal, and that it has not been added by any "betterer" trying to mend the metres of the text is demonstrated by the fact that the metre would be improved by the absence of the word *aptr.*

Meanwhile it appears with certainty from Fjölsvinnsmal that Svipdag never before had seen the castle within whose walls Menglad has *riki, eign ok audsölum* (str. 7,

8). He stands before its gate as a wondering stranger, and puts question after question to Fjölsvin in regard to the remarkable sights before his eyes. It follows that Menglad did not have her halls within this citadel, but dwelt somewhere else, at the time when she on a previous occasion met Svipdag and became assured that he loved her.

In this other place she must have resided when Svipdag's stepmother commanded him to find *Menglödum,* that is to say, Menglad, but also some one else to whom the epithet "ornament-glad" might apply. This is confirmed by the fact that this other person to whom Grogalder's words refer is not at all mentioned in Fjölsvinnsmal. It is manifest that many things had happened, and that Svipdag had encountered many adventures, between the episode described in Grogalder, when he had just been commanded by his stepmother to find "those loving ornaments," and the episode in Fjölsvinnsmal, when he seeks Menglad again in Asgard itself.

Where can he have met her before? Was there any time when Freyja did not dwell in Asgard? Völuspa answers this question, as we know, in the affirmative. The event threatening to the gods and to the existence of the world once happened that the goddess of fertility and love came into the power of the giants. Then all the high-holy powers assembled to consider "who had mixed the air with corruption and given Od's maid to the race of giants." But none of our Icelandic mythic records mentions how and by whom Freyja was liberated from the hands of the powers of frost. Under the name

Svipdag our hero is mentioned only in Grogalder and Fjölsvinnsmal; all we learn of him under the name *Ódr* and *Óttarr* is that he was Freyja's lover and husband (Völuspa, Hyndluljod) ; that he went far, far away; that Freyja then wept for him, that her tears became gold, that she sought him among unknown peoples, and that she in her search assumed many names: *Mardöll, Hörn, Gefn, Syr* (Younger Edda, 114). To get further contributions to the Svipdag myth we must turn to Saxo, where the name Svipdag should be found as Svipdagerus, *Óttar* as Otharus or Hotharus, and *Ódr* as Otherus or Hotherus.*

There cannot be the least doubt that Saxo's Otharus is a figure borrowed from the mythology and from the heroic sagas therewith connected, since in the first eight books of his *History* not a single person can be shown who is not originally found in the mythology. But the mythic records that have come down to our time know only one *Ottarr,* and he is the one who wins Freyja's heart. This alone makes it the duty of the mythologist to follow this hint here given and see whether that which Saxo relates about his Otharus confirms his identity with Svipdag-Ottar.

The Danish king Syvaldus had, says Saxo, an uncommonly beautiful daughter, Syritha, who fell into the hands of a giant. The way this happened was as follows: A woman who had a secret understanding with

*In Saxo, as in other sources of about the same time, aspirated names do not usually occur with aspiration. I have already referred to the examples Handuuanus, Andvani, Helias, Elias, Hersbernus, Esbjörn, Hevindus, Eyvindr, Horvendillus, Orvandill, Hestia, Estland, Holandia, Oland.

the giant succeeded in nestling herself in Syritha's confidence, in being adopted as her maidservant, and in enticing her to a place where the giant lay in ambush. The latter hastened away with Syritha and concealed her in a wild mountain district. When Otharus learned this he started out in search of the young maiden. He visited every recess in the mountains, found the maiden and slew the giant. Syritha was in a strange condition when Otharus liberated her. The giant had twisted and pressed her locks together so that they formed on her head one hard mass which hardly could be combed out except with the aid of an iron tool. Her eyes stared in an apathetic manner, and she never raised them to look at her liberator. It was Otharus' determination to bring a pure virgin back to her kinsmen. But the coldness and indifference she seemed to manifest toward him was more than he could endure, and so he abandoned her on the way. While she now wandered alone through the wilderness she came to the abode of a giantess. The latter made the maiden tend her goats. Still, Otharus must have regretted that he abandoned Syritha, for he went in search of her and liberated her a second time. The mythic poem from which Saxo borrowed his story must have contained a song, reproduced by him in Latin paraphrases, and in which Otharus explained to Syritha his love, and requested her, "whom he had suffered so much in seeking and finding," to give him a look from her eyes as a token that under his protection she was willing to be brought back to her father and mother. But her eyes continually stared on the ground, and apparently she remained as cold and indifferent as before. Otharus then abandoned her for the second time. From the thread of the story it appears that they were then not far from that border which separates Jotunheim from the other realms of the world. Otharus crossed that water, which in the old records is probably called the Elivagar rivers, on the opposite side of which was his father's home. Of Syritha Saxo, on the other hand, says cautiously and obscurely that "she in a manner that sometimes happened in antiquity hastened far away down the rocks"—*more pristino decursis late scopulis (Hist., 333)*—an expression which leads us to suppose that in the mythic account she had flown away in the guise of a bird. Meanwhile fate brought her to the home of Otharus' parents. Here she represented herself to be a poor traveller, born of parents who had nothing. But her refined manners contradicted her statement, and the mother of Otharus received her as a noble guest. Otharus himself had already come home. She thought she could remain unknown to him by never raising the veil with which she covered her face. But Otharus well knew who she was. To find out whether she really had so little feeling for him as her manners seemed to indicate, a pretended wedding between Otharus and a young maiden was arranged, whose name and position Saxo does not mention. When Otharus went to the bridal bed, Syritha was probably near him as bridesmaid, and carried the candle. The light or the flame burnt down, so that the fire came in contact with her hand, but she felt no pain, for there was in her heart a still more burning pain. When Otharus then requested her to take care of her hand, she finally raised her gaze from the ground, and their eyes met. Therewith the spell resting on Syritha was broken: it was plain that they loved each other and the pretended wedding was changed into a real one between Syritha and Otharus. When her father learned this he became exceedingly wroth; but after his daughter had made a full explanation to him, his anger was transformed into kindness and graciousness, and he himself thereupon married a sister of Otharus.

In regard to the person who enticed Syritha into the snare laid by the giant, Saxo is not quite certain that it was a woman. Others think, he says, that it was a man in the guise of a woman.

It has long since attracted the attention of mythologists that in this narrative there are found two names, Otharus and Syritha, which seem to refer to the myth concerning Freyja. Otharus is no doubt a Latinised form of Ottar, and, as is well known, the only one who had this name in the mythology is, as stated, Freyja's lover and husband. Syritha, on the other hand, may be a Latinised form of Freyja's epithet Syr, in which Saxo presumably supposed he had found an abbreviated form of Syri (Siri, Sigrid). In Saxo's narrative Syritha is abducted by a giant (*gigas*), with the aid of an ally whom he had procured among Freyja's attendants. In the mythology Freyja is abducted by a giant, and, as it appears from Völuspa's words, likewise by the aid of some ally who was in Freyja's service, for it is there said that the gods hold council as to who it could have been who "gave," delivered Freyja to the race of the giants (*hverr hefdi ætt jötuns Óds mey gefna*). In Saxo Otharus is of lower descent than Syritha. Saxo has not made him a son of a king, but a youth of humble birth as compared with his bride; and his courage to look up to Syritha, Saxo remarks, can only be explained by the great deeds he had performed or by his reliance on his agreeable manners and his eloquence (*sive gestarum rerum magnitudine sive comitatis et facundiæ fiducia accensus*). In the mythology Ódr was of lower birth than Freyja: he did not by birth belong to the number of higher gods; and Svipdag had, as we know, never seen Asgard before he arrived there under the circumstances described in Fjölsvinnsmal. That the most beautiful of all the goddesses, and the one second in rank to Frigg alone, she who is particularly desired by all powers, the sister of the harvest god Frey, the daughter of Njord, the god of wealth, she who with Odin shares the privilege of choosing heroes on the battlefield—that she does not become the wife of an Asa-god, but "is married to the man called *Odr*," would long since have been selected by the mythologist as a question both interesting and worthy of investigation had they cared to devote any attention to epic coherence and to premises and *dénouement* in the mythology in connection with the speculations on the signification of the myths as symbols of nature or on their ethical meaning. The view would then certainly have been reached that this *Odr* in the epic of the mythology must have been the author of exploits which balanced his humbler descent, and the mythologists would thus have been driven to direct the investigation first of all to the question whether Freyja, who we know was for some time in the power of the giants, but was rescued therefrom, did not find as her liberator this very *Odr,* who afterwards became her husband, and whether *Odr* did not by this very act gain her love and become entitled to obtain her hand. The adventure which Saxo relates actually dovetails itself into and fills a gap in that chain of events which are the result of the analysis of Grogalder and Fjölsvinnsmal. We understand that the young Svipdag is alarmed, and considers the task imposed on him by the stepmother to find Menglad far too great for his strength, if it is necessary to seek Menglad in Jotunheim and rescue her thence. We understand why on his arrival at Asgard he is so kindly received, after he has gone through the formality of giving his name, when we know that he comes not only as the feared possessor of the Volund sword, but also as the one who has restored to Asgard the most lovely and most beautiful asynje. We can then understand why the gate, which holds fast every uninvited guest, opens as of itself for him, and why the savage wolf-dogs lick him. That his words: *thadan* (from his paternal home) *rákumk vinda kalda vegu,* are to Menglad a sufficient answer to her question in regard to his previous journeys can be understood if Svipdag has, as Ottar, searched through the frost-cold Jotunheim's eastern mountain districts to find Menglad; and we can then see that Menglad in Fjölsvinnsmal can speak of her meeting with Svipdag at the gate of Asgard as a "meeting again," although Svipdag

778

never before had been in Asgard. And that Menglad receives him as a husband to whom she is already married, with whom she is now to be "united for ever" (Fjölsvinnsmal, 58), is likewise explained by the improvised wedding which Otharus celebrated with Syritha before she returns to her father.

The identity of Otharus with the *Ottarr-Odr-Svipdagr* of the mythology further appears from the fact that Saxo gives him as father an Ebbo, which a comparative investigation proves to be identical with Svipdag's father Orvandel. Of the name Ebbo and the person to whom it belongs I shall have something to say in Nos. 108 and 109. Here it must be remarked that if Otharus is identical with Svipdag, then his father Ebbo, like Svipdag's father, should appear in the history of the mythic patriarch Halfdan and be the enemy of the latter (see Nos. 24, 33). Such is also the case. Saxo produces Ebbo on the scene as an enemy of Halfdan Berggram (*Hist.*, 329, 330). A woman, Groa, is the cause of the enmity between Halfdan and Orvandel. A woman, Sygrutha, is the cause of the enmity between Halfdan and Ebbo. In the one passage Halfdan robs Orvandel of his betrothed Groa; in the other passage Halfdan robs Ebbo of his bride Sygrutha. In a third passage in his *History* (p. 138) Saxo has recorded the tradition that Horvendillus (Orvandel) is slain by a rival, who takes his wife, there called Gerutha. Halfdan kills Ebbo. Thus it is plain that the same story is told about Svipdag's father Orvandel and about Ebbo the father of Otharus and that Groa, Sygrutha, and Gerutha are different versions of the same dis of vegetation.

According to Saxo, Syritha's father was afterwards married to a sister of Otharus. In the mythology Freyja's father Njord marries Skade, who is the foster-sister and *systrunga* (sister's child) of Ottar-Svipdag (see Nos. 108, 113, 114, 115).

Freyja's surname *Hörn* (also *Horn*) may possibly be explained by what Saxo relates about the giant's manner of treating her hair, which he pressed into one snarled, stiff, and hard mass. With the myth concerning Freyja's locks, we must compare that about Sif's hair. The hair of both these goddesses is subject to the violence of the hands of giants, and it may be presumed that both myths symbolised some feature of nature. Loke's act of violence on Sif's hair is made good by the skill and goodwill of the ancient artists Sindre and Brok (Younger Edda, i. 340). In regard to Freyja's locks, the skill of a "dwarf" may have been resorted to, since Saxo relates that an iron instrument was necessary to separate and comb out the horn-hard braids. In Völuspa's list of ancient artists there is a smith by name *Hornbori,* which possibly has some reference to this.

Reasons have already been given in No. 35 for the theory that it was Gulveig-Heid who betrayed Freyja and delivered her into the hands of the giants. When Saxo says that this treachery was committed by a woman, but also suggests the possibility that it was a man in the guise of a woman, then this too is explained by the mythology, in which Gulveig-Heid, like her fellow culprit, has an androgynous nature. Loke becomes "the possessor of the evil woman" (*kvidugr af konu illri*). In

Fjölsvinnsmal we meet again with Gulveig-Heid, born again and called Aurboda, as one of Freyja's attendants, into whose graces she is nestled for a second time.

101.

SVIPDAG IN SAXO'S ACCOUNT OF HOTHERUS.

From the parallel name Otharus, we must turn to the other parallel name Hotherus. It has already been shown that if the Svipdag synonym *Odr* occurs in Saxo, it must have been Latinised into Otherus or Hotherus. The latter form is actually found, but under circumstances making an elaborate investigation necessary, for in what Saxo narrates concerning this Hotherus, he has to the best of his ability united sketches and episodes of two different mythic persons, and it is therefore necessary to separate these different elements borrowed from different sources. One of these mythic persons is *Hödr* the Asagod, and the other is *Odr*-Svipdag. The investigation will therefore at the same time contain a contribution to the researches concerning the original records of the myth of Balder.

Saxo's account of Hotherus (*Hist.*, 110, &c.), is as follows:

"Hotherus, son of Hothbrodus (Hödbrodd), was fostered in the home of Nanna's father, King Gevarus (Gevarr; see Nos. 90-92), and he grew up to be a stately youth, distinguished as a man of accomplishments among the contemporaries of his age. He could swim, was an excellent archer and boxer, and his skill on various musical instruments was so great that he had the human passions under his control, and could produce, at pleasure, gladness, sorrow, sympathy, or hate. Nanna, the daughter of Gevarus, fell in love with the highly gifted youth and he with her.

Meanwhile, fate brought it to come to pass that Balder, the son of the idol Odin, also fell in love with Nanna. He had once seen her bathing, and had been dazzled by the splendour of her limbs. In order to remove the most dangerous obstacle between himself and her, he resolved to slay Hotherus.

As Hotherus on a foggy day was hunting in the woods he got lost and came to a house, where there sat three wood-nymphs. They greeted him by name, and in answer to his question they said they were the maids who determine the events of the battle, and give defeat or success in war. Invisible they come to the battlefield, and secretly give help to those whom they wish to favour. From them Hotherus learned that Balder was in love with Nanna, but they advised him not to resort to weapons against him, for he was a demigod born of supernatural seed. When they had said this, they and the house in which Hotherus had found them disappeared, and to his joy he found himself standing on a field under the open sky.

When he arrived home, he mentioned to Gevarus what he had seen and heard, and at once demanded the hand of his daughter. Gevarus answered that it would have been a pleasure to him to see Hotherus and Nanna united, but Balder had already made a similar request, and he did not dare to draw the wrath of the latter down upon himself, since not even iron could harm the conjured body of the demigod.

But Gevarus said he knew of a sword with which Balder could be slain, but it lies locked up behind the strongest bars, and the place where it is found is scarcely accessible to mortals. The way thither—if we may use the expression where no road has been made—is filled with obstacles, and leads for the greater part through exceedingly cold regions. But behind a span of swift stags one ought to be able to get safe across the icy mountain ridges. He who keeps the sword is the forest-being Mimingus, who also has a wonderful wealth-producing arm-ring. If Hotherus gets there, he should place his tent in such a manner that its shadow does not fall into the cave where Mimingus dwells, for at the sight of this strange eclipse the latter would withdraw farther into the mountain. Observing these rules of caution, the sword and arm-ring might possibly be secured. The sword is of such a kind that victory never fails to attend it, and its value is quite inestimable.

Hotherus, who carefully followed the advice of Gevarus, succeeded in securing the sword and the ring, which Mimingus, surprised and bound by Hotherus, delivered as a ransom for his life.

When Gelder, the king of Saxony, learned that the treasure of Mimingus had been robbed, he resolved to make war against Hotherus. The foreknowing Gevarus saw this in advance, and advised Hotherus to receive the rain of javelins from the enemy patiently in the battle, and not to throw his own javelins before the enemy's supply of weapons was exhausted. Gelder was conquered, and had to pray for peace. Hotherus received him in the most friendly manner, and now he conquered him with his kindness as he had before done with his cunning as a warrior.

Hotharus also had a friend in Helgo, the king of Halogaland. The chieftain of the Finns and of the Bjarmians, Cuso (Guse), was the father of Thora, whose hand Helgo sought through messengers. But Helgo had so ugly a blemish on his mouth that he was ashamed to converse, not only with strangers, but also with his own household and friends. Cuso had already refused his offer of marriage, but as he now addressed himself to Hotherus asking for assistance, the latter was able to secure a hearing from the Finnish chieftain, so that Helgo secured the wife he so greatly desired.

While this happened in Halogaland, Balder had invaded the territory of Gevarus with an armed force, to demand Nanna's hand. Gevarus referred him to his daughter, who was herself permitted to determine her fate. Nanna answered that she was of too humble birth to be the wife of a husband of divine descent. Gevarus informed Hotherus of what had happened, and the latter took counsel with Helgo as to what was now to be done. After having considered various things, they finally resolved on making war.

And it was a war in which one should think men fought with gods. For Odin, Thor, and the hosts sanctified by the gods fought on Balder's side. Thor had a

784

heavy club, with which he smashed shields and coats-of-mail, and slew all before him. Hotherus would have seen his retreating army defeated had he not himself succeeded in checking Thor's progress. Clad in an impenetrable coat-of-mail, he went against Thor, and with a blow of his sword he severed the handle from Thor's club and made it unfit for use. Then the gods fled. Thereupon the warriors of Hotherus rushed upon Balder's fleet and destroyed and sank it. In the same war Gelder fell and his body was laid in his ship on a pile of his fallen warriors and burned but his ashes were afterwards deposited with great solemnity in a magnificent grave-mound by Hotherus who then returned to Gevarus, celebrated his wedding with Nanna, and made great presents to Helgo and Thora.

But Balder had no peace. Another war was declared, and this time Balder was the victor. The defeated Hotherus took refuge with Gevarus. In this war a water-famine occurred in Balder's army, but the latter dug deep wells and opened new fountains for his thirsty men. Meanwhile Balder was afflicted in his dreams by ghosts which had assumed Nanna's form. His love and longing so consumed him that he at last was unable to walk, but had to ride in a chariot on his journeys.

Hotherus had fled to Sweden, where he retained the royal authority; but Balder took possession of Seeland, and soon acquired the devotion of the Danes, for he was regarded as having martial merits, and was a man of great dignity. Hotherus again declared war against Balder, but was defeated in Jutland, and was obliged to re-

turn to Sweden alone and abandoned. Despondent on
account of his defeats, weary of life and the light of day,
he went into the wilderness and traversed most desolate
forests, where the fall of mortal feet is seldom heard.
Then he came to a cave in which sat three strange women.
From such women he had once received the impenetrable
coat-of-mail, and he recognised them as those very persons. They asked him why he had come to these regions, and he told them how unsuccessful he had been in
his last battle. He reproached them, saying that they
had deceived him, for they had promised him victory,
but he had a totally different fate. The women responded
that he nevertheless had done his enemies great harm,
and assured him that victory would yet perch on his ban-
ners if he should succeed in finding the wonderful nourishment which was invented for the increasing of Balder's strength. This was sufficient to encourage him to
make another war, although there were those among his
friends who dissuaded him therefrom. From different
sides men were gathered, and a bloody battle was fought,
which was not decided at the fall of night. The uneasi-
ness of Hotherus hindered him from sleeping, and he
went out in the darkness of the night to reconnoitre the
condition and position of the enemy. When he had
reached the camp of the enemy he perceived that three
dises, who were wont to prepare Balder's mysterious
food, had just left. He followed their footprints in the
bedewed grass and reached their abode. Asked by them
who he was, he said he was a player on the cithern. One
of them then handed him a cithern, and he played for them

magnificently. They had three serpents, with whose venom Balder's food was mixed. They were now engaged in preparing this food. One of them had the goodness to offer Hotherus some of the food; but the eldest said: "It would be treason to Balder to increase the strength of his foe." The stranger said that he was one of the men of Hotherus, and not Hotherus himself. He was then permitted to taste the food.* The women also presented him with a beautiful girdle of victory.

On his way home Hotherus met his foe and thrust a weapon into his side, so that he fell half-dead to the ground. This produced joy in the camp of Hotherus, but sorrow in the Danish camp. Balder, who knew that he was going to die, but was unwilling to abide death in his tent, renewed the battle the following day, and had himself carried on a stretcher into the thickest of the fight. The following night Proserpina (the goddess of death) came to him and announced to him that he should be her guest the next day. He died from his wound at the time predicted, and was buried in a mound with royal splendour. Hotherus took the sceptre in Denmark after Balder.

Meanwhile it had happened that King Gevarus had been attacked and burned in his house by a jarl under him, by name Gunno. Hotherus avenged the death of Gevarus, and burnt Gunno alive on a funeral pyre as a punishment for his crime.

Rinda and Odin had a son by name Bous. The lat-

---

*According to Gheysmer's synopsis. Saxo himself says nothing of the kind. The present reading of the passage in Saxo is distinctly mutilated.

ter, to avenge the death of his brother Balder, attacked Hotherus, who fell in the conflict. But Bous himself was severely wounded and died the following day from his wounds. Hotherus was followed on the Danish throne by his son Röricus.

In the examination of this narrative in Saxo there is no hope of arriving at absolutely positive results unless the student lays aside all current presuppositions and, in fact, all notions concerning the origin and age of the Balder-myth, concerning a special Danish myth in opposition to a special Norse-Icelandic, &c. If the latter conjecture based on Saxo is correct, then this is to appear as a result of the investigation; but the conjecture is not to be used as a presupposition.

That which first strikes the reader is that the story is not homogeneous. It is composed of elements that could not be blended into one harmonious whole. It suffers from intrinsic contradictions. The origin of these contradictions must first of all be explained.

The most persistent contradiction concerns the sword of victory of which Hotherus secured possession.* We are assured that it is of immense value (*ingens præmium*), and is attended with the success of victory (*belli fortuna comitaretur*), and Hotherus is, in fact, able with the help of this sword to accomplish a great exploit: put Thor and other gods to flight. But then Hotherus is conquered again and again by Balder, and finally also defeated by Bous and slain, in spite of the fact that Gevarus had as-

---

*This Bugge, too, has observed, and he rightly assumes that the episode concerning the sword has been interpolated from some other source.

sured him that this sword should always be victorious. To be sure, Hotherus succeeds after several defeats in giving Balder his death-wound, but this is not done in a battle, and can hardly be counted as a victory; and Hotherus is not able to commit this secret murder by aid of this sword alone, but is obliged to own a belt of victory and to eat a wonderful food, which gives Balder his strength, before he can accomplish this deed.

There must be some reason why Saxo fell into this contradiction, which is so striking, and is maintained throughout the narrative. If Hotherus-*Hödr* in the mythology possessed a sword which always gives victory and is able to conquer the gods themselves, then the mythology can *not* have contained anything about defeats suffered by him after he got possession of this sword, nor can he then have fallen in conflict with Odin's and Rind's son. The only way in which this could happen would be that Hotherus-*Hödr,* after getting possession of the sword of victory, and after once having used it to advantage, in some manner was robbed of it again. But Saxo has read nothing of the sort in his sources, otherwise he would have mentioned it, if for no other reason than for the purpose of giving a cause for the defeat suffered by his hero, and it is doubtless his opinion that the sword with which Balder is mortally wounded is the same as the one Hotherus took from Mimingus. Hence, either *Hödr* has neither suffered the defeats mentioned by Saxo nor fallen by the sword of the brother-avenging son of Odin and Rind, or he has never possessed the sword of victory here mentioned. It is not necessary to point out in which of these alternatives we have the mythological fact. *Hödr* has never possessed the irresistible sword.

But Saxo has not himself invented the episode concerning the sword of victory, nor has he introduced this episode in his narrative about Hotherus without thinking he had good reason therefor.

It follows with certainty that the episode belongs to the saga of another hero, and that things were found in that saga which made it possible for Saxo to confound him with *Hödr*.

The question then arises who this hero was. The first thread the investigation finds, and has to follow, is the name itself, Hotherus, within which Latin form Oder can lie concealed as well as *Hödr*.

In the mythology *Odr*, like *Hödr,* was an inhabitant of Asgard, but nevertheless, like *Hödr,* he has had hostile relations to Asgard, and in this connection he has fought with Thor (see No. 103). The similarity of the names and the similiarity of the mythological situation are sufficient to explain the confusion on the part of Saxo. But there are several other reasons, of which I will give one. The weapon with which Hoder slew Balder in the mythology was a young twig, *Mistelteinn.* The sword of victory made by Volund, with hostile intentions against the gods, could, for the very reason that it was dangerous to Asgard, be compared by skalds with the mistletoe, and be so called in a poetic-rhetorical figure. The fact is, that both in Skirnersmal and in Fjölsvinnsmal the Volund sword is designated as a *teinn;* that the *mistletoe*

is included in the list of sword-names in the Younger
Edda; and that in the later Icelandic saga-literature *mistelteinn* is a sword which is owned in succession by Sam-
ing, *Thráinn,* and Romund Greipson; and finally, that all
that is there said about this sword *mistelteinn* is a faithful
echo of the sword of victory made by Volund, though the
facts are more or less confused. Thus we find, for example, that it is *Máni Karl* who informs Romund where
the sword is to be sought, while in Saxo it is the moon-
god Gevar, Nanna's father, who tells Hotherus where it
lies hid. That the god *Máni* and Gevar are identical
has already been proved (see Nos. 90, 91, 92). Already
before Saxo's time the *mistelteinn* and the sword of victory of the mythology had been confounded with each
other, and Hoder's and Oder's weapons had received the
same name. This was another reason for Saxo to confound Hoder and Oder and unite them in Hotherus.
And when he found in some of his sources that a sword
mistelteinn was used by Oder, and in others that a *mistelteinn* was wielded by Hoder, it was natural that he as
a historian should prefer the sword to the fabulous mistletoe (see more below).

The circumstance that two mythical persons are united
into one in Hotherus has given Saxo free choice of making his Hotherus the son of the father of the one or of
the other. In the mythology Hoder is the son of Odin;
Oder-Svipdag is the son of Orvandel. Saxo has made
him a son of Hoddbrodd, who is identical with Orvandel.
It has already been demonstrated (see No. 29) that Helge
Hundingsbane is a copy of the Teutonic patriarch Half-

dan. The series of parallels by which this demonstration was made clear at the same time makes it manifest that Helge's rival Hoddbrodd is Halfdan's rival Orvandel. The same place as is occupied in the Halfdan myth by Orvandel, Hoddbrodd occupies in the songs concerning Helge Hundingsbane. What we had a right to expect, namely, that Saxo, when he did not make Hotherus the son of Hoder's father, should make him a son of Oder's, has actually been done, whence there can be no doubt that Hoder and Oder were united into one in Saxo's Hotherus.

With this point perfectly established, it is possible to analyse Saxo's narrative point by point, resolve it into its constituent parts, and refer them to the one of the two myths concerning Hoder and Oder to which they belong.* It has already been noted that Saxo was unable to unite organically with his narration of Hoder's adventure the episode concerning the sword of victory taken from Mimingus. The introduction of this episode has made the story of Hotherus a chain of contradictions. On the other hand, the same episode naturally adapts itself to the Svipdag-Oder story, which we already know. We have seen that Svipdag descends to the lower world and there gets into possession of the Volund sword. Hence it is Svipdag-Oder, not Hoder, who is instructed by the moon-god Gevar as to where the sword is to be found. It is he who crosses the frost-mountains, penetrates into the *specus* guarded by Mimingus, and there captures the Volund sword and the Volund ring. It is Svipdag, not

---

*This analysis will be given in the second part of this work in the treatise on the Baider-myth.

Hoder, who, thanks to this sword, is able as *thursar thjódar sjóli* to conquer the otherwise indomitable Halfdan—nay, even more, compel Halfdan's co-father and protector, the Asa-god Thor, to yield.

Thus Saxo's accounts about Otharus and Hotherus fill two important gaps in the records preserved to our time in the Icelandic sources concerning the Svipdagmyth. To this is also to be added what Saxo tells us about Svipdag under this very name (see Nos. 24, 33): that he carries on an implacable war with Halfdan after the latter had first secured and then rejected Groa; that after various fortunes of war he conquers him and gives him a mortal wound; that he takes Halfdan's and Groa's son Gudhorm into his good graces and gives him a kingdom, but that he pursues and wars against Halfdan's and Alveig-Signe's son Hadding, and finally falls by his hand.

Hotherus-Svipdag's perilous journey across the frosty mountains, mentioned by Saxo, is predicted by Groa in her seventh incantation of protection over her son:

> thann gel ek thér in sjaunda,
> ef thik sækja kemr
> frost á fjalli há
> hávetrar kuldi
> megit thinu holdi fara,
> ok haldisk æ lik at lidum.

102.

SVIPDAG'S SYNONYM EIREKR.   ERICUS DISERTUS IN SAXO.

We have not yet exhausted Saxo's contributions to the

myth concerning Svipdag. In two other passages in his *Historia Danica* Svipdag reappears, namely, in the accounts of the reigns of Frode III. and of Halfdan Berggram, in both under the name Ericus (*Eirekr*), a name applied to Svipdag in the mythology also (see No. 108).

The first reference showing that Svipdag and Erik are identical appears in the following analogies:

Halfdan (Gram), who kills a Swedish king, is attacked in war by Svipdag.

Halfdan (Berggram), who kills a Swedish king, is attacked in war by Erik.

Svipdag is the son of the slain Swedish king's daughter.

Erik is the son of the slain Swedish king's daughter.

Saxo's account of King Frode is for the greater part the myth about Frey told as history. We might then expect to find that Svipdag, who becomes Frey's brother-in-law, should appear in some *rôle* in Frode's history. The question, then, is whether any brother-in-law of Frode plays a part therein. This is actually the case. Frode's brother-in-law is a young hero who is his general and factotum, and is called Ericns, with the surname *Disertus,* the eloquent. The Ericus who appears as Halfdan's enemy accordingly resembles Svipdag, Halfdan's enemy, in the fact that he is a son of the daughter of the Swedish king slain by Halfdan. The Ericus who is Frode-Frey's general, again, resembles Svipdag in the fact that he marries Frode-Frey's sister. This is another indication that Erik and Svipdag were identical in Saxo's mythic sources.

Let us now pursue these indications and see whether they are confirmed by the stories which Saxo tells of Halfdan's enemy Erik and Frode-Frey's brother-in-law, Erik the eloquent.

Saxo first brings us to the paternal home of Erik the eloquent. In the beginning of the narrative Erik's mother is already dead and his father is married a second time (*Hist.*, 192). Compare with this the beginning of Svipdag's history, where his mother, according to Grogalder, is dead, and his father is married again.

The stepmother has a son, by name Rollerus, whose position in the myth I shall consider hereafter. Erik and Roller leave their paternal home to find Frode-Frey and his sister Gunvara, a maiden of the most extraordinary beauty. Before they proceed on this adventurous journey Erik's stepmother, Roller's mother, has given them a wisdom-inspiring food to eat, in which one of the constituent parts was the fat of three serpents. Of this food the cunning Erik knew how to secure the better part, really intended for Roller. But the half-brothers were faithful friends.

From Saxo's narrative it appears that Erik had no desire at all to make this journey. It was Roller who first made the promise to go in search for Frode and his sister, and it was doubtless Erik's stepmother who brought about that Erik should assist his brother in the accomplishment of the task. Erik himself regarded the resolve taken by Roller as surpassing his strength (*Hist.*, 193).

This corresponds with what Grogalder tells us about

795

Svipdag's disinclination to perfom the task imposed on him by his stepmother. This also gives us the key to Grogalder's words, that Svipdag was commanded to go and find not only "the one fond of ornaments," but *"those fond of ornaments"* (*koma móti Menglödum*). The plural indicates that there is more than one "fond of ornaments" to be sought. It is necessary to bring back to Asgard not only Freyja, but also Frey her brother, the god of the harvests, for whom the ancient artists made ornaments, and who as a symbol of nature is the one under whose supremacy the forces of vegetation in nature decorate the meadows with grass and the fields with grain. He, too, with his sister, was in the power of the giant-world in the great fimbul-winter (see below).

The food to which serpents must contribute one of the constituent parts reappears in Saxo's account of Hotherus (*Hist.*, 123; No. 101), and is there described with about the same words. In both passages three serpents are required for the purpose. That Balder should be nourished with this sort of food is highly improbable. The serpent food in the stories about Hotherus and Ericus has been borrowed from the Svipdag-myth.

The land in which Frode and his beautiful sister live is difficult of access, and magic powers have hitherto made futile every effort to get there. The attendants of the brother and sister there are described as the most savage, the most impudent, and the most disagreeable that can be conceived. They are beings of the most disgusting kind, whose manners are as unrestrained as their words. To get to this country it is necessary to cross an ocean, where storms, conjured up by witchcraft, threaten every. sailor with destruction.

Groa has predicted this journey, and has sung a magic song of protection over her son against the dangers which he is to meet on the magic sea:

thann gel ek thér inn sétta
ef thú á sjó kemr
meira en menn viti:
logn ok lögr
gangi thér i lúdr saman
ok ljái thér æ friddrjúgrar farar.

When Erik and Roller, defying the storms, had crossed this sea and conquered the magic power which hindered the approach to the country, they entered a harbour, near which Frode and Gunvara are to be sought. On the strand they meet people who belong to the attendants of the brother and sister. Among them are three brothers, all named Grep, and of whom one is Gunvara's pressing and persistent suitor. This Grep, who is a poet and orator of the sort to be found in that land, at once enters into a discussion with Erik. At the end of the discussion Grep retires defeated and angry. Then Erik and Roller proceed up to the abode where they are to find those whom they seek. Frode and Gunvara are met amid attendants who treat them as princely persons, and look upon them as their court-circle. But the royal household is of a very strange kind, and receives visitors with great hooting, barking of dogs, and insulting manners. Frode occupies the high-seat in the hall, where a great fire is burning as a protection against the bitter cold.

It is manifest from Saxo's description that Frode and Gunvara, possibly by virtue of the sorcery of the giants, are in a spiritual condition in which they have almost forgotten the past, but without being happy in their present circumstances. Frode feels unhappy and degraded. Gunvara loathes his suitor Grep. The days here spent by Erik and Roller, before they get an opportunity to take flight with Gunvara, form a series of drinking-bouts, vulgar songs, assaults, fights, and murders. The jealous Grep tries to assassinate Erik, but in this attempt he is slain by Roller's sword. Frode cannot be persuaded to accompany Erik, Roller, and Gunvara on this flight. He feels that his life is stained with a spot that cannot be removed, and he is unwilling to appear with it among other men. In the mythology it is left to Njord himself to liberate his son. In another passage (*Hist.,* 266, 267) Saxo says that King Fridlevus (Njord) liberated a princely youth who had been robbed by a giant. In the mythology this youth can hardly be anyone else than the young Frey, the son of the liberator. Erik afterwards marries Gunvara.

Among the poetical paraphrases from heathen times are found some which refer to Frey's and Freyja's captivity among the giants. In a song of the skald Kormak the mead of poetry is called *jastrin fontanna Sýrar Greppa,* "the seething flood of the sea ranks (of the skerry) of Syr (of Freyja) of the Greps." This paraphrase evidently owes its existence to an association of ideas based on the same myth as Saxo has told in his way. *Sýr,* as we know, is one of Freyja's surnames, and as to its meaning, one which she must have acquired during her sojourn in Jotunheim, for it is scarcely applicable to her outside of Jotunheim. *Greppr,* ,the poet there, as we have already seen, is Freyja's suitor. He has had brothers also called *Greppr,* whence the plural expression *Sýrs Greppa* ("Syr's Greps"), wherein Freyja's surname is joined with more than one Grep, receives its mythological explanation. The giant abode where Frode and Gunvara sojourn, is according to Saxo, situated not far from the harbour where Erik and Roller entered (*portum a quo Frotho non longe deversabatur—Hist.,* 198). The expression "the Greps of Syr's skerries" thus agrees with Saxo.

A northern land uninhabited by man is by Eyvind Skaldaspiller called *utröst Belja dolgs,* "the most remotely situated abode of Bele's enemy (Frey)." This paraphrase is also explained by the myth concerning Frey's and Freyja's visit in Jotunheim. *Beli* is a giant-name, and means "the howler." Erik and Roller, according to Saxo, are received with a horrible howl by the giants who attend Frey. "They produced horrible sounds like those of howling animals" (*ululantium more horrisonas dedere voces*). To the myth about how Frey fell into the power of the giants I shall come later (see Nos. 109, 111, 112).

Erik is in Saxo called *disertus,* the eloquent. The Svipdag epithet *Ódr* originally had a meaning very near to this. The impersonal *ódr* means partly the reflecting element in man, partly song and poetry, the ability of expressing one's self skilfully and of joining the words in an agreeable and persuasive manner (cp. the Gothic *weit-wodan,* to convince). Erik demonstrates the propriety of his name. Saxo makes him speak in proverbs and sentences, certainly for the reason that his Northern source has put them on the lips of the young hero. The same quality characterises Svipdag. In Grogalder his mother sings over him: "Eloquence and social talents be abundantly bestowed upon you;" and the description of him in Fjölsvinnsmal places before our eyes a nimble and vivacious youth who well understands the watchman's veiled words, and on whose lips the speech develops into proverbs which fasten themselves on the mind. Compare *augna gamans,* &c. (str. 5), and the often quoted *Urdar ordi kvedr engi madr* (str. 47).

Toward Gunvara Erik observes the same chaste and chivalrous conduct as Otharus toward Syritha (*intacta illi pudicitia manet*—p. 216). As to birth, he occupies the same subordinate position to her as *Ódr* to Freyja, Otharus to Syritha, Svipdag to Menglad.

The adventures related in the mythology from Svipdag's journey, when he went in search of Freyja-Menglad, are by Saxo so divided between Ericus Disertus and Otharus that of the former is told the most of what happened to Svipdag during his visit in the giant abode, of the latter the most of what happened to him on his way thence to his home.

Concerning Erik's family relations, Saxo gives some facts which, from a mythological point of view, are of great value. It has already been stated that Erik's mother, like Svipdag's, is dead, and that his father, like

Svipdag's, is married a second time where his saga begins. The father begets with his second wife a son, whom Saxo calls Rollerus. When Erik's father also is dead, Roller's mother, according to Saxo, marries again, and this time a powerful champion called Brac (*Hist.*, 217), who in the continuation of the story (p. 217, &c.) proves himself to be *Asa-Brage,* the god Thor (cp. No. 105), to whom she brings her son Roller. In our mythological records we learn that Thor's wife was Sif, the goddess of vegetation, and that Sif had been married and had had a son, by name *Ullr,* before she became the wife of the Asa-god, and that she brought with her to Asgard this son, who became adopted among the gods. Thus the mythic records and Saxo correspond in these points, and it follows that Rollerus is the same as Uller, whom Saxo elsewhere (*Hist.*, 130, 131; cp. No. 36) mentions as Ollerus. The forms Ollerus and Rollerus are to each other as *Olfr* to *Hrólfr. Hrólfr* is a contraction of *Hród-úlfr;* Rollerus indicates a contraction of *Hród-Ullr, Hríd-Ullr.* The latter form occurs in the paraphrase *Hrídullr hrotta,* "the sword's storm-Ull," a designation of a warrior (Grett., 20, 1). It has already been pointed out that in the great war between Odin's clan and the Vans, Ull, although Thor's stepson, takes the side of the Vans and identifies his cause with that of Frey and Svipdag. Saxo also describes the half-brothers as faithfully united, and, in regard to Roller's reliable fraternity, makes Erik utter a sentence which very nearly corresponds to the Danish:

"End svige de Sorne
og ikke de Baarne"

(*Hist.,* 207—*optima est affinium opera opis indigo*).
Saxo's account of Erik and Roller thus gives us the key
to the mythological statements, not otherwise intelligible,
that though Ull has in Thor a friendly stepfather (cp.
the expression *gulli Ullar*—Younger Edda, i. 302), and
in Odin a clan-chief who distinguishes him (cp. *Ullar
hylli,* &c.—Grimnersmal, 42), nevertheless he contends
in this feud on the same side as Erik-Svipdag, with whom
he once set out to rescue Frey from the power of the
giants. The mythology was not willing to sever those
bonds of fidelity which youthful adventurers shared in
common had established between Frey, Ull, and Svipdag. Both the last two therefore associate themselves
with Frey when the war breaks out between the Asas and
Vans.

It follows that Sif was the second wife of Orvandel
the brave before she became Thor's and that Ull is Orvandel's son. The intimate relation between Orvandel on
the one side and Thor on the other has already been
shown above. When Orvandel was out on adventures
in Jotunheim his first wife Groa visited Thor's halls as
his guest, where the dis of vegetation might have a safe
place of refuge during her husband's absence. This feature preserved in the Younger Edda is of great mythological importance, and, as I shall show further on, of
ancient Aryan origin. Orvandel, the great archer and
star-hero, reappears in Rigveda and also in the Greek
mythology—in the latter under the name Orion, as Vigfusson has already assumed. The correctness of the assumption is corroborated by reasons, which I shall present later on. 802

103.

THE SVIPDAG SYNONYM EIRIKR (*continued*).

We now pass to that Erik whom Saxo mentions in his narrative concerning Halfdan-Berggram, and who, like Svipdag, is the son of a Swedish king's daughter. This king had been slain by Halfdan. Just as Svipdag undertakes an irreconcilable war of revenge against Halfdan-Gram, so does Erik against Halfdan-Berggram. In one of their battles Halfdan was obliged to take flight, despite his superhuman strengh and martial luck. More than this, he has by his side the "champion Thoro," and Saxo himself informs us that the latter is no less a personage than the Asa-god Thor, but he too must yield to Erik, Thor's Mjolner and Halfdan's club availed nothing against Erik. In conflict with him their weapons seemed edgeless (*Hist.*, 323, 324).

Thus not only Halfdan, but even Thor himself, Odin's mighty son, he who alone outweighs in strength all the other descendants and clansmen of Odin, was obliged to retreat before a mythical hero; and that his lightning hammer, at other times irresistible, Sindre's wonderful work, is powerless in this conflict, must in the mythology have had particular reasons. The mythology has scarcely permitted its favourite, "Hlodyn's celebrated son," to be subjected to such a humiliation more than once, and this fact must have had such a motive, that the event might be regarded as a solitary exception. It must therefore be borne in mind that, in his narrative concerning Hotherus, Saxo states, that after the latter had acquired the sword of victory guarded by Mimingus, he meets the Asa-god Thor in a battle and forces him to yield, after the former has severed the hammer from its handle with a blow of the sword (*Hist.,* 118; see No. 101). It has already been shown that *Ódr*-Svipdag, not *Hödr,* is the Hotherus who captured the sword of victory and aecomplished this deed (see No. 101). Erik accordingly has, in common with Svipdag, not only those features that he is the daughter-son of a Swedish king whom Halfdan had slain, and that he persists in making war on the latter, but also that he accomplished the unique deed of putting Thor to flight.

Thus the hammer Mjolner is found to have been a weapon which, in spite of its extraordinary qualities, is inferior to the sword of victory forged by Volund (see Nos. 87, 98). Accordingly the mythology has contained two famous judgments on products of the ancient artists. The first judgment is passed by the Asa-gods in solemn consultation, and in reference to this very hammer, Mjolner, explains that Sindre's products are superior to those of Ivalde's sons. The other judgment is passed on the field of battle, and confirms the former judgment of the gods. Mjolner proves itself useless in conflict with the sword of victory. If now the Volund of the heroic traditions were one of the Ivalde sons who fails to get the prize in the mythology, then an epic connection could be found between the former and the latter judgment: the insulted Ivalde son has then avenged himself on the gods and re-established his reputation injured by them. I shall recur to the question whether Volund was a son of Ivalde or not.

The wars between Erik and Halfdan were, according to Saxo, carried on with changing fortunes. In one of these conflicts, which must have taken place before Erik secured the irresistible sword, Halfdan is victorious and takes Erik prisoner; but the heart of the victor is turned into reconciliation toward the inexorable foe, and he offers Erik his life and friendship if the latter will serve his cause. But when Erik refuses the offered conciliation, Halfdan binds him fast to a tree in order to make him the prey of the wild beasts of the forest and abandons him to his fate. Halfdan's desire to become reconciled with Erik, and also the circumstance that he binds him, is predicted, in Grogalder (strs. 9, 10), by Svipdag's mother among the fortunes that await her son:

thann gel ek thér inn fjórda
ef thik fjándr standa
görvir á galgvegi:
bugr theim hverfi
til handa ther mætti,
ok snuisk theim til sátta sefi.

thann gel ek pér inn fimta
ef thér fjöturr verdr
borinn at boglimum:
Leifnis elda læt ek thér
fyr legg of kvedinn,
ok stökkr thá láss af limum,
en af fótum fjöturr.

The Svipdag synonyms so far met with are: Ódr (Hotherus), Óttarr (Otharus), and Eirekr (Ericus).

It is remarkable, but, as we shall find later, easy to explain that this saga-hero, whom the mythology made

Freyja's husband, and whose career was adorned with such strange adventures, was not before the ninth century, and that in Sweden, accorded the same rank as the Asa-gods, and this in spite of the fact that he was adopted in Asgard, and despite the fact that his half-brother Ull was clothed with the same dignity as that of the Asa-gods. There is no trace to show that he who is Freyja's husband and Frey's brother-in-law was generally honoured with a divine title, with a temple, and with sacrifices. He remained to the devotees of the mythology what he was —a brilliant hero, but nothing more; and while the saga on the remote antiquity of the Teutons made him a ruler of North Teutonic tribes, whose leader he is in the war against Halfdan and Hadding (see Nos. 33, 38), he was honoured as one of the oldest kings of the Scandinavian peoples, but was not worshipped as a god. As an ancient king he has received his place in the middle-age chronicles and genealogies of rulers now under the name Svipdag, now under the name Erik. But, at the same time, his position in the epic was such that, if the Teutonic Olympus was ever to be increased with a divinity of Asa-rank, no one would have a greater right than he to be clothed with this dignity. From this point of view light is shed on a passage in ch. 26 of *Vita Ansgarii.* It is there related, that before Ansgarius arrived in Birka, where his impending arrival was not unknown, there came thither a man (doubtless a heathen priest or skald) who insisted that he had a mission from the gods to the king and the people. According to the man's statement, the gods had held a meeting, at which he himself had been present,

IDUN BROUGHT BACK TO ASGARD.

(From an etching by Lorenz Frölich.)

N pursuance of a promise made by Loke to secure his release, he beguiled Idun out of Asgard and into the power of giant Thjasse. Idun was keeper of the apples upon which the gods d to renew their youth and her disappearance from Asgard was, therefore, followed by rapid ageing, into decrepitude, of the gods. They discovered that Loke was the scoundrel who had caused Idun's betrayal and threatened him with death if he failed to bring her back. Accordingly Loke borrowed Freyja's falcon plumage and flew to Jotunheim—home of the giants. Thjasse was at sea fishing, so Loke quickly found Idun, whom he transformed into a nut and hastened with her to Asgard. Thjasse soon learned what had happened and on eagle wings he pursued the fleeing Loke but his coming was seen by Heim-dal, warder of Asgard's gate, and by his orders a fire was quickly made on the walls, which scorched Thjasse's wings as he flew over and he fell into the power of the gods who promptly slew him.

See pages 890, 959, 809, 960.

Freyja's husband, and whose mother was
such strange adventures, was not before
tury, and that in Sweden, accorded the same rank as the
Asa-gods, and this in spite of the fact that he was adopted
in Asgard, and despite the fact that his half-brother Ull
was clothed with the same dignity as that of the Asa-gods.
There is no trace to show that he who is Freyja's husband
and Frey's brother-in-law was generally honoured with a
divine title, with a temple, and with sacrifices.
remained sons of Asgard and once the power of giants
—a being which upon which the saga
on the realm most importance from Asgard
of North

one would have be clothed
with this dignity. From a Swedish point of view light is shed
on a passage in ch. 26 of his Asgard. It is there related, that before Asgard's
impending arrival was not unknown, there came thither
a man (doubtless a heathen
that he had a mission from the gods
people. According to the man's statement, the gods
had held a meeting, at which he himself had been present,

and in which they unanimously had resolved to adopt in their council that King Erik who in antiquity had ruled over the Swedes, so that he henceforth should be one of the gods (*Ericum, quondam regem vestrum, nos unanimes in collegiam nostrum ascisimus, ut sit unus de numero deorum*); this was done because they had perceived that the Swedes were about to increase the number of their present gods by adopting a stranger (Christ) whose doctrine could not be reconciled with theirs, and who accordingly did not deserve to be worshipped. If the Swedes wished to add another god to the old ones, under whose protection the country had so long enjoyed happiness, peace, and plenty, they ought to accord to Erik, and not to the strange god, that honour which belongs to the divinities of the land. What the man who came to Birka with this mission reported was made public, and created much stir and agitation. When Ansgarius landed, a temple had already been built to Erik, in which supplications and sacrifices were offered to him. This event took place at a time foreboding a crisis for the ancient Odinic religion. Its last bulwarks on the Teutonic continent had recently been levelled with the ground by Charlemagne's victory over the Saxons. The report of the cruelties practised by the advocates of the doctrine, which invaded the country from the south and the west for the purpose of breaking the faith of the Saxon Odin worshippers towards their religion, had certainly found its way to Scandinavia, and doubtless had its influence in encouraging that mighty effort made by the northern peoples in the ninth century to visit and conquer on their own territory their Teutonic kinsmen who had been converted to Christianity. It is of no slight mythological interest to learn that zealous men among the Swedes hoped to be able to inspire the old doctrine with new life by adopting among the gods Freyja's husband, the most brilliant of the ancient mythic heroes and the one most celebrated by the skalds. I do not deem it impossible that this very attempt made Erik's name hated among some of the Christians, and was the reason why "Old Erik" became a name of the devil. *Vita Ansgarii* says that it was the devil's own work that Erik was adopted among the gods.

The Svipdag synonym Erik reappears in the Christian saga about Erik Vidforle (the far-travelled), who succeeded in finding and entering *Odainsakr* (see No. 44). This is a reminiscence of Svipdag's visit in Mimer's realm. The surname *Vidförli* has become connected with two names of Svipdag: we have *Eirikr hinn vidförli* and *Ódr* (*Oddr*) *hinn vidförli* in the later Icelandic sagas.

104.

THE LATER FORTUNES OF THE VOLUND SWORD.

I have now given a review of the manner in which I have found the fragments of the myth concerning Svipdag up to the point where he obtains Freyja as his wife. The fragments dove-tail into each other and form a consecutive whole. Now, a few words in regard to the part afterwards played by the Volund sword, secured by Svipdag in the lower world, in the mythology, and in the saga. The sword, as we have seen, is the prize for which Asgard opens its gate and receives Svipdag as Freyja's husband. We subsequently find it in Frey's possession. Once more the sword becomes the price of a bride, and passes into the hands of the giant Gymer and his wife. It has already been demonstrated that Gymer's wife is the same Angerboda who, in historical times and until Ragnarok, dwells in the Ironwood (see No. 35). Her shepherd, who in the woods watches her monster flocks, also keeps the sword until the fire-giant Fjalar shall appear in his abode in the guise of the red cock and bring it to his own father Surt, in whose hand it shall cause Frey's death, and contribute to the destruction of the world of gods.

A historian, Priscus, who was Attila's contemporary, relates that the Hun king got possession of a divine sword that a shepherd had dug out of the ground and presented to him as a gift. The king of the Huns, it is added, rejoiced in the find; for, as the possessor of the sword that had belonged to the god "Mars," he considered himself as armed with authority to undertake and carry on successfully any war he pleased (see Jordanes, who quotes Priscus).

On the Teutonic peoples the report of this pretended event must have made a mighty impression. It may be that the story was invented for this purpose; for their myths told of a sword of victory which was owned by that god who, since the death of Balder, and since Tyr became one-handed, was, together with Thor, looked upon as the bravest of the warlike gods, which sword had been carried away from Asgard to the unknown wildernesses of the East, where it had been buried, not to be produced again before the approach of Ragnarok, when it was to be exhumed and delivered by a shepherd to a foe of mankind. Already, before this time, the Teutons had connected the appearance of the Huns with this myth. According to Jordanes, they believed that evil troll-women, whom the Gothic king Filimer had banished from his people, had taken refuge in the wildernesses of the East, and there given birth to children with forest giants ("satyres"), which children became the progenitors of the Huns. This is to say, in other words, that they believed the Huns were descended from Angerboda's progeny in the Ironwood, which, in the fulness of time, were to break into Midgard with the monster Hate as their leader. The sword which the god Frey had possessed, and which was concealed in the Ironwood, becomes in Jordanes a sword which the god "Mars" had owned, and which, thereafter, had been concealed in the earth. Out of Angerboda's shepherd, who again brings the sword into daylight and gives it to the world-hostile Fjalar, becomes a shepherd who exhumes the sword and gives it to Attila, the foe of the Teutonic race.

The memory of the sword survived the victory of Christianity, and was handed down through the centuries in many variations. That Surt at the end of the world was to possess the sword of course fell away, and instead now one and then another was selected as the hero who was to find and take it; that it was watched by a woman and by a man (in the mythology Angerboda and Egg-ther); and that the woman was an even more disgusting being than the man, were features that the saga retained both on the Continent and in England.

The Beowulf poem makes a monster, by name Grendel ("the destroyer"), dwell with his mother under a marsh in a forest, which, though referred to Denmark and to the vicinity of the splendid castle of a Danish king, is described in a manner which makes it highly probable that the prototype used by the Christian poet was a heathen skald's description of the Ironwood. There is, says he, the mysterious land in which the wolf conceals himself, full of narrow valleys, precipices, and abysses, full of dark and deep forests, marshes shrouded in gloom, lakes shaded with trees, nesses lashed by the sea, mountain torrents and bogs, which in the night shine as of fire, and shelter demoniac beings and dragons in their turbid waves. The hunted game prefers being torn into pieces by dogs to seeking its refuge on this unholy ground, from which raging storms chase black clouds until the heavens are darkened and the rain pours down in torrents. The English poet may honestly have located the mythological Ironwood in Denmark. The same old border-land, which to this very day is called "Dänische wold," was still in the thirteenth century called by the Danes Jarnwith, the Ironwood. From his abode in this wilderness Grendel makes nightly excursions to the Danish royal castle, breaks in there, kills sleeping champions with his iron hands, sucks out their blood, and carries their corpses to the enchanted marsh in order to eat them there. The hero, Beowulf, who has heard of this, proceeds to Denmark, penetrates into the awful forest, dives, armed with

Denmark's best sword, down into the magic marsh to Grendel's and his mother's hall, and kills them after a conflict in which the above-mentioned sword was found useless. But down there he finds another which Grendel and his mother kept concealed, gets possession of it, and conquers with its aid.

Of this remarkable sword it is said that it was "rich in victory," that it hailed from the past, that "it was a good and excellent work of a smith," and that the golden hilt was the work of the "wonder-smith." On the blade was risted (engraved) "that ancient war" when "the billows of the raging sea washed over the race of giants," and on a plate made of the purest gold was written in runes "the name of him for whom this weapon was first made." The Christian poet found it most convenient for his purpose not to name this name for his readers or hearers. But all that is here stated is applicable to the mythological sword of victory. "The Wonder-smith" in the Old English tale is Volund (Weland). The coat of mail ⊾ borne by Beowulf is "Welandes geweorc." "Deor the Scald's Complaint" sings of Weland, and King Alfred in his translation of Boethius speaks of "the wise Weland, the goldsmith, who, in ancient times, was the most celebrated." That the Weland sword was "the work of a ⌐ giant" corresponds with the Volund myth (see below); and as we here learn that the blade was engraved with pictures representing the destructions of the ancient giant-artists in the waves of the sea (the blood of the primeval giant Ymer), then this illustrates a passage in Skirnersmal where it is likewise stated that the sword was risted with images and "that it fights of itself against the giant race" (Skirnersmal, 8, 23, 25; see No. 60). This expression is purposely ambiguous. One meaning is emphasised by Frey's words in Skirnersmal, that it fights of itself "if it is a wise man who owns it" (*ef sá er horscr er hefir*). The other meaning of the expression appears from the Beowulf poem. The sword itself fights against the giant race in the sense that the "wonder-smith" (Weland), by the aid of pictures on the blade of the sword itself, represented that battle which Odin and his brothers fought against the primeval giants. when the former drowned the latter in the blood of their progenitor, the giant Ymer.

Grendel is the son of the troll-woman living in the marsh, just as Hate is Angerboda's. The author identifies Grendel with Cain banished from the sight of his Creator, and makes giants, thurses, and "elves" the progeny of the banished one. Grendel's mother is a "she-wolf of the deep" and a mermaid (*merewif*). Angerboda is the mother of the wolf progeny in the Ironwood and "drives the ships into Ægir's jaws." What "Beowulf" tells about Grendel reminds us in some of the details so strongly of Völuspa's words concerning Hate that the question may be raised whether the English author did not have in mind a strophe resembling the one in Völuspa which treats of him. Völuspa's Hate *fyllisk fjörvi feigra manna,* "satiates himself with the vital force of men selected for death." Beowulf's Grendel sucks the blood of his chosen victims until life ebbs out of them. Völuspa's Hate *rydr ragna sjöt raudum dreyra,* "colours the princely abode with red blood from the wounds." Grendel steals into the royal castle and stains it with blood. The expression here reappears almost literally. Völuspa's *ragna sjöt* and *dreyri* corres- pond perfectly to "Beowulf's" *driht-sele* and *dreor.* ⊬

In Vilkinasaga we read that Nagelring, the best sword in the world was concealed in a forest, and was there watched by a woman and a man. The man had the strength of twelve men, but the woman was still stronger. King Thidrek and his friend Hildebrand succeeded after a terrible combat in slaying the monster. The woman had to be slain thrice in order that she should not come to life again. This feature is also borrowed from the myth about Angerboda, the thrice slain.

Historia Pontificum (from the middle of the twelfth century) informs us that Duke Wilhelm of Angoulême (second half of the tenth century) possessed an extra- ordinary sword made by Volund. But this was not the real sword of victory. From Jordane's history it was known in the middle age that this sword had fallen into Attila's hands, and the question was naturally asked what afterwards became of it. Sagas answered the ques- tion. The sword remained with the descendants of the Huns, the Hungarians. The mother of the Hungarian king Solomon gave it to one Otto of Bavaria. He lent it to the margrave of Lausitz, Dedi the younger. After the murder of Dedi it came into the hands of Emperor Henry IV., who gave it to his favourite, Leopold of Merseburg. By a fall from his horse Leopold was wounded by the point of the sword, and died from the

wound. Even in later times the sword was believed to
exist, and there were those who believed that the Duke of
Alba bore it at his side.

105.

THE SVIPDAG EPITHET SKIRNER.   THE VOLUND SWORD'S NAME GAMBANTEIN.

After Svipdag's marriage with Freyja the saga of his
life may be divided into two parts—the time before his
visit in Asgard as Freyja's happy husband and Frey's
best friend, and the time of his absence from Asgard and
his change and destruction.

To the former of these divisions belongs his journey,
celebrated in song, to the abode of the giant Gymer,
whither he proceeds to ask, on Frey's behalf, for the hand
of Gerd, Gymer's and Aurboda's fair daughter. It has
already been pointed out that after his marriage with
Gunvara-Freyja, Erik-Svipdag appears in Saxo as
Frotho-Frey's right hand, ready to help and a trusted
man in all things. Among other things the task is also
imposed on him to ask, on behalf of Frotho, for the hand
of a young maid whose father in the mythology doubtless
was a giant. He is described as a deceitful, treacherous
being, hostile to the gods, as a person who had laid a
plan with his daughter as a bait to deceive Frotho and
win Gunvara for himself. The plan is frustrated by
Svipdag (Ericus), Ull (Rollerus), and Thor (Bracus),
the last of whom here appears in his usual *rôle* as the con-

815

queror of giants. At the very point when Frotho's intended father-in-law thinks he has won the game Thor rushes into his halls, and the schemer is compelled to save himself by flight (*Hist.,* 221, &c.). In the excellent poem Skirnersmal, the Icelandic mythic fragments have preserved the memory of Frey's courtship to a giant-maid, daughter of Aurboda's terrible husband, the giant-chief Gymer. Here, as in Saxo, the Vana-god does not himself go to do the courting, but sends a messenger, who in the poem is named by the epithet Skirner. All that is there told about this Skirner finds its explanation in Svipdag's saga. The very epithet *Skirnir,* "the shining one," is justified by the fact that Solbjart-Orvandel, the star-hero, is his father. Skirner dwells in Asgard, but is not one of the ruling gods. The one of the gods with whom he is most intimately united is Frey. Thus his position in Asgard is the same as Svipdag's. ' Skirner's influence with Freyja's brother is so great that when neither Njord nor Skade can induce the son to reveal the cause of the sorrow which afflicts him, they hope that Skirner may be able to do so. Who, if not Svipdag, who tried to rescue Frey from the power of the giants, and who is his brother-in-law, and in Saxo his all in all, would be the one to possess such influence over him? Skirner also appeals to the fact that Frey and he have in days past had adventures together of such a kind that they ought to have faith in each other, and that Frey ought not to have any secret which he may not safely confide to so faithful a friend (str. 5). Skirner is wise and poetic, and has proverbs on his lips like Svipdag-Erik (cp. str. 13 in Skirnersmal with str. 47 in Fjölsvinnsmal). But the conclusive proof of their identity is the fact that Skirner, like Svipdag, had made a journey to the lower world, had been in Mimer's realm at the foot of Ygdrasil, and there had fetched a sword called Gambantein, which is the same sword as the one Frey lays in his hand when he is to go on his errand of courtship—the same sword as Frey afterwards parts with as the price paid to Gymer and Aurboda for the bride. When Gerd refuses to accept the courtship-presents that Skirner brings with him, he draws his sword, shows its blade to Gerd, threatens to send her with its edge to Nifelhel, the region below the Na-gates, the Hades-dwelling of Hrimner, Hrimgrimner, and of other giants of antiquity, the abode of the furies of physical sicknesses (see No. 60), and tells her how this terrible weapon originally came into his possession:

> Til holtz ec gecc
> oc til brás vidar
> gambantein at geta,
> gambantein ec gat.

> "I went to Holt
> And to the juicy tree
> Gambantein to get,
> Gambantein I got."

The word *teinn*, a branch, a twig, has the meaning of sword in all the compounds where it occurs: *benteinn, bifteinn, eggteinar, hœvateinn (homateinn), hjörteinn, hrœteinn, sárteinn, valteinn.* *Mistelteinn* has also become the name of a sword (Younger Edda, i. 564; Fornald., i, 416, 515; ii. 371; cp. No. 101), and the same weapon as is here called *gambanteinn* is called *hævateinn, homateinn* (see further No. 116) in Fjölsvinnsmal.

In the mythology there is only one single place which is called Holt. It is *Mimis holt, Hoddmimis holt,* the subterranean grove, where the children who are to be the parents of the future race of man have their secure abode until the regeneration of the world (see Nos. 52, 53), living on the morning-dew which falls from the world-tree, *hrár vidr,* "the tree rich in sap" (see No. 89). Mimer-Nidhad also comes from Holt when he imprisons Volund (Volund., 14). It has already been proved above that, on his journey in the lower world, Svipdag also came to *Mimis holt,* and saw the citadel within which the *ásmegir* have their asylum.

Saxo has known either the above-cited strophe or another resembling it, and when his Erik-Svipdag speaks of his journey in ambiguous words (*obscura umbage*), Saxo makes him say: *Ad trunca sylvarum robora penetravi . . . ibi cuspis a robore regis excussa est* (*Hist.,* 206). With the expression *ad robora sylvarum penetravi* we must compare *til holtz ec gecc.* The words *robur regis* refer to the tree of the lower world king, Mimer *Mimameidr,* the world-tree. Erik-Svipdag's purpose with his journey to this tree is to secure a weapon. Saxo calls this weapon *cuspis.* Fjölsvinnsmal calls it, with a paraphrase, *broddr. Cuspis* is a translation of *broddr.*

Thus there can be no doubt concerning the identity of Skirner with Svipdag.

106.

SVIPDAG'S LATER FORTUNES. HIS TRANSFORMATION AND
DEATH. FREYJA GOES IN SEARCH OF HIM. FREY-
JA'S EPITHET MARDÖLL. THE SEA-KIDNEY, BRIS-
INGAMEN. SVIPDAG'S EPITHET HERMÓDR.

When the war between the Asas and the Vans had
broken out, Svipdag, as we have learned, espouses the
cause of the Vans (see Nos. 33, 38), to whom he naturally belongs as the husband of the Vana-dis Freyja and
Frey's most intimate friend. The happy issue of the war
for the Vans gives Svipdag free hands in regard to Halfdan's hated son Hadding, the son of the woman for
whose sake Svipdag's mother Groa was rejected. Meanwhile Svipdag offers Hadding reconciliation, peace, and
a throne among the Teutons (see No. 38). When Hadding refuses to accept gifts of mercy from the slayer of
his father, Svipdag persecutes him with irreconcilable
hate. This hatred finally produces a turning-point in
Svipdag's fortunes and darkens the career of the brilliant
hero. After the Asas and Vans had become reconciled
again, one of their first thoughts must have been to put an
end to the fued between the Teutonic tribes, since a continuation of the latter was not in harmony with the
peace restored among the gods (see No. 41), nevertheless
the war was continued in Midgard (see No. 41), and the
cause is Svipdag. He has become a rebel against both
Asas and Vans, and herein we must look for the reason
why, as we read in the Younger Edda, he disappeared

from Asgard (Younger Edda, 114). But he disappears not only from the world of the gods, but finally also from the terrestrial seat of war, and that god or those gods who were to blame for this conceal his unhappy and humiliating fate from Freyja. It is at this time that the faithful and devoted Vana-dis goes forth to seek her lover in all worlds *med ukunnum thjódum.*

Saxo gives us two accounts of Svipdag's death—the one clearly converted into history, the other corresponding faithfully with the mythology. The former reports that Hadding conquered and slew Svipdag in a naval battle (*Hist.,* 42). The latter gives us the following account (*Hist.,* 48):

While Hadding lived in exile in a northern wilderness, after his great defeat in conflict with the Swedes, it happened, on a sunny, warm day, that he went to the sea to bathe. While he was washing himself in the cold water he saw an animal of a most peculiar kind (*bellua inauditi generis*), and came into combat with it. Hadding slew it with quick blows and dragged it on shore. But while he rejoiced over this deed a woman put herself in his way and sang a song, in which she let him know that the deed he had now perpetrated should bring fearful consequences until he succeeded in reconciling the divine wrath which this murder had called down upon his head. All the forces of nature, wind and wave, heaven and earth, were to be his enemies unless he could propitiate the angry gods, for the being whose life he had taken was a celestial being concealed in the guise of an animal, one of the super-terrestrial:

Quippe unum e superis alieno corpore tectum
Sacrilegæ necuere manus: sic numinis almi
Interfector ades.

It appears, however, from the continuation of the narrative, that Hadding was unwilling to repent what he had done, although he was told that the one he had slain was a supernatural being, and that he long refused to propitiate those gods whose sorrow and wrath he had awakened by the murder. Not until the predictions of the woman were confirmed by terrible visitations does Hadding make up his mind to reconcile the powers in question. And this he does by instituting the sacrificial feast, which is called Frey's offering, and thenceforth was celebrated in honour of Frey (*Fro deo rem divinam furvis hostiis fecit*).

Hadding's refusal to repent what he had done, and the defiance he showed the divine powers, whom he had insulted by the murder he had committed, can only be explained by the fact that these powers were the Vanagods who long gave succour to his enemies (see No. 39), and that the supernatural being itself, which, concealed in the guise of an animal, was slain by him, was some one whose defeat gave him pleasure, and whose death he considered himself bound and entitled to cause. This explanation is fully corroborated by the fact that when he learns that Odin and the Asas, whose favourite he was, no longer hold their protecting hands over him, and that the propitiation advised by the prophetess becomes a necessity to him, he institutes the great annual offering to Frey, Svipdag's brother-in-law. That this god especially must be propitiated can, again, have no other reason than the fact that Frey was a nearer kinsman than any of the Asa-gods to the supernatural being, from whose slayer he (Frey) demanded a ransom, And as Saxo has already informed us that Svipdag perished in a naval engagement with Hadding, all points to the conclusion that in the celestial person who was concealed in the guise of an animal and was slain in the water we must discover Svipdag Freyja's husband.

Saxo does not tell us what animal guise it was. It must certainly have been a purely fabulous kind, since Saxo designates it as *bellua inauditi generis.* An Anglo-Saxon record, which is to be cited below, designates it as *uyrm* and *draca.* That Svipdag, sentenced to wear this guise, kept himself in the water near the shore of a sea, follows from the fact that Hadding meets and kills him in the sea where he goes to bathe. Freyja, who sought her lost lover everywhere, also went in search for him to the realms of *Ægir* and *Rán.* There are reasons for assuming that she found him again, and, in spite of his transformation and the repulsive exterior he thereby got, she remained with him and sought to soothe his misery with her faithful love. One of Freyja's surnames shows that she at one time dwelt in the bosom of the sea. The name is *Mardöll.* Another proof of this is the fragment preserved to our time of the myth concerning the conflict between Heimdal and Loke in regard to Brisingamen. This neck- and breast-ornament, celebrated in song both among the Teutonic tribes of England and those of Scandinavia, one of the most splendid works of the ancient artists, belonged to Freyja (Thrymskvida, Younger

Edda). She wore it when she was seeking Svipdag and found him beneath the waves of the sea; and the splendour which her Brisingamen diffused from the deep over the surface of the sea is the epic intepretation of the name *Mardöll* from *marr,* "sea," and *döll,* feminine of *dallr* (old English *deall*), "glittering" (compare the names Heimdallr and Delling). *Mardöll* thus means "the one diffusing a glimmering in the sea." The fact that Brisingamen, together with its possessor, actually was for a time in Æger's realm is proved by its epithet *fagrt hafnýra,* "the fair kidney of the sea," which occurs in a strophe of Ulf Uggeson (Younger Edda, 268). There was also a skerry, *Vágasker, Singasteinn,* on which Brisingamen lay and glittered, when Loke, clad in the guise of a seal tried to steal it. But before he accomplished his purpose, there crept upon the skerry another seal, in whose looks—persons in disguise were not able to change their eyes—the evil and cunning descendant of Farbaute must quickly have recognised his old opponent Heimdal. A conflict arose in regard to the possession of the ornament, and the brave son of the nine mothers became the victor and preserved the treasure for Asgard.

To the Svipdag synonyms *Ódr* (Hotharus), *Ottar* (Otharus), *Eirekr* (Ericus), and *Skirnir,* we must finally add one more, which is, perhaps, of Anglo-Saxon origin: *Hermodr, Heremod.*

From the Norse mythic records we learn the following in regard to Hermod:

(*a*) He dwelt in Asgard, but did not belong to the number of ruling gods. He is called Odin's *sveinn* (Younger

Edda, 174), and he was the Asa-father's favourite, and received from him helmet and cuirass (Hyndluljod, 2).

(*b*) He is called *enn hvati* (Younger Edda, 174), the rapid. When Frigg asks if anyone desires to earn her favour and gratitude by riding to the realm of death and offering Hel a ransom for Balder, Hermod offers to take upon himself this task. He gets Odin's horse Sleipner to ride, proceeds on his way to Hel, comes safely to that citadel in the lower world, where Balder and Nanna abide the regeneration of the earth, spurs Sleipner over the castle wall, and returns to Asgard with Hel's answer, and with the ring Draupner, and with presents from Nanna to Frigg and Fulla (Younger Edda, 180).

From this it appears that Hermod has a position in Asgard resembling Skirner's; that he, like Skirner, is employed by the gods as a messenger when important or venturesome errands are to be undertaken; and that he, like Skirner, then gets that steed to ride, which is able to leap over vaferflames and castle-walls. We should also bear in mind that Skirner-Svipdag had made celebrated journeys in the same world to which Hermod is now sent to find Balder. As we know, Svipdag had before his arrival in Asgard travelled all over the lower world, and had there fetched the sword of victory. After his adoption in Asgard, he is sent by the gods to the lower world to get the chain Gleipner.

(*c*) In historical times Hermod dwells in Valhal, and is one of the chief einherjes there. When Hakon the Good was on the way to the hall of the Asa-father, the latter sent Brage and Hermod to meet him:

Hermódr ok Bragi
kvad Hroptatýr
gangit i gegn grami
thvi at konungr ferr
sá er kappi thykkir,
til hallar binnig (Hakonarmal).

This is all there is in the Norse sources about Hermod. Further information concerning him is found in the Beowulf poem, which in two passages (str. 1747, &c., and 3419, &c.) compares him with its own unselfish and blameless hero, Beowulf, in order to make it clear that the latter was in moral respects superior to the famous hero of antiquity. Beowulf was related by marriage to the royal dynasty then reigning in his land, and was reared in the king's halls as an older brother of his sons. The comparisons make these circumstances, common to Beowulf and Hermod, the starting-point, and show that while Beowulf became the most faithful guardian of his young foster-brothers, and in all things maintained their rights, Hermod conducted himself in a wholly different manner. Of Hermod the poem tells us:

(*a*) He was reared at the court of a Danish king (str. 1818, &c., 3421, &c.).

(*b*) He set out on long journeys, and became the most celebrated traveller that man ever heard of (*se wæs wreccena wide mærost ofer wer-theóde*—str. 1800-1802).

(*c*) He performed great exploits (str. 1804).

(*d*) He was endowed with powers beyond all other men (str. 3438-39).

(*e*) God gave him a higher position of power than that accorded to mortals (str. 3436, &c.).

(*f*) But although he was reared at the court of the Danish king, this did not turn out to the advantage of the Skjoldungs, but was a damage to them (str. 3422, &c.), for there grew a bloodthirsty heart in his breast.

(*g*) When the Danish king died (the poem does not say how) he left young sons.

(*h*) Hermod, betrayed by evil passions that got the better of him, was the cause of the ruin of the Skjoldungs, and of a terrible plague among the Danes, whose fallen warriors for his sake covered the battlefields. His table-companions at the Danish court he consigned to death in a fit of anger (str. 3426, &c.).

(*i*) The war continues a very long time (str. 1815, &c., str. 3447).

(*k*) At last there came a change, which was unfavourable to Hermod, whose superiority in martial power decreased (str. 1806).

(*l*) Then he quite unexpectedly disappeared (str. 3432) from the sight of men.

(*m*) This happened against his will. He had suddenly been banished and delivered to the world of giants, where "waves of sorrow" long oppressed him (str. 1809, &c.).

(*n*) He had become changed to a dragon (*wyrm, draca*).

(*o*) The dragon dwelt near a rocky island in the sea *under harne stan* (beneath a grey rock).

(*p*) There he slew a hero of the Volsung race (in the Beowulf poem Sigemund—str. 1747, &c.).

All these points harmonise completely with Svipdag's

saga, as we have found it in other sources. Svipdag is the stepson of Halfdan the Skjoldung, and has been reared in his halls, and dwells there until his mother Groa is turned out and returns to Orvandel. He sets out like Hermod on long journeys, and is doubtless the most famous traveller mentioned in the mythology; witness his journey across the Elivagar, and his visit to Jotunheim while seeking Frey and Freyja; his journey across the frosty mountains, and his descent to the lower world, where he traverses Nifelheim, sees the Eylud mill, comes into Mimer's realm, procures the sword of victory, and sees the glorious castle of the *ásmegir;* witness his journey over Bifrost to Asgard, and his warlike expedition to the remote East (see also Younger Edda, i. 108, where Skirner is sent to *Svartalfaheim* to fetch the chain Glitner). He is, like Hermod, endowed with extraordinary strength, partly on account of his own inherited character, partly on account of the songs of incantation sung over him by Groa, on account of the nourishment of wisdom obtained from his stepmother and finally on account of the possession of the indomitable sword of victory. By being adopted in Asgard as Freyja's husband, he is, like Hermod, elevated to a position of power greater than that which mortals may expect. But all this does not turn out to be a blessing to the Skjoldungs, but is a misfortune to them. The hatred he had cherished toward the Skjoldung Halfdan is transferred to the son of the latter, Hadding, and he persecutes him and all those who are faithful to Hadding, makes war against him, and is unwilling to end the long war, although the gods demand it. Then he suddenly disappears, the divine wrath having clothed him with the guise of a strange animal, and relegated him to the world of water-giants, where he is slain by Hadding (who in the Norse heroic saga becomes a Volsung, after Halfdan, under the name Helge Hundingsbane, was made a son of the Volsung Sigmund).

Hermod is killed on a rocky island *under harne stan.* Svipdag is killed in the water, probably in the vicinity of the *Vágasker* and the *Singasteinn,* where the Brisingamen ornament of his faithful Mardol is discovered by Loke and Heimdal.

Freyja's love and sorrow may in the mythology have caused the gods to look upon Svipdag's last sad fate and death as a propitiation of his faults. The tears which the Vana-dis wept over her lover were transformed, according to the mythology, into gold, and this gold, the gold of a woman's faithfulness, may have been regarded as a sufficient compensation for the sins of her dear one, and doubtless opened to Svipdag the same Asgard-gate which he had seen opened to him during his life. This explains that Hermod is in Asgard in the historical time, and that, according to a revelation to the Swedes in the ninth century, the ancient King Erik was unanimously elevated by the gods as a member of their council.

Finally, it should be pointed out that the Svipdag synonym *Odr* has the same meaning as *môd* in Heremôd, and as *ferhd* in Svidferhd, the epithet with which Hermod is designated in the Beowulf strophe 1820. *Odr* means "the one endowed with spirit," *Heremôd* "the one endowed with martial spirit," *Svidherhd,* "the one endowed with mighty spirit." 828

Heimdal's and Loke's conflict in regard to Brisingamen has undoubtedly been an episode in the mythic account of Svipdag's last fortunes and Freyja's abode with him in the sea. There are many reasons for this assumption. We should bear in mind that Svipdag's closing career constituted a part of the great epic of the first world war, and that both Heimdal and Loke take part in this war, the former on Hadding's, the latter on Gudhorm-Jormunrek's and Svipdag's side (see Nos. 38, 39, 40). It should further be remembered that, according to Saxo, at the time when he slays the monster, Hadding is wandering about as an exile in the wildernesses, and that it is about this time that Odin gives him a companion and protector in Liserus-Heimdal (see No. 40). The unnamed woman, who after the murder had taken place puts herself in Hadding's way, informs him whom he has slain, and calls the wrath of the gods and the elements down upon him, must be Freyja herself, since she witnessed the deed and knew who was concealed in the guise of the dragon. So long as the latter lived Brisingamen surely had a faithful watcher, for it is the nature of a dragon to brood over the treasures he finds. After being slain and dragged on shore by Hadding, his "bed," the gold, lies exposed to view on Vagasker, and the glimmer of Brisingamen reaches Loke's eyes. While the woman, in despair on account of Svipdag's death, stands before Hadding and speaks to him, the ornament has no guardian, and Loke finds the occasion convenient for stealing it. But Heimdal, Hadding's protector, who in the mythology always keeps his eye on the acts of Loke and on his kinsmen

9 829

hostile to the gods, is also present, and he too has seen Brisingamen. Loke has assumed the guise of a seal, while the ornament lies on a rock in the sea, *Vágasker,* and it can cause no suspicion that a seal tries to find a resting-place there. Heimdal assumes the same guise, the seals fight on the rock, and Loke must retire with his errand unperformed. The rock is also called Singastein (Younger Edda, i. 264, 268), a name in which I see the Anglo-Saxon *Sincastân,* "the ornament rock." An echo of the combat about Brisingamen reappears in the Beowulf poem, where Heimdal (not Hamdir) appears under the name Hâma, and where it is said that "Hâma has brought to the weapon-glittering citadel (Asgard) *Brosingamene,*" which was "the best ornament under heaven;" whereupon it is said that Hâma fell "into Eormenric's snares," with which we should compare Saxo's account of the snares laid by Loke, Jormenrek's adviser, for Liserus-Heimdal and Hadding.*

107.

REMINISCENCES OF THE SVIPDAG-MYTH.

The mythic story about Svipdag and Freyja has been handed down in popular tales and songs, even to our time, of course in an ever varying and corrupted form. Among the popular tales there is one about *Mærthöll,* put in writ-

---

*As Jordanes confounded the mythological Gudhorm-Jormunrek with the historical Ermanarek, and connected with the history of the latter the heroic saga of Ammius-Hamdir, it lay close at hand to confound Hamdir with Heimdal, who, like Hamdir, is the foe of the mythical Jormunrek.

ing by Konrad Maurer, and published in *Modern Icelandic Popular Tales.*

The wondrous fair heroine in this tale bears Freyja's well-known surname, Mardol, but little changed. And as she, like Freyja, weeps tears that change into gold, it is plain that she is originally identical with the Vana-dis, a fact which Maurer also points out.

Like Freyja, she is destined by the norn to be the wife of a princely youth. But when he courted her, difficulties arose which remind us of what Saxo relates about Otharus and Syritha.

As Saxo represents her, Syritha is bound as it were by an enchantment, not daring to look up at her lover or to answer his declarations of love. She flies over the mountains *more pristino,* "in the manner usual in antiquity," consequently in all probability in the guise of a bird. In the Icelandic popular tale Marthol shudders at the approaching wedding night, since she is then destined to be changed into a sparrow. She is about to renounce the embrace of her lover, so that he may not know anything about the enchantment in which she is fettered.

In Saxo the spell resting on Syritha is broken when the candle of the wedding night burns her hand. In the popular tale Marthol is to wear the sparrow guise for ever if it is not burnt on the wedding night or on one of the two following nights.

Both in Saxo and in the popular tale another maiden takes Mardol's place in the bridal bed on the wedding night. But the spell is broken by fire, after which both the lovers actually get each other.

831

The original identity of the mythological Freyja-Mardol, Saxo' Syritha, and the *Mærthöll* of the Icelandic popular tale is therefore evident.

In Danish and Swedish versions of a ballad (in Syv, Nyerup, Arwidsson, Geijer and Afzelius, Grundtvig, Dybeck, Hofberg; compare Bugge's Edda, p. 352, &c.) a young Sveidal (Svedal, Svendal, Svedendal, Silfverdal) is celebrated, who is none other than Svipdag of the mythology. Svend Grundtvig and Bugge have called attention to the conspicuous similarity between this ballad on the one hand, and Grogalder and Fjölsvinnsmal on the other. From the various versions of the ballad it is necessary to mention here only those features which best preserve the most striking resemblance to the mythic prototype. Sveidal is commanded by his stepmother to find a maiden "whose sad heart had long been longing." He then goes first to the grave of his deceased mother to get advice from her. The mother speaks to him from the grave and promises him a horse, which can bear him over sea and land, and a sword hardened in the blood of a dragon and resembling fire. The narrow limits of the ballad forbade telling how Sveidal came into possession of the treasures promised by the mother or giving an account of the exploits he performed with the sword. This plays no part in the ballad; it is only indicated that events not recorded took place before Sveidal finds the longing maid. Riding through forests and over seas, he comes to the country where she has her castle. Outside of this he meets a shepherd, with whom he enters into conversation. The shepherd informs him that within is found a young maiden who has long been longing for a young man by name Sveidal, and that none other than he can enter there, for the timbers of the castle are of iron, its gilt gate of steel, and within the gate a lion and a white bear keep watch. Sveidal approaches the gate; the locks fall away spontaneously; and when he enters the open court the wild beasts crouch at his feet, a linden-tree with golden leaves bends to the ground before him, and the young maiden whom he seeks welcomes him as her husband.

One of the versions makes him spur his horse over the castle wall; another speaks of seven young men guarding the wall, who show him the way to the castle, and who in reality are "god's angels under the heaven, the blue."

The horse who bears his rider over the salt sea is a reminiscence of Sleipner, which Svipdag rode on more than one occasion; and when it is stated that Sveidal on this horse galloped over the castle wall, this reminds us of Skirner-Svipdag when he leaps over the fence around Gymer's abode, and of Hermod-Svipdag when he spurs Sleipner over the wall to Balder's lower-world castle. The shepherds, who are "god's angels," refers to the watchmen mentioned in Fjölsvinnsmal, who are gods; the wild beasts in the open court to the two wolf-dogs who guard Asgard's gate; the shepherd whom Sveidal meets outside of the wall to Fjölsvin; the linden-tree with the golden leaves to *Mimameidr* and to the golden grove growing in Asgard. One of the versions make two years pass while Sveidal seeks the one he is destined to marry.

In Germany, too, we have fragments preserved of the myth about Svipdag and Freyja. These remnants are, we admit, parts of a structure built, so to speak, in the style of the monks, but they nevertheless show in the most positive manner that they are borrowed from the fallen and crumbled arcades of the heathen mythology. We rediscover in them the old medieval poem about "Christ's unsewed grey coat."

The hero of the poem is Svipdag, here called by his father's name Orendel, Orentel—that is, Orvandel. The father himself, who is said to be a king in Trier, has received another name, which already in the most ancient heathen times was a synonym of Orvandel, and which I shall consider below. This in connection with the circumstance that the younger Orentel's (Svipdag's) patron saint is called "the holy Wieland," and thus he has the name of a person who, in the mythology, as shall be shown below, was Svipdag's uncle (father's brother) and helper, and whose sword is Svipdag's protection and pledge of victory, proves that at least in solitary instances not only the events of the myth but also its names and family relations have been preserved in a most remarkable and faithful manner through centuries in the minds of the German people.

In the very nature of things it cannot in the monkish poem be the task of the young Svipdag-Orentel to go in search of the heathen goddess Freyja and rescue her from the power of the giants. In her stead appears a "Frau Breyde," who is the fairest of all women, and the only one worthy to be the young Orentel's wife. In the heathen poem the goddess of fate Urd, in the German medieval poem God Himself, resolves that Orentel is to have the fairest woman as his bride. In the heathen poem Freyja is in the power of giants, and concealed somewhere in Jotunheim at the time when Svipdag is commanded to find her, and it is of the greatest moment for the preservation of the world that the goddess of love and fertility should be freed from the hands of the powers of frost. In the German poem, written under the influence of the efforts of the Christian world to reconquer the Holy Land, Frau Breyde is a princess who is for the time being in Jerusalem, surrounded and watched by giants, heathens, and knights templar, the last of whom, at the time when the poem received its present form, were looked upon as worshippers of the devil, and as persons to be shunned by the faithful. To Svipdag's task of liberating the goddess of love corresponds, in the monkish poem, Orentel's task of liberating Frau Breyde from her surrounding of giants, heathens, and knights templar, and restoring to Christendom the holy grave in Jerusalem. Orentel proceeds thither with a fleet. But although the journey accordingly is southward, the mythic saga, which makes Svipdag journey across the frost-cold Elivagar, asserts itself; and as his fleet could not well be hindered by pieces of ice on the coast of the Holy Land, it is made to stick fast in "dense water," and remain there for three years, until, on the supplication of the Virgin Mary, it is liberated therefrom by a storm. The Virgin Mary's prayers have assumed the same place in the Christian poems as Groa's incantations in the heathen. The fleet, made free from the "dense water," sails to a land which is governed by one Belian, who is conquered by Orentel in a naval engagement. This Belian is the mythological *Beli,* one of those "howlers" who surrounded Frey and Freyja during their sojourn in Jotunheim and threatened Svipdag's life. In the Christian poem Bele was made a king in Great Babylonia, doubtless for the reason that his name suggested the biblical "Bel in Babel." Saxo also speaks of a naval battle in which Svipdag-Ericus conquers the mythic person, doubtless a storm-giant, who by means of witchcraft prepares the ruin of sailors approaching the land where Frotho and Gunvara are concealed. After various other adventures Orentel arrives in the Holy Land, and the angel Gabriel shows him the way to Frau Breyde, just as "the seven angels of God" in one of the Scandinavian ballads guide Sveidal to the castle where his chosen bride abides. Lady Breyde is found to be surrounded by none but foes of Christianity—knights templar, heathens, and giants— who, like Gunvara's giant surroundings in Saxo, spend their time in fighting, but still wait upon their fair lady as their princess. The giants and knights templar strive to take Orentel's life, and, like Svipdag, he must constantly be prepared to defend it. One of the giants slain by Orental is a "banner-bearer." One of the giants, who in the mythology tries to take Svipdag's life, is Grep, who, according to Saxo, meets him in derision with a banner on the top of whose staff is fixed the head of an ox.

Meanwhile Lady Breyde is attentive to Orentel. As Menglad receives Svipdag, so Lady Breyde receives

Orentel with a kiss and a greeting, knowing that he is destined to be her husband.

When Orental has conquered the giants he celebrates a sort of wedding with Lady Breyde, but between them lies a two-edged sword, and they sleep as brother and sister by each other's side. A wedding of a similar kind was mentioned in the mythology in regard to Svipdag and Menglad before they met in Asgard and were finally united. The chaste chivalry with which Freyja is met in the mythology by her rescuer is emphasised by Saxo both in his account of Ericus-Svipdag and Gunvara and in his story about Otharus and Syritha. He makes Ericus say of Gunvara to Frotha: *Intacta illi pudicitia manet* (*Hist.*, 126). And of Otharus he declares: *Neque puellam stupro violare sustinuit, nec splendido loco natam obscuro concubitus genere macularet* (*Hist.*, 331). The first wedding of Orentel and Breyde is therefore as if it had not been, and the German narrative makes Orentel, after completing other warlike adventures, sue for the hand of Breyde for the second time. In the mythology the second and real wedding between Svipdag and Freyja must certainly have taken place, inasmuch as he became reunited with her in Asgard.

The sword which plays so conspicuous a part in Svipdag's fortunes has not been forgotten in the German medieval tale. It is mentioned as being concealed deep down in the earth, and as a sword that is always attended by victory.

On one occasion Lady Breyde appears, weapon in hand, and fights by the side of Orentel, under circumstances which remind us of the above-cited story from Saxo (see No. 102), when Ericus-Svipdag, Gunvara-Freyja, and Rollerus-Ull are in the abode of a treacherous giant, who tries to persuade Svipdag to deliver Gunvara to him, and when Bracus-Thor breaks into the giant abode, and either slays the inmates or puts them to flight. Gunvara then fights by the side of Ericus-Svipdag, *muliebri corpore virilem animum æquans* (*Hist.*, 222).

In the German Orentel saga appears a "fisherman," who is called master Yse. Orentel has at one time been wrecked, and comes floating on a plank to his island, where Yse picks him up. Yse is not a common fisherman. He has a castle with seven towers, and eight hundred fishermen serve under him. There is good reason for assuming that this mighty chieftain of fishermen originally was the Asa-god Thor, who in the northern ocean once had the Midgard-serpent on his hook, and that the episode of the picking up of the wrecked Orentel by Yse has its root in a tradition concerning the mythical adventure, when the real Orvandel, Svipdag's father, feeble and cold, was met by Thor and carried by him across the Elivagar. In the mythology, as shall be shown hereafter, Orvendel the brave was Thor's "sworn" man, and fought with him against giants before the hostility sprang up between Ivalde's sons and the Asa-gods. In the Orentel saga Yse also regards Orentel as his "thrall." The latter emancipates himself from his thraldom with gold. Perhaps this ransom is a reference to the gold which Freyja's tears gave as a ransom for Svipdag.

Orentel's father is called Eigel, king in Trier. In

Vilkinasaga we find the archer Egil, Volund's brother, mentioned by the name-variation Eigill. The German Orentel's patron saint is Wieland, that is, Volund. Thus in the Orentel saga as in the Volundarkvida and in Vilkinasaga we find both these names Egil and Volund combined, and we have all the more reason for regarding King Eigel in Trier as identical with the mythological Egil, since the latter, like Orvandel, is a famous archer. Below, I shall demonstrate that the archer Orvandel and the archer Egil actually were identical in the mythology.

But first it may be in order to point out the following circumstances. Tacitus tells us in his *Germania* (3): "Some people think, however, that Ulysses, too, on his long adventurous journeys was carried into this ocean (the Germanic), and visited the countries of Germany, and that he founded and gave name to Asciburgium, which is situated on the Rhine, and is still an inhabited city; nay, an altar consecrated to Ulysses, with the name of his father Laertes added, is said to have been found there." To determine the precise location of this Asciburgium is not possible. Ptolemy (ii. 11, 28), and after him Marcianus Heracleota (*Peripl.*, 2, 36), inform us that an Askiburgon was situated on the Rhine, south of and above the delta of the river. *Tabula Peutingeriana* locates Asceburgia between Gelduba (Gelb) and Vetera (Xanten). But from the history of Tacitus it appears (iv. 33) that Asciburgium was situated between Neuss and Mainz (Mayence). Read the passage: *Aliis a Novæsio, aliis a Mogontiaco universas copias advenisse credentibus.*

The passage refers to the Roman troops sent to Asciburgium and there attacked—those troops which expected to be relieved from the nearest Roman quarters in the north or south. Its location should accordingly be looked for either on or near that part of the Rhine, which on the east bordered the old archbishopric Trier.

Thus the German Orentel saga locates King Eigel's realm and Orentel's native country in the same regions, where, according to Tacitus' reporter, Ulysses was said to have settled for some time and to have founded a citadel. As is well known, the Romans believed they found traces of the wandering Ulysses in well-nigh all lands, and it was only necessary to hear a strange people mention a far-travelled mythic hero, and he was at once identified either as Ulysses or Hercules. The Teutonic mythology had a hero *à la* Ulysses in the younger Orentel, Odr-Svipdag-Heremod, whom the Beowulf poem calls "incomparably the most celebrated traveller among mankind" (*wreccena wide mærost ofer wer-theóde*). Mannhardt has already pointed out an episode (Orentel's shipwreck and arrival in Yse's land) which calls to mind the shipwreck of Odysseus and his arrival in the land of the Pheaces. Within the limits which the Svipdag-myth, according to my own investigations, proves itself to have had, other and more conspicuous features common to both, but certainly not borrowed from either, can be pointed out, for instance Svipdag's and Oydsseus' descent to the lower world, and the combat in the guise of seals between Heimdal and Loke, which reminds us of the conflict of Menelaos clad in seal-skin with the seal-watcher Proteus

(*Odyss.*, iv., 404, &c.). Just as there are words in the Aryan languages that in their very form point to a common origin, but not to a borrowing, so there are also myths in the Aryan religions which in their very form reveal their growth from an ancient common Aryan root, but produce no suspicion of their being borrowed. Among these are to be classed those features of the Odysseus and Svipdag myths which resemble each other.

It has already been demonstrated above, that *Germannia's* Mannus is identical with Halfdan of the Norse sources, and that Yngve-Svipdag has his counterpart in Ingævo (see No. 24). That informer of Tacitus who was able to interpret Teutonic songs about Mannus and his sons, the three original race heroes of the Teutons, must also in those very songs have heard accounts of Orvandel's and Svipdag's exploits and adventures, since Orvandel and Svipdag play a most decisive part in the fortunes of Mannus-Halfdan. If the myth about Svipdag was composed in a later time, then Mannus-Halfdan's saga must have undergone a change equal to a complete transformtion after the day of Tacitus, and for such an assumption there is not the slightest reason. Orvandel is not a mythic character of later make. As already pointed out, and as shall be demonstrated below, he has ancient Aryan ancestry. The centuries between Tacitus and Paulus Diaconus are unfortunately almost wholly lacking in evidence concerning the condition of the Teutonic myths and sagas; but where, as in Jordanes, proofs still gleam forth from the prevailing darkness, we find mention of *Arpantala, Amala, Fridigernus, Vidigoia* (Jord., v.).

Jordanes says that in the most ancient times they were celebrated in song and described as heroes who scarcely had their equals (*quales vix heroas fuisse miranda jactat antiquitas*). Previous investigators have already recognized in Arpantala Orvandel, in Amala Hamal, in Vidigoia Wittiche, Wieland's son (Vidga Volundson), who in the mythology are cousins of Svipdag (see No. 108). Fridigernus, *Fridgjarn,* means "he who strives to get the beautiful one," an epithet to which Svipdag has the first claim among ancient Teutonic heroes, as Freyja herself has the first claim to the name *Frid* (beautiful). In Fjölsvinnsmal it belongs to a dis, who sits at Freyja's feet, and belongs to her royal household. This is in analogy with the fact that the name *Hlin* belongs at the same time to Frigg herself (Völuspa), and to a goddess belonging to her royal household (Younger Edda, i. 196).

What Tacitus tells about the stone found at Asciburgium, with the names of Ulysses and Laertes inscribed thereon, can of course be nothing but a conjecture, based on the idea that the famous Teutonic traveller was identical with Odysseus. Doubtless this idea has been strengthened by the similarity between the names *Odr,* Goth. *Vods,* and Odysseus, and by the fact that the name Laertes (acc. Laerten) has sounds in common with the name of Svipdag's father. If, as Tacitus seems to indicate, Asciburgium was named after its founder, we would find in *Asc-* an epithet of Orvandel's son, common in the first century after Christ and later. In that case it lies nearest at hand to think of *aiska* (Fick. iii. 5), the English "ask," the Anglo-Saxon *ascian,* the Swedish *äska,* "to seek," "search for," "to try to secure," which easily adapted itself to Svipdag, who goes on long and perilous journeys to look for Freyja and the sword of victory. I call attention to these possibilities because they appear to suggest an ancient connection, but not for the purpose of building hypotheses thereon. Under all circumstances it is of interest to note that the Christian medieval Orentel saga locates the Teutonic migration hero's home to the same part of Germany where Tacitus in his time assumed that he had founded a citadel. The tradition, as heard by Tacitus, did not however make the regions about the Rhine the native land of the celebrated traveller. He came thither, it is said in *Germania,* from the North after having navigated in the Northern Ocean. And this corresponds with the mythology, which makes Svipdag an Inguæon, and Svion, a member of the race of the Skilfing-Ynglings, makes him in the beginning fight on the side of the powers of frost against Halfdan, and afterwards lead not only the north Teutonic (Inguæonian) but also the west Teutonic tribes (the Hermiones) against the east Teutonic war forces of Hadding (see Nos. 38-40).

Memories of the Svipdag-myth have also been preserved in the story about Hamlet, Saxo's Amlethus (Snæbjorn's *Amlodi*), son of Horvendillus (Orvandel). In the medieval story Hamlet's father, like Svipdag's father in the mythology, was slain by the same man, who marries the wife of the slain man, and, like Svipdag in the myth, Hamlet of the medieval saga becomes the avenger of his father Horvendillus and the slayer of his stepfather. On more than one occasion the idea occurs in the Norse sagas that a lad whose stepfather has slain his father broods over his duty of avenging the latter, and then plays insane or half idiot to avoid the suspicion that he may become dangerous to the murderer. Svipdag, Orvandel's son, is reared in his stepfather's house amid all the circumstances that might justify or explain such a hypocrisy. Therefore he has as a lad received the epithet *Amlodi,* the meaning of which is "insane," and the myth having at the same time described him as highly-gifted, clever, and sharp-witted, we have in the words which the mythology has attributed to his lips the key to the ambiguous words which make the cleverness, which is veiled under a stupid exterior, gleam forth. These features of the mythic account of Svipdag have been transferred to the middle-age saga anent Hamlet—a saga which already in Saxo's time had been developed into an independent narrative. I shall return to this theme in a treatise on the heroic sagas. Other reminiscences of the Svipdag-myth reappear in Danish, Swedish, and Norwegian ballads. The Danish ballads, which, with surprising fidelity, have preserved certain fundamental traits and details of the Svipdag-myth even down to our days, I have already discussed. The Norwegian ballad about "Hermod the Young" (*Landstad Norske Folkeviser,* p. 28), and its Swedish version, "Bergtrollet," which corresponds still more faithfully with the myth (Arvidson, i. 123), have this peculiar interest in reference to mythological synonymics and the connection of the mythic fragments preserved, that Svipdag appears in the former as in the Beowulf poem and in the Younger Edda under the name Hermod, and that both versions have for their theme a story, which Saxo tells about his Otharus when he describes the flight of the latter through Jotunheim with the rediscovered Syritha. It has already been stated above (No. 100) that after Otharus had found Syritha and slain a giant in whose power she was, he was separated from her on their way home, but found her once more and liberated her from a captivity into which she had fallen in the abode of a giantess. This is the episode which forms the theme of the ballad about "Hermod the Young," and of the Swedish version of it. Brought together, the two ballads give us the following contents:

The young Hermod secured as his wife a beautiful maiden whom he liberated from the hands of a giantess. She had fallen into the hands of giants through a witch, "gigare," originally *gýgr,* a troll-woman, Aurboda, who in a great crowd of people had stolen her out of a church (the divine citadel Asgard is changed into a "house of God"). Hermod hastens on skees "through woods and caverns and recesses," comes to "the wild sea-strand" (Elivagar) and to the "mountain the blue," where the giantess resides who conceals the young maiden in her abode. It is Christmas Eve. Hermod asks for lodgings for the night in the mountain dwelling of the giantess and gets it. Resorting to cunning, he persuades the giantess the following morning to visit her neighbours, liberates the fair maiden during her absence, and flies on his skees with her "over the high mountains and down the low ones." When the old giantess on her return home

10   845

finds that they have gone she hastens (according to the Norwegian version accompanied by eighteen giants) after those who have taken flight through dark forests with a speed which makes every tree bend itself to the ground. When Hermod with his young maiden had come to the salt fjord (Elivagar), the giantess is quite near them, but in the decisive moment she is changed to a stone, according to the Norse version, by the influence of the sun, which just at that time rose; according to the Swedish version, by the influence of a cross which stood near the fjord and its "long bridge."

The Swedish version states, in addition to this, that Hermod had a brother; in the mythology, Ull the skilful skee-runner. In both the versions, Hermod is himself an excellent skee-man. The refrains in both read: "He could so well on the skees run." Below, I shall prove that Orvandel, Svipdag's and Ull's father, is identical with Egil, the foremost skee-runner in the mythology, and that Svipdag is a cousin of Skade, "the dis of the skees." Svipdag-Hermod belongs to the celebrated skee-race of the mythology, and in this respect, too, these ballads have preserved a genuine trait of the mythology.

In their way, these ballads, therefore, give evidence of Svipdag's identity with Hermod, and of the latter's identity with Saxo's Otherus.

Finally, a few words about the Svipdag synonyms. Of these, *Odr* and *Hermodr* (and in the Beowulf poem *Svidferhd*) form a group which, as has already been pointed out above, refer to the qualities of his mind. Svipdag ("the glimmering day") and Skirner ("the shining one") form another group, which refers to his birth as the son of the star-hero Orvandel, who is "the brightest of stars," and "a true beam from the sun" (see above). Again, anent the synonym *Eirekr,* we should bear in mind that Svipdag's half-brother Gudhorm had the epithet *Jormunrekr,* and the half-brother of the latter, Hadding, the epithet *thódrekr.* They are the three half-brothers who, after the patriarch Mannus-Halfdan, assume the government of the Teutons, and as each one of them has large domains, and rules over many Teutonic tribes, they are, in contradistinction to the princes of the separate tribes, great kings or emperors. It is the dignity of a great king which is indicated, each in its own way, by all these parallel names—*Eirekr, Jormunrekr,* and *thjódrekr.*

108.

SVIPDAG'S FATHER ORVANDEL. EVIDENCE THAT HE IS IDENTICAL WITH VOLUND'S BROTHER EGIL. THE ORVANDEL SYNONYM EBBO (EBUR, IBOR).

Svipdag's father, Orvandel, must have been a mortal enemy of Halfdan, who abducted his wife Groa. But hitherto it is his son Svipdag whom we have seen carry out the feud of revenge against Halfdan. Still, it must seem incredible that the brave archer himself should remain inactive and leave it to his young untried son to fight against Thor's favourite, the mighty son of Borgar. The epic connection demands that Orvandel also should take part in this war, and it is necessary to investigate whether our mythic records have preserved traces of the satisfaction of this demand in regard to the mythological epic.

As his name indicates, Orvandel was a celebrated archer. That *Ör-* in Orvandel, in heathen times, was conceived tq be the word *ör,* "arrow"—though this meaning does not therefore need to be the most original one—is made perfectly certain by Saxo, according to whom *Örvandill's* father was named *Geirvandill* (Gervandillus, *Hist.,* 135). Thus the father is the one "busy with the spear," the son "the one busy with the arrow."

Taking this as the starting point, we must at the very threshold of our investigation present the question: Is there among Halfdan's enemies mentioned by Saxo anyone who bears the name of a well-known archer?

This is actually the fact. Halfdan Berggram has to contend with two mythic persons, Toko and Anundus, who with united forces appear against him (*Hist.,* 325). Toko, *Toki,* is the well-known name of an archer. In another passage in Saxo (*Hist.,* 265, &c.) one Anundus, with the help of Avo (or Ano) *sagittarius,* fights against one Halfdan. Thus we have the parallels:

The archer Orvandel is an enemy of Halfdan.'

The man called archer Toko and Anundus are enemies of Halfdan.

The archer Avo and Anundus are enemies of Halfdan.

What at once strikes us is the fact that both the one called Toko (an archer's name) and the archer Avo have as comrade one Anundus in the war against Halfdan. Whence did Saxo get this Anundus? We are now in the domain of mythology related as history, and the name Anund must have been borrowed thence. Can any other source throw light on any mythic person by this name?

There was actually an Anund who held a conspicuous place in mythology, and he is none other than Volund. Volundarkvida informs us that Volund was also called Anund. When the three swan-maids came to the Wolfdales, where the three brothers, Volund, Egil, and Slagfin, had their abode, one of them presses Egil "in her white embrace," the other is Slagfin's beloved, and the third "lays her arms around Anund's white neck."

> enn in thrithia
> theirra systir
> varthi hvitan
> hals Onondar.

Volund is the only person by name Anund found in our mythic records. If we now eliminate—of course only for the present and with the expectation of confirmatory evideuce—the name Anund and substitute Volund, we get the following parallels:

Volund and Toko (the name of an archer) are enemies of Halfdan.

Volund and the archer named Avo are enemies of Halfdan.

The archer Orvandel is an enemy of Halfdan.

From this it would appear that Volund was very intimately associated with one of the archers of the mythology, and that both had some reason for being enemies of Halfdan. Can this be corroborated by any other source?

Volund's brothers are called *Egill* and *Slagfidr* (*Slag-finnr*) in Volundarkvida. The Icelandic-Norwegian poems from heathen times contain paraphrases which prove that the mythological Egil was famous as an archer and skee-runner. The bow is "Egil's weapon," the arrows are "Egil's weapon-hail" (Younger Edda, 422), and "the swift herring of Egil's hands" (*Har. Gr.,* p. 18). A ship is called Egil's skees, originally because he could use his skees also on the water. In Volundarkvida he makes hunting expeditions with his brothers on skees. Vilkinasaga also (29, 30) knows Egil as Volund's brother, and speaks of him as a wonderfully skilful archer.

The same Volund, who in Saxo under the name Anund has Toko (the name of an archer) or the archer Avo by his side in the conflict with Halfdan, also has the archer Egil as a brother in other sources.

Of an archer Toko, who is mentioned in *Hist.,* 487-490, Saxo tells the same exploit as Vilkinasaga attributes to Volund's brother Egil. In Saxo it is Toko who performs the celebrated masterpiece which was afterwards attributed to William Tell. In Vilkinasaga it is Egil. The one like the other, amid similar secondary circumstances, shoots an apple from his son's head. Egil's skill as a skee-runner and the serviceableness of his skees on the water have not been forgotten in Saxo's account of Toko. He runs on skees down the mountain, sloping precipitously down to the sea, Kullen in Scania, and is said to have saved himself on board a ship. Saxo's Toko was therefore without doubt identical with Volund's brother Egil, and Saxo's Anund is the same Volund of whom the Volundarkvida testifies that he also had this name in the mythology.

Thus we have demonstrated the fact that Volund and Egil appeared in the saga of the Teutonic patriarch Half-dan as the enemies of the latter, and that the famous archer Egil occupied the position in which we would expect to find the celebrated archer Orvandel, Svipdag's father. Orvandel is therefore either identical with Egil, and then it is easy to understand why the latter is an enemy of Halfdan, who we know had robbed his wife Groa; or he is not identical with Egil, and then we know no motive for the appearance of the latter on the same side as Svipdag, and we, moreover, are confronted by the improbability that Orvandel does nothing to avenge the insult done to him.

Orvandel's identity with Egil is completely confirmed by the following circumstances.

Orvandel has the Elivagar and the coasts of Jotunheim as the scene of his exploits during the time in which he is the friend of the gods and the opponent of the giants. To this time we must refer Horvendillus' victories over Collerus (Kollr) and his sister Sela (cp. the name of a monster *Selkolla*—Bisk S., i. 605) mentioned by Saxo (*Hist.*, 135-138). His surname *inn frækni,* the brave, alone is proof that the myth refers to important exploits carried out by him, and that these were performed against the powers of frost in particular—that is to say, in the service of the gods and for the good of Midgard—is plain from the narrative in the Younger Edda (276, 277). This shows, as is also demanded by the epic connection,

851

that the Asa-god Thor and the archer Orvandel were at least for a time confidential friends, and that they had met each other on their expeditions for similar purposes in Jotunheim. When Thor, wounded in his forehead, returns from his combat with the giant *Hrungnir* to his home, *thrúdvángr* (*thrúdvángar, thrudheimr,*) Orvandel's wife Groa was there and tried to help him with healing sorcery, wherein she would also have succeeded if Thor could have made himself hold his tongue for a while concerning a report he brought with him about her husband, and which he expected would please her. And Groa did become so glad that she forgot to continue the magic song and was unable to complete the healing. The report was, as we know, that, on the expedition to Jotunheim from which he had now come home, Thor had met Orvandel, carried him in his basket across the Elivagar, and thrown a toe which the intrepid adventurer had frozen up to heaven and made a star thereof. Thor added that before long Orvandel would come "home;" that is to say, doubtless, "home to Thor," to fetch his wife Groa. It follows that, when he had carried Orvandel across the Elivagar, Thor had parted with him somewhere on the way, in all probability in Orvandel's own home, and that while Orvandel wandered about in Jotunheim, Groa, the dis of growth, had a safe place of refuge in the Asa-God's own citadel. A close relation between Thor and Orvandel also appears from the fact that Thor afterwards marries Orvandel's second wife Sif, and adopts his son Ull, Svipdag's half-brother (see No. 102), in Asgard.

Consequently Orvandel's abode was situated south of

the Elivagar (Thor carried him *nordan or Jötunheimum* —Younger Edda, 276), in the direction Thor had to travel when going to and from the land of the giants, and presumably quite near or on the strand of that mythic water-course over which Thor on this occasion carried him. When Thor goes from Asgard to visit the giants he rides the most of the way in his chariot drawn by the two goats *Tanngnjóstr* and *Tanngrisnir.* In the poem Haustlaung there is a particularly vivid description of his journey in his thunder chariot.through space when he proceeded to the meeting agreed upon with the giant Hrungner, on the return from which he met and helped Orvandel across Elivagar (Younger Edda, 276). But across this water and through Jotunheim itself Thor never travels in his car. He wades across the Elivagar, he travels on foot in the wildernesses of the giants, and encounters his foe face to face, breast to breast, instead of striking from above with lightning. In this all accounts of Thor's journeys to Jotunheim agree. Hence south of the Elivagar and somewhere near them there must have been a place where Thor left his chariot and his goats in safety before he proceeded farther on his journey. And as we already know that the archer Orvandel, Thor's friend, and like him hostile to the giants, dwelt on the road traveled by the Asa-god, and south of the Elivagar, it lies nearest at hand to assume that Orvandel's castle was the stopping place on his journey, and the place where he left his goats and car.

Now in Hymerskvida (7, 37, 38) we actually read that Thor, on his way to Jotunheim, had a stopping-place, where his precious car and goats were housed and taken care of by the host, who accordingly had a very important task, and must have been a friend of Thor and the Asa-gods in the mythology. The host bears the archer name Egil. From Asgard to Egil's abode, says Hymers-kvida, it is about one day's journey for Thor when he rides behind his goats on his way to Jotunheim. After this day's journey he leaves the draught-animals, decorated with horns, with Egil, who takes care of them, and the god continues his journey on foot. Thor and Tyr being about to visit the giant Hymer—

> Foro drivgom
> dag thann fram
> Asgardi fra,
> unz til Egils quomo;
> hirdi hann hafra
> horngaufgasta
> hurfo at haullo
> er Hymir átti.

("Nearly all the day they proceeded their way from Asgard until they came to Egil's. He gave the horn-strong goats care. They (Thor and Tyr) continued to the great hall which Hymer owned.")

From Egil's abode both the gods accordingly go on foot. From what is afterwards stated about adventures on their way home, it appears that there is a long distance between Egil's house and Hymer's (cp. str. 35—*foro lengi, adr.*, &c.). It is necessary to journey across the Elivagar first—*byr fyr austan, Elivága hundviss Hymir* (str. 5). In the Elivagar Hymer has his fishing-grounds, and there he is wont to catch whales on hooks (cp. str. 17—*a vâg roa*) ; but still he does not venture far out upon the water (see str. 20), presumably because he has enemies on the southern strand where Egil dwells. Between the Elivagar and Hymer's abode there is a considerable distance through woody mountain recesses (*holtrid*—str. 27) and past rocks in whose caverns dwell monsters belonging to Hymer's giant-clan (str. 35). Thor resorts to cunning in order to˘secure a safe retreat. After he has been out fishing with the giant, instead of making his boat fast in its proper place on the strand, as Hymer requests him to do, he carries the boat with its belongings all the difficult way up to Hymer's hall. He is also attacked on his way home by Hymer and all his giant-clan, and, in order to be able to wield Mjolner freely, he must put down the precious kettle which he has captured from the˙ frost-giant and was carrying on his broad shoulders (str. 35, 36). But the undisturbed retreat across the Elivagar he has secured by the above-mentioned cunning.

Egil is called *hraunbúi* (str. 38), an epithet the ambiguous meaning of which should not be unobserved. It is usually translated with rock-dweller, but it here means "he who lives near or at *Hraunn*" (*Hrönn*). *Hraunn* is one of the names of the Elivagar (see Nos. 59, 93; cp. Younger Edda, 258, with Grimnersmal, 38).

After their return to Egil's, Thor and Tyr again seat themselves in the thunder-chariot and proceed to Asgard with the captured kettle. But they had not driven far before the strength of one of the horn-decorated draught

animals failed, and it was found that the goat was lame
(str. 37). A misfortune had happened to it while in
Egil's keeping, and this had been caused by the cunning
Loke (str. 37). The poem does not state the kind of
misfortune—the Younger Edda gives us information on
this point—but if it was Loke's purpose to make enmity
between Thor and his friend Egil he did not succeed this
time. Thor, to be sure, demanded a ransom for what
had happened, and the ransom was, as Hymerskvida
informs us, two children who were reared in Egil's house.
But Thor became their excellent foster-father and protector, and the punishment was therefore of such a kind
that it was calculated to strengthen the bond of friendship instead of breaking it.

Gylfaginning also (Younger Edda, i. 142, &c.) has
preserved traditions showing that when Thor is to make a
journey from Asgard to Jotunheim it requires more than
one day, and that he therefore puts up in an inn at the
end of the first day's travel, where he eats his supper and
stops over night. There he leaves his goats and travels
the next day eastward (north), "across the deep sea"
(*hafit that hit djúpa*), on whose other side his giant foes
have their abode. The sea in question is the Elivagar,
and the tradition correctly states that the inn is situated
on its southern (western) side.

But Gylfaginning has forgotten the name of the host
in this inn. Instead of giving his name it simply calls
him a *buandi* (peasant); but it knows and states on the
other hand the names of the two children there reared,
Thjalfe and Roskva; and it relates how it happened that

one of Thor's goats became lame, but without giving Loke the blame for the misfortune. According to Gylfaginning the event occurred when Thor was on his way to Utgard-Loke. In Gylfaginning, too, Thor takes the two children as a ransom, and makes Thjalfe (*thjálfi*) a hero, who takes an honourable part in the exploits of the god.

As shall be shown below, this inn on the road from Asgard to Jotunheim is presupposed as well known in Eilif Gudrunson's Thorsdrapa, which describes the adventures Thor met with on his journey to the giant Geirrod. Thorsdrapa gives facts of great mythological importance in regard to the inhabitants of the place. They are the "sworn" helpers of the Asa-gods, and when it is necessary Thor can thence secure brave warriors, who accompany him across Elivagar into Jotunheim. Among them an archer plays the chief part in connection with Thjalfe (see No. 114).

On the north side of Elivagar dwell accordingly giants hostile to gods and men; on the south side, on the other hand, beings friendly to the gods and bound in their friendship by oaths. The circumstance that they are bound by oaths to the gods (see Thorsdrapa) implies that a treaty has been made with them and that they owe obedience. Manifestly the uttermost picket guard to the north against the frost-giants is entrusted to them.

This also gives us an explanation of the position of the star-hero Orvandel, the great archer, in the mythological Epic. We can understand why he is engaged to the dis of growth, Groa, as it is his duty to defend Midgard against the destructions of frost; and why he fights on the Elivagar and in Jotunheim against the same enemies as Thor; and why the mythology has made him and the lord of thunder friends who visit each other. With the tenderness of a father, and with the devotion of a fellow-warrior, the mighty son of Odin bears on his shoulders the weary and cold star-hero over the foggy Elivagar, filled with magic terrors, to place him safe by his own hearth south of this sea after he has honoured him with a token which shall for ever shine on the heavens as a monument of Orvandel's exploits and Thor's friendship for him. In the meantime Groa, Orvandel's wife, stays in Thor's halls.

But we discover the same bond of hospitality between Thor and Egil. According to Hymerskvida it is in Egil's house, according to Gylfaginning in the house in which Thjalfe is fostered, where the accident to one of Thor's goats happens. In one of the sources the youth whom Thor takes as a ransom is called simply Egil's child; in the other he is called Thjalfe. Two different mythic sources show that Thjalfe was a waif, adopted in Egil's house, and consequently not a real brother but a foster-brother of Svipdag and Ull. One source is Fornalder-saga (iii. 241), where it is stated that Groa in a *flœdar-mál* found a little boy and reared him together with her own son. *Flœdarmál* is a place which a part of the time is flooded with water and a part of the time lies dry. The other source is the Longobard saga, in which the mythological Egil reappears as Agelmund, the first king of the Longobardians who emigrated from Scandinavia (*Origo Longob.*, Paulus Diac., 14, 15; cp. No. 112). Agelmund, it is said, had a foster-son, Lamicho (*Origo Longob.*), or Lamissio (Paulus Diac.), whom he found in a dam and took home out of pity. Thus in the one place it is a woman who bears the name of the archer Orvandel's wife, in the other it is the archer Egil himself, who adopts as foster-son a child found in a dam or in a place filled with water. Paulus Diaconus says that the lad received the name Lamissio to commemorate this circumstance, "since he was fished up out of a dam or dyke," which in their (the Longobardian) language is called *lama* (cp. *lehm,* mud. The name Thjalfe (*thjálfi*) thus suggests a similar idea. As Vigfusson has already pointed out, it is connected with the English delve, a dyke; with the Anglo-Saxon *delfan;* the Dutch *delven,* to work the ground with a spade, to dig. The circumstances under which the lad was found presaged his future. In the mythology he fells the clay-giant, *Mökkr-kalfi* (Younger Edda, i. 272-274). In the migration saga he is the discoverer of land and circumnavigates islands (Korm., 19, 3; Younger Edda, i. 496), and there he conquers giants (Harbards-ljod, 39) in order to make the lands inhabitable for immigrants. In the appendix to the Gotland law he appears as Thjelvar, who lands in Gotland, liberates the island from trolls by carrying fire, colonises it and becomes the progenitor of a host of emigrants, who settle in southern countries. In Paulus Diaconus he grows up to be a powerful hero; in the mythology he develops into the Asa-god Thor's brave helper, who participates in his and the great archer's adventures on the Elivagar and in Jotunheim. Paulus (ch. 15) says that when Agelmund once came with his Longobardians to a river, "amazons" wanted to hinder him from crossing it. Then Lamissio fought, swimming in the river, with the bravest one of the amazons, and killed her. In the mythology Egil himself fights with the giantess Sela, mentioned in Saxo as an amazon; *piraticis exercita rebus ac bellici perita muneris* (*Hist.*, 138), while Thjalfe combats with giantesses on Hlessey (Harbardslj., 39), and at the side of Thor and the archer he fights his way through the river waves, in which giantesses try to drown him (Thorsdrapa). It is evident that Paulus Diaconus' accounts of Agelmund and Lamissio are nothing but echoes related as history of the myths concerning Egil and Thjalfe, of which the Norse records fortunately have preserved valuable fragments.

Thus Thjalfe is the archer Egil's and Groa's fosterson, as is apparent from a bringing together of the sources cited. From other sources we have found that Groa is the archer Orvandel's wife. Orvandel dwells near the Elivagar and Thor is his friend, and visits him on his way to and from Jotunheim. These are the evidences of Orvandel's and Egil's identity which lie nearest at hand.

It has already been pointed out that Svipdag's father Orvandel appears in Saxo by the name Ebbo (see Nos. 23, 100). It is Otharus-Svipdag's father whom he calls Ebbo (*Hist.*, 329-333). Halfdan slays Orvandel-Ebbo, while the latter celebrates his wedding with a princess Sygrutha (see No. 23). In the mythology Egil had the same fate: an enemy and rival kills him for the sake of a woman. "Franks Casket," an old work of sculpture now preserved in England, and reproduced in George Stephens' great work on the runes,* represents Egil defending his house against a host of assailants who storm it. Within the house a woman is seen, and she is the cause of the conflict. Like Saxo's Halfdan, one of the assailants carries a tree or a branched club as his weapon. Egil has already hastened out, bow in hand, and his three famous arrows have been shot. Above him is written in runes his name, wherefore there can be no doubt about his identity. The attack, according to Saxo, took place, in the night (*noctuque nuptiis superveniens—Hist.*, p. 330).

In a similar manner Paulus Diaconus relates the story concerning Egil Agelmund's death (ch. 16). He is attacked, so it is stated, in the night time by Bulgarians, who slew him and carried away his only daughter. During a part of their history the Longobardians had the Bulgarians as neighbors, with whom they were on a warfooting. In the mythology it was "Borgarians," that is to say, Borgar's son Halfdan and his men, who slew Orvandel. In history the "Borgarians" have been changed into Bulgarians for the natural reason that accounts of wars fought with Bulgarians were preserved in the traditions of the Longobardians.

The very name Ebbo reappears also in the saga of the Longobardians. The brothers, under whose leadership the Longobardians are said to have emigrated from Scandinavia, are in Saxo (*Hist.*, 418) called Aggo and Ebbo; in *Origo Longobardorum*, Ajo and Ybor; in Paulus

---

Runic Monuments, by George Stephens.

(ch. 7), Ajo and Ibor. Thus the name Ebbo is another form for Ibor, the German Ebur, the Norse *Jöfurr*, "a wild boar." The Ibor of the Longobard saga, the emigration leader, and Agelmund, the first king of the emigrants, in the mythology, and also in Saxo's authorities, are one and the same person. The Longobardian emigration story, narrated in the form of history, thus has its root in the universal Teutonic emigration myth, which was connected with the enmity caused by Loke between the gods and the primeval artists—an enmity in which the latter allied themselves with the powers of frost, and, at the head of the Skilfing-Yngling tribes, gave the impetus to that migration southward which resulted in the populating of the Teutonic continent with tribes from South Scandia and Denmark (see Nos. 28, 32).

Nor is the mythic hero Ibor forgotten in the German sagas. He is mentioned in Notker (about the year 1000) and in the Vilkinasaga. Notker simply mentions him in passing as a saga-hero well known at that time. He distinguishes between the real wild boar (Eber) roaming in the woods, and the Eber (Ebur) who "wears the swan-ring." This is all he has to say of him. But, according to Volundarkvida, the mythological Ebur-Egil is married to a swan-maid, and, like his brother Volund, he wore a ring. The signification of the swan-rings was originally the same as that of Draupner: they were symbols of fertility, and were made and owned for this reason by the primeval artists of mythology, who, as we have seen, were the personified forces of growth in nature, and by their beloved or wives, the swan-maids, who represented the saps of vegetation, the bestowers of the mythic "mead" or "ale." The swan-maid who loves Egil is, therefore, in Volundarvida called Olrun, a parallel to the name Olgefion, as Groa, Orvandel's wife, is called in Haustlaung (Younger Edda, i. 282). Saxo, too, has heard of the swan-rings, and says that from three swans singing in the air fell a *cingulum* inscribed with names down to King Fridlevus (Njord), which informed him where he was to find a youth who had been robbed by a giant, and whose liberation was a matter of great importance to Fridlevus. The context shows that the unnamed youth was in the mythology Fridlevus-Njord's own son Frey, the lord of harvests, who had been robbed by the powers of frost. Accordingly, a swan-ring has co-operated in the mythology in restoring the fertility of the earth.

In Vilkinasaga appears Villifer. The author of the saga says himself that this name is identical with Wild-Ebur, wild boar. Villifer, a splendid and noble-minded youth, wears on his arm a gold ring, and is the elder friend, protector, and saviour of Vidga Volundson. Of his family relations Vilkinasaga gives us no information, but the part it gives him to play finds its explanation in the myth, where Ebur is Volund's brother Egil, and hence the uncle of his favourite Vidga.

If we now take into consideration that in the German Orentel saga, which is based on the Svipdag-myth, the father of the hero is called Eigel (Egil), and his patron saint Wieland (Volund), and that in the archer, who in Saxo fights by the side of Anund-Volund against Halfdan, we have re-discovered Egil where we expected Orvandel; then we here find a whole chain of evidence that Ebur, Egil, and Orvandel are identical, and at the same time the links in this chain of evidence, taken as they are from the Icelandic poetry, and from Saxo, from England, Germany, and Italy, have demonstrated how widely spread among the Teutonic peoples was the myth about Orvandel-Egil, his famous brother Volund, and his no less celebrated son Svipdag. The result gained by the investigation is of the greatest importance for the restoration of the epic connection of the mythology. Hitherto the Volundarkvida with its hero has stood in the gallery of myths as an isolated torso with no trace of connection with the other myths and mythic sagas. Now, on the other hand, it appears, and as the investigation progresses it shall become more and more evident, that the Volund-myth belongs to the central timbers of the great epic of Teutonic mythology, and extends branches through it in all directions.

In regard to Svipdag's saga, the first result gained is that the mythology was not inclined to allow Volund's sword, concealed in the lower world, to fall into the hands of a hero who was a stranger to the great artist and his plans. If Volund forged the sword for a purpose hostile to the gods, in order to avenge a wrong done him, or to elevate himself and his circle of kinsmen among the elves at the expense of the ruling gods, then his work was not done in vain. If Volund and his brothers are those Ivalde sons who, after having given the gods beautiful treasures, became offended on account of the decision

864

which placed Sindre's work, particularly Mjolner, higher than their own, then the mythology has also completely indemnified them in regard to this insult. Mjolner is broken by the sword of victory wielded by Volund's nephew; Asgard trembles before the young elf, after he had received the incomparable weapon of his uncle; its gate is opened for him and other kinsmen of Volund, and the most beautiful woman of the world of gods becomes his wife.

109.

FREY FOSTERED IN THE HOME OF ORVANDEL-EGIL AND VOLUND. ORVANDEL'S EPITHET ISOLFR. VOLUND'S EPITHET AGGO.

The mythology has handed down several names of the coast region near the Elivagar, where Orvandel-Egil and his kinsmen dwelt, while they still were the friends of the gods, and were an outpost active in the service against the frost-powers. That this coast region was a part of Alfheim, and the most northern part of this mythic land, appears already from the fact that Volund and his brothers are in Volundarkvida elf-princes, sons of a mythic "king." The rule of the elf-princes must be referred to Alfheim for the same reason as we refer that of the Vans to Vanheim, and that of the Asa-gods to Asgard. The part of Alfheim here in question, where Orvandel-Egil's citadel was situated, was in the mythology called *Ýdalir, Ýsetr* (Grimnersmal, 5; Olaf Trygveson's saga, ch. 21). This is also suggested by the fact that *Ullr*, elevated to the dignity of an Asa-god, he who is the son of Orvandel-Egil, and Svipdag's brother (see No. 102), according to Grimnersmal, has his halls built in *Ýdalir*. Divine beings who did not originally belong to Asgard, but were adopted in Odin's clan, and thus became full citizens within the bulwarks of the Asa-citadel, still retain possession of the land, realm, and halls, which is their udal and where they were reared. After he became a denizen in Asgard, Njord continued to own and to reside occasionally in the Vana-citadel Noatun beyond the western ocean (see Nos. 20, 93). Skade, as an asynje, continues to inhabit her father Thjasse's halls in Thrymheim (Grimnersmal, 11). Vidar's grass and brush-grown realm is not a part of Asgard, but is the large plain on which, in Ragnarok, Odin is to fall in combat with Fenrer (Grimnersmal, 17; see No. 39). When Ull is said to have his halls in Ydaler, this must be based on a similar reason, and Ydaler must be the land where he was reared and which he inherited after his father, the great archer. When Grimnersmal enumerates the homes of the gods, the series of them begins with Thrudheim, Thor's realm, and next thereafter, and in connection with Alfheim, is mentioned Ydaler, presumably for the reason that Thor's land and Orvandel-Egil's were, as we have seen, most intimately connected in mythology.

> Land er heilact,
> er ec liggia se
> asom oc olfom nær;
> en i thrudheimi
> scal thórr vera,
> unz um rivfaz regin.

Ydalir heita.
thar er Ullr hefir
ser úm gorva sali;
Alfheim Frey
gáfo i árdaga
tivar at tannfæ.

Ýdalir means the "dales of the bow" or "of the bows." *Ýsetr* is "the chalet of the bow" or "of the bows." That the first part of these compound words is *ýr*, "a bow," is proved by the way in which the local name *Ýsetr* can be applied in poetical paraphrases, where the bow-holding hand is called Ysetr. The names refer to the mythical rulers of the region, namely, the archer Ull and his father the archer Orvandel-Egil. The place has also been called *Geirvadills setr, Geirvandills setr*, which is explained by the fact that Orvandel's father bore the epithet Geirvandel (Saxo, *Hist.*, 135). Hakon Jarl, the ruler of northern Norway, is called (Fagrsk., 37, 4) *Geirvadills setrs Ullr*, "the Ull of Geirvandel's chalet," a paraphrase in which we find the mythological association of Ull with the chalet which was owned by his father Orvandel and his grandfather Geirvandel. The Ydales were described as rich in gold. *Ysetrs eldr* is a paraphrase for gold. With this we must compare what Volund says (Volundarkvida, 14) of the wealth of gold in his and his kinsmen's home. (See further, in regard to the same passage, Nos. 114 and 115.)

In connection with its mention of the Ydales, Grimnersmal states that the gods gave Frey Alfheim as a toothgift. *Tannfé* (tooth-gift) was the name of a gift which was given (and in Iceland is still given) to a child when it gets its first tooth. The tender Frey is thus appointed by the gods as king over Alfheim, and chief of the elf-princes there, among whom Volund and Orvandel-Egil, judging from the mythic events themselves, must have been the foremost and most celebrated. It is also logically correct, from the standpoint of nature symbolism, that the god of growth and harvests receives the government of elves and primeval artists, the personified powers of culture. Through this arrangement of the gods, Volund and Orvandel become vassals under Njord and his son.

In two passages in Saxo we read mythic accounts told as history, from which it appears that Njord selected a foster-father for his son, or let him be reared in a home under the care of two fosterers. In the one passage (*Hist,.* 272) it is Fridlevus-Njord who selects Avo the archer as his son's foster-father; in the other passage (*Hist.,* 181) it is the tender Frotho, son of Fridlevus and future brother-in-law of Ericus-Svipdag, who receives Isulfus and Aggo as guardians.

So far as the archer Avo is concerned, we have already met him above (see No. 108) in combat by the side of Anundus-Volund against one Halfdan. He is a parallel figure to the archer Toko, who likewise fights by the side of Anundus-Volund against Halfdan, and, as has already been shown, he is identical with the archer Orvandel-Egil.

The name Aggo is borne by one of the leaders of the emigration of the Longobardians, brother of Ebbo-Ibor, in whom we have already discovered Orvandel-Egil.

The name Isolfr, in the Old Norse poetic language,

868

designates the bear (Younger Edda, i. 589; ii. 484). Vil-kinasaga makes Ebbo (Wild-Ebur) appear in the guise of a bear when he is about to rescue Volund's son Vidga from the captivity into which he had fallen. In his shield Ebbo has images of a wild boar and of a bear. As the wild boar refers to one of his names (Ebur), the image of the bear should refer to another (Isolfr).

Under such circumstances there can be no doubt that Orvandel-Egil and one of his brothers, the one desig-nated by the name Aggo (Ajo), be this Volund or Slagfin, were entrusted in the mythology with the duty of foster-ing the young Frey. Orvandel also assumes, as vassal under Njord, the place which foster-fathers held in rela-tion to the natural fathers of their protégés.

Frey, accordingly, is reared in Alfheim, and in the Ydales he is fostered by elf-princes belonging to a circle of brothers, among whom one, namely, Volund, is the most famous artist of mythology. His masterpiece, the sword of victory, in time proves to be superior to Sindre's chief work, the hammer Mjolner. And as it is always Volund whom Saxo mentions by Orvandel-Egil's side among his brothers (see No. 108), it is most reasonable to suppose that it is Volund, not Slagfin, who appears here under the name Aggo along with the great archer, and, like the latter, is entrusted with the fostering of Frey. It follows that Svipdag and Ull were Frey's fos-ter-brothers. Thus it is the duty of a foster-brother they perform when they go to rescue Frey from the power of giants, and when they, later, in the war between the Asas and Vans, take Frey's side. This also throws additional light on Svipdag-Skirner's words to Frey in Skirnersmal, 5:

ungir saman
varom i árdaga,
vel mættim tvæir truasc.

110.

SVIPDAG'S GRANDFATHER IS IVALDE. ORVANDEL, VOLUND,
AND SLAGFIN THEREFORE IDENTICAL WITH IVALDE'S
SONS.

In the mythology we read that elves smithied splendid treasures for Frey (Grimnersmal, 42; Younger Edda, i. 140, 340). Among these treasures were the remarkable ship *Skidbladnir* and the gold-glittering boar *Slidrugtanni,* also called Gullinbursti (Younger Edda, i. 176, 264, 340-344), both clearly symbols of vegetation. The elves that smithied these treasures are called Ivalde's sons, and constitute the same group of brothers whose gifts to the gods, at the instigation of Loke, are subjected to a public examination by the Asas and by them found wanting as compared with Sindre's products. It would be most surprising, nay, quite incredible, if, when other artists made useful presents to Frey, the elf-prince Volund and his brothers did not do likewise, inasmuch as he is the chief smith of them all, and inasmuch as he, with his brother Orvandel-Egil, has taken upon himself the duties of a foster-father toward the young harvest-god, among which duties one was certainly to care for his good and enable him to perform the important task devolving on him in the administration of the world.

From this standpoint already it is more than probable that the same artist who in the heroic saga of the Teutonic tribes, under the name Volund, Wieland, Weland, by the side of Mimer, plays the part of the foremost smith that antiquity knew is the same one as in the mythology was the most excellent smith; that is, the most skilful one among Ivalde's sons. This view is perfectly confirmed as to its correctness by the proofs which I shall now present.

Of Ivalde, Fornspjallsljod says that he had two groups of children, and that Idun, the goddess of vegetation, belonged to one of these groups:

> Álfa ættar
> Ithunni heto
> Ivallds ellri
> ýngsta barna.

Idun is, therefore, a sister of the celebrated artists, the sons of Ivalde. In Volundarkvida, Volund and Slagfin are brothers or half-brothers of the dises of vegetation, who are together with them in the Wolfdales (see str. 2). According to Fornspjallsljod, Idun was for a time absent from Asgard, and stayed in a winter-cold land near Narfe-Mimer's daughter Nat, and in company with persons whose names and epithets indicate that they were smiths, primeval artists (*Rögnir* and *Regin;* see Nos. 113, 115, and the epithet *viggiar,* a synonym of *smidar*—Younger Edda, i. 587). Thus we read precisely the same of Idun as of the swan-maids and vegetation-dises who dwelt for a time in the Wolfdales with Volund and his brothers.

Further on it shall be demonstrated that the name of Volund's father in the introduction of Volundarkvida and the name given to the father of Volund's and Slagfin's swan-maids are synonyms, and refer to one and the same person. But if we for the present leave this proof out, and confine ourselves to the evidences already presented, then the question concerning the identity of the Ivalde sons with the group of brothers Volund, Egil, and Slagfin assumes the following form:

1. (*a*) There is in the mythology a group of brothers, the Ivalde sons, from whose hands the most wonderful works proceeded, works which were presented to the gods, and by the latter were compared with those of the primeval artist Sindre.

(*b*) In the heroic saga there is a group of brothers, to whom Volund belongs, the most celebrated of the smiths handed down from the mythology.

2. (*a*) Ivalde is an elf and his sons elves.

(*b*) Volund, Egil, and Slagfin are elves (Volundarkvida, 32).

3. (*a*) Ivalde's sons are brothers or half-brothers of the goddess of vegetation, Idun.

(*b*) Volund, Egil, and Slagfin are brothers or half-brothers of swan-maids and dises of vegetation.

4. (*a*) Of Idun, the sister of Ivalde's sons, it is stated that she was for a time absent from the gods, and dwelt with the primeval artists in a winter-cold land, near Nat, the daughter of *Narfi*-Mimer.

(*b*) Volund and his brothers' swan-maids dwell for a time in a winter-cold land, which, as my researches have already shown, is situated *fyr nágrindr nedan,* consequently in the lower world, near the realm of Nat.

5. (*a*) Ivalde's sons were intimately associated with Frey and gave him precious treasures.

(*b*) Volund and Egil were intimately associated with Frey, and were his fosterers and wards.

6. (*a*) Ivalde's sons were most deeply insulted by the gods.

(*b*) Volund has been most deeply insulted by the Asas. He and Egil become their foes, and ally themselves with the powers of frost.

7. (*a*) The insult given to Ivalde's sons consisted in the fact that their works were judged inferior as compared with the hammer Mjolner made by Sindre.

(*b*) The best smith-work produced by Volund is a sword of such a quality that it is to prove itself superior to Mjolner in battle.

These circumstances alone force us to assume the identity of Ivalde's sons with Volund and his brothers. We must either admit the identity, or we are obliged to assume that the epic of the mythology contained two such groups of brothers, and made them identical in descent, functions, and fortunes. Besides, it must then have made the one group avenge not an insult offered to itself, but an insult to the other. I have abstained from the latter assumption, because it is in conflict with the best rules for a logical investigation—*causæ non sunt præter necessitatem multiplicandæ.* And the identity gains confirmation from all sides as the investigation progresses.

873

111.

THE RESULTS OF THE JUDGMENT PASSED ON THE WORKS
OF ART PRODUCED BY THE IVALDE SONS. PARALLEL
MYTHS IN RIGVEDA.

In the Younger Edda, which speaks of the judgment
passed by the gods on the art works of the Ivalde sons
(p. 340, &c.), there is nothing said about the consequences
of the judgment; and the mythologists seem therefore to
have assumed that no results followed, although it was
prepared by the "father of misfortunes," the far-calcu-
lating and evil-scheming Loke. The judgment would in
that case be an isolated event, without any influence on
the future, and without any connection with the other
mythic events. On the other hand, no possible explanation was found of Volund's words (Volundarkvida, 28),
which he utters after he has taken his terrible vengeance
on Nidad and is prepared to fly away in eagle guise from
his prison: *Nu hefi ec hefnt harma minna allra nema
einna ivithgjarnra*—"Now I have avenged all the wrongs
done to me, excepting one, which demands a more terrible
vengeance." The wrong here referred to by him is not
done to him by Nidad, and did not happen to him while
he lived as an exile in the wildnerness of the Wolfdales,
but belongs to an earlier time, when he and his brothers
and their kinsmen dwelt in the realm rich in gold, where,
according to Volundarkvida (14), they lived a happy
life. This wrong was not avenged when he and his
brothers left their home abounding in gold, in order that
far from his enemies he might perfect his plan of revenge

by making the sword of victory. Volund's words refer to the judgment passed on the art work of the Ivalde sons, and thus the mythic events unite themselves into a continuous chain.

This judgment was in its consequences too important not to be referred to in Völuspa, which makes all the danger-boding events of the mythology pass one by one before our eyes in the order in which they happened, in order to show how this world from an innocent and happy beginning sank deeper and deeper into the misery which attains its maturity in Ragnarok. That is the plan and purpose of the poem. As I shall show fully and in detail in another part of this work, its purpose is not to speak of Valfather's "art work," but of the treacherous deeds of Loke, "the father of evil" (*Vafodrs vel*—Cod. Hauk.) ; not to speak of "the traditions of the past," but of "the past events full of danger" (*forn spjöll fira*). The happy time during which the Asas *tefldu i túni* and *teitir váru* passes away for ever, and is followed by an epoch in which three dangerous thurs-maidens came from Jotenheim. These thurs-maidens are not the norns, as has usually been assumed. Of the relation of the norns to the gods I have given a full account already. The three thurs-maids are the one who in her unity is triple and is thrice born of different parents. Her name is Heid-Gulveig-Angerboda, and, in connection with Loke, she constitutes the evil principle of Teutonic mythology, like Angra Mainyu, and Jahi in the Iranian mythology (Bundehesh, 3). The misfortune-boding event which happens after the first hypostasis of "the three times born" came from

Jotunheim is mentioned in connection with its couse-
quences in Völuspa (str. 8.) The Asas had not hitherto
suffered from want of works of gold, but now came a
time when such as might be of use or pleasure to the gods
were no longer to be had. Of the gold-metal itself the
gods have never been in want. Their halls glitter with
this metal, and it grows in the bright wood *Glasir*, outside of Valhal (Younger Edda, i. 340). The poem, as
the very words show, means golden works of art, things
made of gold, such as *Gungnir, Draupnir,* Sif's hair, Brisingamen, and *Slidrugtanni,* things the possession of which
increased the power of the gods and the wealth of Midgard. Such ceased to flow into the hands of the gods.
The epoch in which Sindre's and the Ivalde son's gifts
increased Asgard's collection of world-protecting weapons
and fertility-producing ornaments was at an end, when
Loke, through Heid's arrival, found his other ego and
when the evil principle, hitherto barren, could as man
and woman give birth to evil deeds. The consequence
of the first deceitful act was, as we see, that hands skilful
in art—hands which hitherto had made and given such
treasures—refused to serve the gods any longer. The
arrangement whereby Loke gained this end Völuspa does
not mention, but it can be no other than the judgment
brought about by him, which insulted the sons of Ivalde,
and, at the same time, cheated the victorious Sindre out
of the prize agreed on, Loke's head. Both the groups of
artists must have left the divine court angry at the gods.
When we remember that the primeval artists are the creative forces of vegetation personified, then we can also

876

understand the significance of the conflict between them and the gods, whom they hitherto had served. The first part of Völuspa is interpolated partly with strophes from an old song of creation of great mythological importance, partly with its lists of names for the use of young poets. If we remove these interpolations, there remains a chain of primeval mythological mishaps, the first link of which is the event which marks the end of the first epoch during which the primeval artists, amicably united with the gods, made splendid weapons, means of locomotion, and ornaments for the latter. On this conflict followed the blending of the air with harmful elements—in other words, it was the beginning of the great winter. Freyja was betrayed into the hands of the giants; the black art, sown by Heid, was disseminated among mankind; the murder was committed against the one thrice born contrary to promise and oath; there is war between the Asas and Vans; the first great war in the world breaks out, when Asgard is stormed and Midgard is covered with battlefields, on which brothers slay each other; Balder is killed by the mistletoe; the host of monsters are born who, in the Ironwood, await Ragnarok; on account of the sins of men, it became necessary to make places of torture in the lower world. All these terrible events, which happened in time's morning, are the cunning work of the father of misfortunes and of his feminine counterpart. The seeress in Völuspa relates all these events and deeds to show the necessity of the coming destruction and regeneration of the world.

Above (see No. 54), it has already been shown that the

fragments of old Aryan mythology, which Avesta, Zend, and Bundehesh have preserved, speak of a terrible winter, which visited the world. To rescue that which is noblest and best among plants, animals, and men from the coming destruction, Jima arranged in the lower world a separate enclosed domain, within which selected organisms live an uncontaminated life undisturbed by the events of this world, so that they may people a more beautiful and a happier earth in the regenerated world. I have shown that the same myth in all important details reappears in the Teutonic doctrine anent Mimer's grove and the *ásmegir* living there. In the Iranian records, we read that the great winter was the work of the evil spirit, but they do not tell the details or the epic causes of the destruction by the cold. Of these causes we get information in Rigveda, the Indian sister of the Iranian mythology.

Clothed with divine rank, there lives among Rigveda's gods an extraordinary artist, Tvashtar (Tvashtri), often mentioned and addressed in Rigveda's hymns. The word means "the master-workman," "the handi-workman" (Bergaigne, *Relig. Ved.,* iii. 45; Darmesteter, Ormazd, 63, 100). He is the one who forms the organisms in the maternal wombs, the one who prepares and first possesses as his secret the strength- and inspiration-giving soma-drink (Rigv., ii. 53, &c.); it is he that supports the races of men (Rigv., iii. 55, 19). Among the wonderful things made by his hands are mentioned a goblet, which the gods drink from, and which fills itself with blessings (Rigv., iii. 55, 20; x. 53, 9), and Indra's the Hindooic Thor's, thunderbolt, corresponding to Thor's Mjolner.

But among mortals brothers have been reared, themselves mortals, and not of divine rank, but who have educated themselves into artists, whose skill fills the world with astonishment. They are three in number, usually called the *Ribhus,* but also *Anus* and *Ayus,* names which possibly may have some original connection with the Volund names Aunnd and Ajo. Most clever and enterprising in successful artistic efforts is the youngest of the three (Rigv., iv. 34). They are also soma-brewers, skalds, and heroes (Rigv., iv. 36, 5, 7), and one of them, like Volund's brother Orvandel-Egil, is an unsurpassed archer (Rigv., iv. 36, 6). On account of their handiwork, these mortal artists come in contact with the gods (Rigv., iv. 35), and as Volund and Orvandel-Egil become Thor's friends, allies, war-comrades, and servants, so the Ribhus become Indra's (Rigv., i. 51, 2; vii, 37, 7); "with Indra, the helpful, allied themselves the helpers; with Indra, the nimble, the Ribhus." They make weapons, coats-of-mail, and means of locomotion, and make wonderful treasures for the gods. On earth they produce vegetation in the deserts, and hew out ways for the fertilising streams (Rigv., v. 42, 12; iv. 33, 7). With Ivalde's sons, they, therefore, share the qualities of being at the same time creators of vegetation, and smiths at the hearth, and bestowers of precious treasures to the gods.

But some evil tongue persuaded the gods that the Ribhus had said something derogatory of the goblet made by Tvashtar. This made Tvashtar angry, and he demanded their death. The gods then sent the fire-god Agni to the Ribhus. The Ribhus asked: "Why has the most excellent, the most youthful one come to us? On what errand does he come?" Agni told them that it was reported that they had found fault with Tvashtar's goblet; they declared that they had not said anything derogatory, but only talked about the material of which it was made. Agni meanwhile stated the resolution of the gods, to the effect that they were to make from Tvashtar's goblet four others of the same kind. If they were unable to do this, then the gods would doubtless satisfy Tvashtar's request and take their lives; but if they were able to make the goblets, then they should share with the gods the right to receive offerings. Moreover, they were to give the following proof of mastership. They were to smithy a living horse, a living chariot, a living cow, and they were to create a means of rejuvenation and demonstrate its efficacy on two aged and enfeebled beings. The Ribhus informed the gods that they would do what was demanded of them. So they made the wonderful chariot or the chariot-ship, which they gave to the Asvinians—the beautiful twin-gods—on which they ride through the air and on the sea (cp. Skidbladner, Frey's ship, and Hringhorne, Balder's, and probably also Hoder's means of locomotion through the air and on the sea). Of one horse they made two, and presented them to Indra. Out of an empty cow's hide they smithied a cow (cp. Sindre's work of art when he made the boar Slidringtanne out of an empty pig's skin). They made the remedy of rejuvenation, and tested it successfully on their aged parents. Finally, they do the great master-work of producing four goblets of equal excellence from Tvashtar's. Thereupon they appear before the gods who, "w:th insight," test their works. Tvashtar himself could not help being astounded when he saw the goblets. But the result of the test by the gods, and the judgment passed on the art-works of the Ribhus, were fraught with danger for the future. Both Tvashtar and the Ribhus became dissatisfied. Tvashtar abandoned the gods and betook himself to the mountains with the dises of vegetation, in whose company he is often mentioned. The Ribhus refused to accept from the gods the proffered share in morning and noon sacrifices, and went away cursing their adversaries. They proceeded on long journeys, and the gods knew not where to find them (Rigv., i. 161, 1-13; iv. 33, 1-11, &c.).

The result of this trouble between the primeval artists themselves, and between them and the gods, becomes clear from the significance which Tvashtar, he who nourishes the world, and the Ribhus, they who deck the deserts with vegetation, and irrigate the valleys, have as symbols of nature. The beneficent powers of nature, who hitherto had operated in the service of the gods, abandon their work, and over the world are spread that winter of which the Iranian mythology speaks, that darkness, and that reign of giant-monsters which, according to Rigveda, once prevailed, and during which time Indra, at the head of the gods, fought valiantly to restore order and to bring back the sun.

Here we find remarkable points of contact, or rather contact surfaces, between the Asiatic-Aryan groups of myths and the Teutonic. The question is not as to similarity in special details. That kind of similarities may be pointed out in nearly all mythic groups in the world, and, as a rule, altogether too bold hypotheses are built on the feeble foundations they offer. The question here is in regard to identity in great, central, connected collections of myths. Such are: The myths concerning an original harmony between a divine clan on the one hand, and artists subordinate to, and in the service of, the divine clan on the other hand. Artists who produce fertility, ornaments, and weapons for the gods, know how to brew the strength- and inspiration-giving mead, and are closely connected with dises of vegetation, who, as we shall show, appear as swan-maids, not only in the Teutonic mythology but also in the Hindooic; the myths telling how this harmony was frustrated by a judgment in a competition, the contending parties being on the one hand he who in the Hindooic mythology made Indra's thunderbolt, and in the Teutonic Thor's thundering Mjolner; and on the other hand three brothers, of whom one is an excellent archer; the myths concerning the consequences of the judgment, the destruction of nature by frost-powers and giant-monsters; the myths (in the Iranian and Teutonic records of antiquity) concerning the subterranean paradise, in which a selection of the best beings of creation are protected against annihilation, and continue to live uncorrupted through centuries; the myths (in the Iranian and Teutonic records of antiquity) of the destiny of these beings, connected with the myths likewise common to the Iranian and Teutonic mythologies concerning the destruction and regeneration of the world. Common to the Hindooic and Teutonic mythology is also the idea that a cunning, spying, being, in Rigveda Dadhyak (Dadhyank), in the Icelandic sources Loke, has lost his head to an artist who smithied the bolt for Indra and the hammer for Thor, but saves his wager through cunning.

An important observation should here be pointed out. A comparison between different passages in Rigveda shows, that of all the remarkable works of art which were exhibited to the gods for their examination, there was originally not one of metal. Tvashtar's goblet was not made of gold, but of fire and water and a third element. Indra's thunderbolt was made of the bones of the head of Dadhyak's horse, and it is in a later tradition that it becomes bronze. Common to the Aryan-Asiatic and the Teutonic mythology is the ability of the primeval artists to make animals from empty skins of beasts, and of making from *one* work of art several similar ones (the goblet of the Ribhus, Sindre's Draupner). In the Teutonic mythology, Thor's hammer was not originally of metal, but of stone, and the other works produced by Sindre and Ivalde's sons may in the course of centuries have undergone similar changes. It should also be noted that not a trace is to be found in the Asiatic groups of myths of a single one to be compared with that concerning Svipdag and the sword of victory. In the Teutonic heroic saga, Geirvandel, the spear-hero, is the father of Orvandel, the archer, and of him is born Svipdag, the sword-hero (cp. No. 123). The myth concerning the sword of victory seems to be purely Teutonic, and to have sprung into existence during one of the bronze or iron ages, while the myths concerning the judgment passed on the primeval artists, and concerning the fimbul-winter following, must hail from a time when metals were not yet used by the Aryans. In the other event it would be most incredible to suppose that the judgment should concern works of art, of which not a single one originally suggested a product of metal.

<h2 style="text-align:center">112.</h2>

THE CONSEQUENCES OF THE JUDGMENT PASSED ON THE IVALDE SONS (*continued*). NJORD'S EFFORTS TO BRING ABOUT A RECONCILIATION.

It has already been stated that Fridlevus-Njord rescues a princely youth from the power of the giants. According to Saxo, the event was an episode in the feud between Fridlevus-Njord and Anundus (Volund), and Avo, the archer (Orvandel-Egil). This corroborates the theory that the rescued youth was Frey, Volund's and Egil's foster-son. The first one of the gods to be seized by fears on account of the judgment passed on Ivalde's sons, ought, naturally, to be Njord, whose son Frey was at that time in the care and power of Volund and Egil (see No. 109). We also learn from Saxo that Fridlevus took measures to propitiate the two brothers. He first sends messengers, who on his behalf woo the daughter of Anund-Volund, but the messengers do not return. Anund had slain them. Thereupon Fridlevus goes himself, accompanied by others, and among the latter was a "mediator." The name of the mediator was Bjorno, and he was one of those champions who constituted the defence of that citadel, which Fridlevus afterwards captured, and which we have recognised as Asgard (see No. 36). Thus Bjorno is one of the Asas, and there are reasons, which I shall discuss later, for assuming him to be Balder's brother *Hödr*. The context shows that Fridlevus' journey to Ivalde's sons and meeting with them takes place while there was yet hope of reconciliation, and before the latter arrived in the inaccessible Wolfdales, which are situated below the Na-gates in the subterranean Jotunheim. On the way thither they must have been overtaken by Fridlevus, and doubtless the event occurred there which Saxo relates, and of which an account in historical form is preserved in the Longobardian migration saga.

The meeting did not lead to reconciliation, but to war. Avo, the archer (Orvandel-Egil; see Nos. 108, 109) appeared on the one side and challenged Fridlevus-Njord to a duel. Bjorno became angry that a person of so humble descent as this Avo dared to challenge the noble-born Fridlevus, and in his wrath he drew his bow to fell "the plebeian" with an arrow. Thus Bjorno also was an archer. But Avo anticipated him, and an arrow from him severed Bjorno's bow-string from the bow. While Bjorno was tying the string again, there came from Avo a second arrow, which passed between his fingers without hurting him, and then there came a third arrow, which shot away Bjorno's arrow just as he was placing it on the string. Then the Ivalde sons continued their departure. Bjorno let loose a *molossus* he had with him to pursue them, probably the same giant-dog or giant wolf-dog which Saxo describes in a preceding chapter (*Hist.,*

260) as being in Bjorno's possession, and which before had guarded the giant Offote's herds. But this *molossus* was not able to prevent those fleeing from reaching their destination in safety. In all probability Frey had already been delivered by his wards to the giants when this happened. This must have occurred on the way between the abode abounding in gold, where Ivalde's sons had formerly lived in happiness, and the Wolfdales, and so within Jotunheim, where the gods were surrounded by foes.

The story of this adventure on the journey of the emigrating Ivalde sons reappears in a form easily recognised in Paulus Diaconus, where he tells of the emigration of the Longobardians under Ibor (Orvandel-Egil; see No. 108) and Ajo (Volund). In Saxo Avo-Egil, who belongs to the race of elves, becomes a low-born champion, while the Vana-god Njord becomes King Fridlevus. In Paulus the saga is not content with making the great archer of the emigrants a plebeian, but he is made a thrall who challenges a chosen free-born warrior among the foes of the Longobardians. In the mythology and in Saxo the duel was fought with bows and arrows, and the plebeian was found to be far superior to his opponent. Paulus does not name the kind of weapons used, but when it had ended with the victory of "the thrall," an oath was taken on an *arrow* that the thralls were to be freed from their chains by the Longobardians. Consequently the arrow must have been the thrall's weapon of victory. In the mythology, the journey of the Ivalde sons to the Wolfdales was down to the lower world Jotunheim and northward through Nifelhel, inhabited by thurses and monsters. Both in Saxo and Paulus this sort of beings take part in the adventures described. In Saxo, Fridlevus' war-comrade Bjorno sends a monster in the guise of a dog against the sons of Ivalde. In Paulus, according to the belief of their enemies, the emigrants had as their allies "men with dog-heads."

Bjorno is an Asa-god; and he is described as an archer who had confidence in his weapon, though he proved to be inferior to Avo in the use of it. Among the gods of Asgard only two archers are mentioned—*Hödr* and *Ullr.* At the time when this event occurred Ull had not yet been adopted in Asgard. As has been shown above (see No. 102), he is the son of Orvandel-Egil and Sif. His abode is still with his parents when Svipdag, his half-brother, receives instructions from Sif to seek Frey and Freyja in Jotunheim (see No. 102), and he faithfully accompanies Svipdag through his adventures on this journey. Thus Ull is out of the question—the more so as he would in that case be opposing his own father. Hoder (*Hödr*) is mentioned as an archer both in the Beowulf poem, where he, under the name Hædcyn, shoots Balder-Herebeald accidentally with his "horn-bow," and in Saxo (*arcus peritia pollebat—Hist.,* 111), and in Christian tales based on myths, where he appears by the name *Hedinn.* That Bjorno, mentioned by Saxo as a beautiful youth, is Hoder is confirmed by another circumstance. He is said to be *sequestris ordinis vir* (*Hist.,* 270), an expression so difficult to interpret that scholars have proposed to change it into *sequioris* or *equestris ordinis vir.*

The word shows that Bjorno in Saxo's mythological authorities belonged to a group of persons whose functions were such that they together might be designated as a *sequestris ordo*. *Sequester* means a mediator in general, and in the law language of Rome it meant an impartial arbitrator to whom a dispute might be referred. The Norse word which Saxo, accordingly, translated with *sequestris ordo*, "the mediators," "the arbitrators," can have been none other than the plural *ljónar*, a mythological word, and also an old legal term, of which it is said in the Younger Edda: *Ljónar heita their menn, er ganga um sættir manna*, "*ljónar* are called those men whose business it is to settle disputes." That this word *ljónar* originally designated a certain group of Asa-gods whose special duty it was to act as arbitrators is manifest from the phrase *ljóna kindir*, "the children of the peacemakers," an expression inherited from heathendom and applied to mankind far down in Christian times; it is an expression to be compared with the phrase *megir Heimdallar*, "Heimdal's sons," which also was used to designate mankind. In Christian times the phrase "children of men" was translated with the heathen expression *ljóna kindir;* and when the recollection of the original meaning of *ljónar* was obliterated, the word, on account of this usage, came to mean men in general (*viri, homines*), a signification which it never had in the days of heathendom.

Three Asa-gods are mentioned in our mythological records as peacemakers—Balder, Hoder, and Balder's son, Forsete. Balder is mentioned as judge in the Younger Edda (90). As such he is *liksamastr*—that is, "the most infliential peacemaker.'" Of Forsete, who inherits his father's qualities as judge, it is said in Grimnersmal (15) that he *svefer allar sacir,* "settles all disputes." Hoder, who both in name and character appears to be a most violent and thoughtless person, seems to be the one least qualified for this calling. Nevertheless he performed the duties of an arbitrator by the side of Balder and probably under his influence. Saxo (*Hist.,* 122) speaks of him as a judge to whom men referred their disputes—*consueverat consulenti populo plebiscita depromere*—and describes him as gifted with great talents of persuasion. He had *eloquentiæ suavitatem,* and was able to subdue stubborn minds with *benignissimo sermone* (*Hist.,* 116, 117). In Völuspa (60) the human race which peoples the renewed earth is called *burir brodra tvegia,* "the sons of the two brothers," and the two brothers mentioned in the preceding strophe are Balder and Hoder. Herewith is to be compared *ljóna kindir* in Völuspa (14). In Harbardsljod (42) the insolent mocker of the gods, Harbard, refers to the miserable issue of an effort made by *jafnendr,* "the arbitrator," to reconcile gods with certain ones of their foes. I think it both possible and probable that the passage refers to the mythic event above described, and that it contains an allusion to the fact that the effort to make peace concerned the recovery of Frey and Freyja, who were delivered as "brides" to naughty giants, and for which "brides" the peacemakers received arrows and blows as compensation. Compare the expression *bæta mundi baugi* and Thor's astonishment, expressed in the next strophe, at the insulting words, the worst of the kind he ever heard. Saxo describes the giant in whose power Frey is, when he is rescued by his father, as a cowardly and enervated monster whose enormous body is a *moles destituta rubore* (*Hist.*, 268). In this manner ended the effort of the gods to make peace. The three sons of Ivalde continue their journey to the Wolfdales, inaccessible to the gods, in order that they thence might send ruin upon the world.

113.

PROOFS THAT IVALDE'S SONS ARE IDENTICAL WITH OLVALDE'S.

Observations made in the course of my investigations anent Ivalde and his sons have time and again led me to the unexpected result that Ivalde's sons, Slagfin, Egil, and Volund, are identical with Olvalde-Alvalde's sons, who, in the Grotte-song, are called *Idi, Urnir* or *Aurnir* (*Ornir*), and *thjazi,* and in the Younger Edda (p. 214) *thjazi, Idi,* and *Gángr.* This result was unexpected and, as it seemed to me in the beginning, improbable, for the reason that where Thjasse is mentioned in the Elder Edda, he is usually styled a giant, while Volund is called a prince or chief of elves in Volundarkvida. In Grimnersmal (11) Thjasse is designated as *inn amátki iotunn;* in Harbardsljod (19) as *enn thrudmothgi iotunn;* in Hyndluljod (30) as a kinsman of Gymer and Aurboda. The Grotte-song (9) says that Thjasse, Ide, and Aurnir were brothers of those mountain giants who were the fathers of Menja and Fenja. In the Younger Edda he is also called a *jötunn.* In the beginning of my researches, and before Volund's position in the mythology was clear to me, it appeared to me highly improbable that a prince among the elves and one of the chief artists in the mythology could be characterised as a giant. Indeed I was already then aware that the clan-names occurring in the mythology—*áss, vanr, álfr, dvergr,* and *jötunn*—did not exclusively designate the descent of the beings, but could also be applied to them on account of qualities developed or positions acquired, regardless of the clan to which they actually belonged by their birth. In Thrymskvida (15), so to speak in the same breath, Heimdal is called both *áss* and *vanr*—*"thá quath that Heimdallr, hvitastr ása, vissi han vel fram sem vanir áthrir."* And Loke is designated both as *áss* and *jötunn,* although the Asas and giants represent the two extremes. Neither Heimdal nor Loke are of the Asa-clan by birth; but they are adopted in Asgard, that is, they are adopted Asas, and this explains the appellation. Elves and dwarfs are doubtless by descent different classes of beings, but the word dwarf, which in the earliest Christian times became the synonym of a being of diminutive stature, also meant an artist, a smith, whence both Vans and elves, nay, even Fjalar, could be incorporated in the Völuspa dwarf-list. When, during the progress of my investigations, it appeared that Volund and his brothers in the epic of the mythology were the most dangerous foes of the gods and led the powers of frost in their efforts to destroy the world, it could no longer surprise me that Volund, though an elf prince, was characterised as *inn ámátki iotunn, enn thrudmothgi*

891

iotunn. But there was another difficulty in the way: according to Hyndluljod and the Grotte-song, Thjasse and his brothers were kinsmen of giants, and must therefore undoubtedly have had giant-blood in their veins. But there are kinsmen of the giants among the Asas too; and when in the progress of the investigation it appears that Thjasse's mother is a giantess, but his father a *hapt,* a god of lower rank, then his maternal descent, and his position as an ally and chief of the giants, and as the most powerful foe of Asgard and Midgard, are sufficient to explain the apparent contradiction that he is at the same time a giant and a kinsman of the giants, and still identical with the elf-prince, Volund. It should also be observed that, as shall be shown below, the tradition has preserved the memory of the fact that Volund too was called a giant and had kinsmen among the giants.

The reasons which, taken collectively, prove conclusively at least to me, that Ivalde's sons and Olvalde's are identical are the following:

(1) In regard to the names themselves, we note in the first place that, as has already been pointed out, the name of the father of Ide, as Aurnir-Gang, and of Thjasse appears with the variations *Allvaldi, Ölvaldi,* and *Audvaldi.* To persons speaking a language in which the prefixes *I-, Id-,* and *All-* are equivalents and are substituted for one another, and accustomed to poetics, in which it was the most common thing to substitute equivalent nouns and names (for example, *Grjótbjörn* for *Arinbjörn, Fjallgyldir* for *Ásólfr,* &c.), it was impossible to see in *Ivaldi* and *Allvaldi* anything but names designating the same person.

892

(2) Anent the variation Olvalde we have already seen that its equivalents Olmodr and Sumbl (Finnakonungr, *phinnorum rex*) allude to Slagfin's, Orvandel-Egil's, and Volund's father, while Olvalde himself is said to be the father of Ide, Aurnir, and Thjasse.

(3) Ajo's and Ibor's mother is called *Gambara* in *Origo Longobardorum* and in Paulus Diaconus. Aggo's and Ebbo's mother is called *Gambaruc* in Saxo. In Ibor-Ebbo and Ajo-Aggo we have re-discovered Egil and Volund. The Teutonic stem of which the Latinised Gambara was formed is in all probability *gambr, gammr,* a synonym of *gripr* (Younger Edda, ii. 572), the German *Greif*. According to the Younger Edda (i. 314), Thjasse's mother is the giantess *Greip,* daughter of *Geirrŏdr*. The forms *grip,* neuter and *greip,* feminine, are synonyms in the Old Norse language, and they surely grew out of the same root. While Gambara thus is Volund's mother, Thjasse's mother bears a name to which Gambara alludes.

(4) The variation *Audvaldi* means "the one presiding over riches," and the epithet finds its explanation in the Younger Edda's account of the gold treasure left by Thjasse's father, and of its division among his sons (p. 214. It is there stated that Thjasse's father was *mjök gullaudigr.* Ivalde's sons, who gave the gods golden treasures, were likewise rich in gold, and in Volundar-kvida Volund speaks of his and his kinsmen's golden wealth in their common home.

(5) Of the manner in which Thjasse and his brothers divided the golden treasure the Younger Edda contains,

in the above passage, the following statement: "When Olvalde died and his sons were to divide the inheritance, they agreed in the division to measure the gold by taking their mouths full of gold an equal number of times. Hence gold is called in poetry the words or speech of these giants."

It is both possible and assumable that in the mythology the brothers divided the gold in silence and in harmony. But that it should have been done in the manner here related may be doubted. There is reason to suspect that the story of the division of the gold in the manner above described was invented in Christian times in order to furnish an explanation of the phrase *thingskil thjaza* in Bjarkamal, of *Idja glysmál* in the same source, and of *idja ord,* quoted in *Malskrudsfrædi.* More than one pseudo-mythic story, created in the same manner and stamped by the same taste, is to be found in the Younger Edda. It should not be forgotten that all these phrases have one thing in common, and that is, a public deliberation, a judicial act. *Mál* and *ord* do not necessarily imply such an allusion, for in addition to the legal meaning, they have the more common one of speech and verbal statements in general; but to get at their actual significance in the paraphrases quoted we must compare them with *thingskil,* since in these paraphrases all the expressions, *thingskil, glysmál,* and *ord,* must be founded on one and the same mythic event. With *thingskil* is meant that which can be produced before a court by the defendant in a dispute to clear up his case; and as gold ornaments are called Thjasse's *thingskil* in Bjarkamal, it should follow that some judicial act was mentioned in the mythology, in which gold treasures made or possessed by Thjasse were produced to clear up a dispute which, in some way or other, touched him. From the same point of view Ide's *glysmál* and Ide's *ord* are to be interpreted. Ide's *glysmál* are Ide's "glittering pleadings;" his *ord* are the evidence or explanation presented in court by the ornaments made by or belonging to him. Now, we know from the mythology a court act in which precious works of the smiths, "glittering pleadings," were produced in reference to the decision of a case. The case or dispute was the one caused by Loke, and the question was whether he had forfeited his head to Sindre or not. As we know, the decision of the dispute depended on a comparison between Brok's and Sindre's works on the one hand, and those of the Ivalde sons on the other. Brok had appeared before the high tribunal, and was able to plead his and his brother's cause. Ivalde's sons, on the other hand, were not present, but the works done by them had to speak in their behalf, or rather for themselves. From this we have, as it seems to me, a simple and striking explanation of the paraphrases *thjaza thingskil, Idja glysmál, Idja ord.* Their works of art were the glittering but mute pleadings which were presented, on their part, for the decision of the case. That gold carried in the mouth and never laid before the tribunal should be called *thingskil* I regard as highly improbable. From heathen poems we cannot produce a single positive proof that a paraphrase of so distorted and inadequate a character was ever used.

(6) Saxo relates that the same Fridlevus-Njord who

fought with Anund-Volund and Avo-Egil wooed Anund's daughter and was refused, but was married to her after Anund's death. Thus it would seem that Njord married a daughter of Volund. In the mythology he marries Thjasse's daughter Skade. Thus Volund and Thjasse act the same part as father-in-law of Njord.

(7) Saxo further relates that Freyja-Syritha's father was married to the *soror* of Svipdag-Otharus. *Soror* means sister, but also foster-sister and playmate. If the word is to be taken in its strictest sense, Njord marries a daughter of Volund's brother; if in its modified sense, Volund's daughter.

(8) In a third passage (*Hist.,* 50, 53), Skade's father appears under the name Haquinus. The same name belongs to a champion (*Hist.,* 323) who assists Svipdag-Ericus in his combat with the Asa-god Thor and his favourite Halfdan, and is the cause that Thor's and Halfdan's weapons prove themselves worthless against the Volund sword wielded by Svipdag-Ericns. There is, therefore, every reason for regarding Haquinus as one of Saxo's epithets for Volund. The name *Hákon,* of which Haquinus has been supposed to be the Latinised form, never occurs in the Norse mythic records, but Haquinus is in this case to be explained as a Latinisation with the aspirate usual in Saxo of the Old German Aki, the Middle German Ecke, which occurs in the compositions Eckenbrecht, Eckehard, and Eckesachs. In "Rosengarten," Eckenbrecht is a celebrated weapon-smith. In Vilkinasaga, Eckehard is, like Volund, a smith who works for Mimer; and Eckesachs is a sword made by the three

dwarfs, of which in part the same story is told as of Volund's sword of victory. Thus while Haquinus and what is narrated of Haquinus refers to the smith Volund, a person who in Saxo is called Haquinus assumes the place which belongs to Thjasse in his capacity of Skade's father.

(9) In Lokasenna (17), Loke reproaches Idun that she has embraced the slayer of her own brother:

> thic queth ec allra quenna
> vergjarnasta vera,
> sitztu arma thina
> lagdir itrthvegna
> um thinn brothurbana.

Idun is a daughter of Ivalde (Forspjallsljod), and hence a sister or half-sister of the famous smiths, Ivalde's sons. From the passage it thus appears that one of Ivalde's sons was slain, and Loke insists that Idun had given herself to the man who was the cause of his death.

There is not the slightest reason to doubt that in this instance, as in so many other cases, Loke boasts of the evil deeds he has committed, and of the successes he has had among the asynjes, according to his own assurances. With the reproaches cast on Idun we should compare what he affirms in regard to Freyja, in regard to Tyr's wife, in regard to Skade and Sif, in reference to all of whom he claims that they have secretly been his mistresses. Against Idun he could more easily and more truthfully bring this charge, for the reason that she was at one time wholly in his power, namely, when he stole into Thjasse's halls and carried her away thence to Asgard (Younger Edda, i.

210-214). Under such circumstances, that slayer of Idun's brother, whom she is charged with embracing, can be none other than Loke himself. As a further allusion to this, the author of the poem makes Loke speak of a circumstance connected with the adventure—namely, that Idun, to sweeten the pleasure of the critical hour, washed her arms shining white—a circumstance of which none other than herself and her secret lover could know. Thus Loke is the cause of the slaying of one of the famous artists, Ivalde's sons. The murders of which Loke boasts in the poem are two only, that of Balder and that of Thjasse. He says that he advised the killing of Balder, and that he was the first and foremost in the killing of Thjasse (*fyrstr oc ofstr*). Balder was not Idun's brother. So far as we can make out from the mythic records extant, the Ivalde son slain must have been identical with Thjasse, the son of Alvalde. There is no other choice.

(10) It has already been shown above that Volund and the swan-maid who came to him in the Wolfdales were either brother and sister or half-brother and half-sister. From what has been stated above, it follows that Thjasse and Idun were related to each other in the same manner.

(11) Thjasse's house is called *Brunn-akr* (Younger Edda, i. 312). In Volundarkvida (9) Volund is called *Brunni*.

(12) Idun has the epithet *Snót* (Younger Edda, 306), "the wise one," "the intelligent one." Volund's swan-maid has the epithet *Alvitr*, "the much-knowing one," "the very intelligent one" (Volundarkvida, 1).

Volund has the epithet *Asólfr* (Hyndluljod; cp. No. 109). Thjasse has the epithet *Fjallgylder* (Younger Edda, 308), which is a paraphrase of *Asólfr* (*áss=fjöll, olfr=gyldir*).

(13) One of Volund's brothers, namely Orvandel-Egil, had the epithet "Wild boar" (Ibor, Ebur). One of Thjasse's brothers is called *Urnir, Aurnir.* This name means "wild boar." Compare the Swedish and Norwegian peasant word *orne,* and the Icelandic word *runi* (a boar), in which the letters are transposed.

(14) At least one of Alvalde's sons was a star-hero, viz., Thjasse, whose eyes Odin and Thor fastened on the heavens (Harbardsljod, 18; Younger Edda, i. 318, 214). At least one of Ivalde's sons was a star-hero, viz., Orvandel-Egil (Younger Edda, i. 276, &c.). No star-hero is mentioned who is not called a son of Alvalde or is a son of Ivalde, and not a single name of a star or of a group of stars can with certainty be pointed out which does not refer to Alvalde's or Ivalde's sons. From the Norse sources we have the names *Örvandilstá thjaza augu Lokabrenna* and *Reid Rögnis.* Lokabrenna, the Icelandic name of Sirius, can only refer to the *brenna* (fire) caused by Loke when Thjasse fell into the vaferflames kindled around Asgard. In *Reid Rögnis,* Rogner's car, Rogner is, as shall be shown below, the epithet of a mythic person, in whom we rediscover both Volund and Thjasse. In Old English writings the Milky Way is called Vætlinga-stræt, Watlingestræt. The Watlings or Vætlings can only be explained as a patronymic meaning Vate's sons. Vate is one of the names of the father of Volund and his

brothers (see No. 110). Another old English name of star-group is Eburthrung, Eburthring. Here Egil's surname Ebur, "wild boar," reappears. The name Ide, borne by a brother of Thjasse, also seems to have designated a star-hero in England.

At least two of these figures and names are very old and of ancient Aryan origin. I do not know the reasons why Vigfusson assumes that Orvandel is identical with Orion, but the assumption is corroborated by mythological facts. Orion is the most celebrated archer and hunter of Greek mythology, just as Orvandel is that of the Teutonic. Like Orvandel-Egil, he has two brothers of whom the one Lykos (wolf) has a Telchin name, and doubtless was originally identical with the Telchin Lykos, who, like Volund, is a great artist and is also endowed with powers to influence the weather. Orion could, so it is said, walk on the sea as well as on the land. Orvandel-Egil has skees, with which he travels on the sea as well as on the snow-fields, whence small ships are called *Egil's andrar*, Egil's skees (Kormak, 5). Orion wooes a daughter of Oinopion. The first part of the word is *oinos* (wine); and as Oinopion is the son of Bacchus, there is no room for doubt that he originally had a place in the Aryan myth in regard to the mead. Orvandel-Egil woos a daughter of Sumbl (Olvalde), the king of the Finns, who in the Teutonic mythology is Oinopion's counterpart. Orion is described as a giant, a tall and exceedingly handsome man, and is said to be a brother of the Titans. His first wife, the beautiful Sida, he soon lost by death; just as Orvandel lost Groa. Sida, *Sida* with its Dorian variation Rhoa, *Roa,* means fruit. The name Groa refers, like Sida, Rhoa, to vegetation, growth. After Sida's decease, Orion woos Oinopion's daughter just as Orvandel-Egil woos the daughter of the Finnish king Sumbl after Groa's death. He has a third erotic alliance with Eos. According to one record he is said to have been killed because, in his love of the chase, he had said that he would exterminate all game on earth. This statement may have its origin in the myth preserved by the Teutons about Volund's and Orvandel-Egil's effort to destroy all life on the earth by the aid of the powers of frost. Hesiod says that the Pleiades (which set when Orion rises above the horizon) save themselves from Orion in the stream of the ocean. The above-mentioned Old English name of a constellation Eburthrung may refer to the Pleiades, since the part *thrung, drying,* refers to a dense cluster of stars. The first part of the word, Ebur, as already stated, is a surname of Orvandel-Egil. It should be added that the points of similarity between the Orion and Orvandel myths are of such a nature that they exclude all idea of being borrowed one from the other. Like the most of the Greek myths in the form in which they have been handed down to us, the Orion myth is without any organic connection with any epic whole. The Orvandel myth, on the other hand, dovetails itself as a part into a mythological epic which, in grand and original outlines, represents the struggle betweeen gods, patriarchs, ancient artists, and frost-giants for the control of the world.

The name Thjasse, *thjazi,* in an older and uncorrupted form *thizi,* I regard to be most ancient like the person that bears it. According to my opinion, Thjasse is identical with the star-hero mentioned in Rigveda, *Tishya*, the *Tistrya* of the Iranians, who in Rigveda (x. 64, 8) is worshipped together with an archer, who presumably was his brother. The German middle-age poetry has preserved the name Thjasse in the form *Desen* (which is related to *thjazi* as *Delven* is to *thialfi*). In "Dieterichs Flucht" Desen is a king, whose daughter marries Dieterich-Hadding's father. In the Norse sources a sister of Thjasse (Alveig-Signe, daughter of Sumbl, the king of the Finns) marries Hadding's father, Halfdan. Common to the German and Norse traditions is, therefore, that Hadding's father marries a near kinswoman of Thjasse.

(15) In the poem Haustlaung Thjasse's adventure is mentioned, when he captured Loke with the magic rail. Here we get remarkable, hitherto misunderstood, facts in regard to Thjasse's personality.

That they have been misunderstood is not owing to lack of attention or acumen on the part of the interpreters. On the contrary, acumen has been lavished thereon.* In some cases the scholars have resorted to text-changes in order to make the contents intelligible, and this was necessary on account of the form in which our mythology hitherto has been presented, and that for good reasons, since important studies of another kind, especially of accurate editions of the Teutonic mythological texts, have claimed the time of scholars and compelled them to neglect the study of the epic connection of the myths and of their exceedingly rich and abundant synonymics. As a

---

*See for example Th. Wisén's investigations and Finnur Jonsson's *Krit. Stud.* (Copenhagen, 1884).

matter of course, an examination of the synonymics and of the epic connection could not fail to shed another light than that which could be gained without this study upon a number of passages in the old mythological poems, and upon the paraphrases based on the myths and occurring in the historical songs.

In Haustlaung Thjasse is called *fadir mörna,* "the father of the swords." Without the least reason it has been doubted that a mythic person, that is so frequently called a giant, and whose connection with the giant world and whose giant nature are so distinctly held forth in our mythic sources, could be an artist and a maker of swords. Consequently the text has been changed to *fadir mornar* or *fadir morna,* the father of consumption or of the strength-consuming diseases, or of the feminine thurses representing these diseases. But so far as our mythic records give us any information, Thjasse had no other daughter than Skade, described as a proud, bold, powerful maid, devoted to achievements, who was elevated to the rank of an asynje, became the wife of the god of wealth, the tender stepmother of the lord of harvests (Skirners-mal), Frigg's *elja,* and in this capacity the progenitress of northern rulers, who boasted their descent from her. That Thjasse had more daughters is indeed possible, but they are not mentioned, and it must remain a conjecture on which nothing can be built; and even if such were the case, it must be admitted that as Skade was the foremost and most celebrated among them, she is the first one to be thought of when there is mention of a daughter or of daughters of Thjasse. But that Skade should be spoken

of as a *morn,* a consumption-witch, and that Hakon Jarl
should be regarded as descended from a demon of consumption, and be celebrated in song as the scion of such a
person, I do not deem possible. The text, as we have it,
tells us that Thjasse was the father of swords (*mörnir=*
sword; see Younger Edda, i. 567; ii. 560, 620). We
must confine ourselves to this reading and remember that
this is not the only passage which we have hitherto met
with where his name is put in connection with works of a
smith. Such a passage we have already met with in
thjaza thingskil.

(16) In the same poem, Haustlaung, Thjasse is called
hapta snytrir, "the one who decorated the gods," furnished them with treasures. This epithet, too, appeared
unintelligible, so long as none of the artists of antiquity
was recognised in Thjasse; hence text-changes were also
resorted to in this case in order to make sense out of the
passage.

The situation described is as follows: Odin and *Hænir,*
accompanied by Loke are out on a journey. They have
traversed mountains and wildernesses (Bragaraedur, 2),
and are now in a region which, to judge from the context, is situated within Thjasse's domain, Thrymheim.
The latter, who is *margspakr* and *lómhugadr* (Haustl.,
3, 12), has planned an ambush for Loke in the very place
which they have now reached: a valley (Bragaraedur, 2)
overgrown with oak-trees (Haustl., 6), and the more in-
viting as a place of refreshment and rest, inasmuch as the
Asas are hungry after their long journey (Bragaraedur,
21), and see a herd of "yoke-bears" pasturing in the grass

near by. Thjasse has calculated on this and makes one of the bears act the part of a decoy (*tálhreinn*=a decoy reindeer—Haustlaung, 3; see Vigfusson's Dict., 626), which permits itself to be caught by the travellers. That the animal belongs to Thjasse's herds follows from the fact that it (str. 6) is said to belong to the "dis of the bowstring," Skade, his daughter. The animal is slaughtered and a fire is kindled, over which it is to be roasted. Near the place selected for the eating of the meal there lies, as it were accidentally, a rail or stake. It resembles a common rail, but is in fact one of Thjasse's smith-works, having magic qualities. When the animal is to be carved, it appears that the "decoy reindeer was quite hard between the bones for the gods to cut" (*tálhreinn var medal beina tormidladr tífum*—str. 3). At the same time the Asas had seen a great eagle flying toward them (str. 2), and alighting near the place where they prepared their feast (str. 3). From the context it follows that they took it for granted that the eagle guise concealed Thjasse, the ruler of the region. The animal being found to be so hard to carve, the Asas at once guess that Thjasse, skilled in magic arts, is the cause, and they immediately turn to him with a question, which at the same time tells him that they know who he is:

> Hvat, quotho, bapta snytrir
> hjálmfaldinn, thvi valda?

"They (the gods) said (*quotho*): Why cause this (*hvat thvi valda*) thou ornament-giver of the gods (*hjálmfaldinn hapta snytrir*), concealed in a guise (eagle

guise) ?" He at once answers that he desires his share
of the sacred meal of the gods, and to this Odin gives his
consent. Nothing indicates that Odin sees a foe in
Thjasse. There is then no difficulty in regard to the roast;
and when it is ready and divided into four parts Thjasse
flies down, but, to plague Loke, he takes so much that the
latter, angry, and doubtless also depending on Odin's protection if needed, seizes the rail lying near at hand and
strikes the eagle a blow across the back. But Loke could
not let go his hold of the rail; his hand stuck fast to one
end while the other end clung to the eagle, and Thjasse
flew with him and did not let go of him before he had
forced him to swear an oath that he would bring Idun into
Thjasse's hands.

So long as it was impossible to assume that Thjasse
had been the friend of the gods before this event happened,
and in the capacity of ancient artist had given them valuable products of his skill, and thus become a *hapta snytrir,* it was also impossible to see in him, though he was
concealed in the guise of an eagle, the *hjálmfaldinn* here
in question, since *hjálmfaldinn* manifestly is in apposi-
tion to *hapta snytrir,* "the decorator of the gods." (The
common meaning of *hjálmr,* as is well known, is a covering, a garb, or which *hjálmr* in the sense of a helmet is a
specification.) It therefore became necessary to assume
that Odin was meant by *hjálmfaldinn* and *hapta snytrir.*
This led to the changing of *quotho* to *quad,* and to the in-
sertion in the manuscripts of a *mun* not found there, and
to the exclusion of a *thvi* found there. The result was,
moreover, that no notice was taken of the use made of the

expressions *hjálmfaldinn* and *snytrir* in a poem closely related to Haustlaung, and evidently referring to its description of Thjasse. This poem is Einar Skalaglam's "Vellekla," which celebrates Hakon Jarl, the Great. Hakon Jarl regarded himself as descended from Thjasse through the latter's daughter, Skade (Háleygjatal), and on this account Vellekla contains a number of allusions to the mythic progenitor. The task (from a poetic and rhetorical point of view) which Einar has undertaken is in fact that of taking, so far as possible, the kernel of those paraphrases with which he celebrates Hakon Jarl (see below) from the myth concerning Thjasse, and the task is performed with force and acumen. In the execution of his poem Einar has had before him that part of Thjodulf's Haustlaung which concerned Thjasse. In str. 6 he calls Thjasse's descendant *thjódar snytrir,* taking his cue from Haustlaung, which calls Thjasse *hapta snytrir.* In str. 8 he gives Hakon the epithet *hjálmi faldinn,* having reference to Haustlaung, which makes Thjasse appear *hjálm faldinn.* In str. 10 Hakon is a *gard-Rögnir,* just as Thjasse is a *ving-Rögnir* in Haustlaung. In str. 11 Hakon is a *midjungr,* just as Thjasse is a *midjungr* in Haustlaung. In str. 16 an allusion is made in the phrase *vildi Yggsnidr fridar bildja* to Haustlaung's *málunautr hváts mátti fridar bidja.* In str. 21 Hakon is called *hlym-Narfi,* just as Thjasse in Haustlaung is called *grjót Nidadr* (*Narfi* and *Nidadr* are epithets of Mimer; see Nos. 85, 87). In str. 22 Hakon is called *fangsæll,* and Thjasse has the same epithet in Haustlaung. Some of the paraphrases in Vellekla, to which the myth about Thjasse furnishes the kernel, I shall discuss below. There can, therefore, be no doubt whatever that Einar in Haustlaung's *hjálmfaldinn* and *hapta snytrir* saw epithets of Thjasse, and we arrive at the same result if we interpret the text in its original reading and make no emendations.

Thus we have already found three paraphrases which inform us that Thjasse was an ancient artist, one of the great smiths of mythology: (1) *thiaza thingskil,* golden treasures produced as evidence in court owned or made by Thjasse; (2) *hapta snytrir,* he who gave ornaments to the gods; (3) *fadir mörna,* the father of the swords.

Thjasse's claim to become a table-companion of the gods and to eat with them, *af helgu skutli,* points in all probability to an ancient mythological fact of which we find a counterpart in the Iranian records. This fact is that, as a compensation for the services he had rendered the gods, Thjasse was anxious to be elevated to their rank and to receive sacrifices from their worshippers. This demand from the Teutonic star-hero Thjasse is also made by the Iranian star-hero Tistrya, Rigveda's Tishya. Tistrya complains in Avesta that he has not sufficient strength to oppose the foe of growth, Apaosha, since men do not worship him, Tistrya, do not offer sacrifices to him. If they did so, it is said, then he would be strong enough to conquer. Tishya-Tistrya does not appear to have obtained complete rank as a god; but still he is worshipped in Rigveda, though very seldom, and in cases of severe dry weather the Iranians were commanded to offer sacrifices to him.

(17) In Haustlaung Thjasse is called *ving-Rögnir*

vagna, "the Rogner of the winged cars," and *fjardar-blads leik-Regin,* "the Regin of the motion of the feather-leaf (the wing)." In the mythology Thjasse, like Volund, wears an eagle guise. In an eagle guise Volund flies away from his prison at Mimer- *Nidadr's.* When Thjasse, through Loke's deceit, is robbed of Idun, he hastens in wild despair, with the aid of his eagle guise, after the robber, gets his wings burned in the vaferflames kindled around Asgard, falls pierced by the javelins of the gods, and is slain by Thor. The original meaning of *Regin* is maker, creator, arranger, worker. The meaning has been preserved through the ages, so that the word *regin,* though applied to all the creative powers (Völsupa), still retained even in Christian times the signification of artist, smith, and reappears in the heroic traditions in the name of the smith *Reginn.* When, therefore, Thjasse is called "the Regin of the motion of the feather-leaf," there is no reason to doubt that the phrase alludes not only to the fact that he possessed a feather guise, but also to the idea that he was its "smith;" the less so as we have already seen him characterised as an ancient artist in the phrases *thiaza thingskil, hapta snytrir,* and *fadir mörna.* Thus we here have a fourth proof of the same kind. The phrase "the Rognir of the winged cars" connects him not only with a single vehicle, but with several. "Wing-car" is a paraphrase for a guise furnished with wings, and enabling its owner to fly through the air. The expression "wing-car" may be applied to several of the strange means used by the powers for locomotion through the air and over the sea, as, for instance, the cars of Thor and Frey, Balder's ship Ringhorn, Frey's ship Skidbladner, and the feather garbs of the swan-maids. The mythology which knew from whose hands Skidbladner proceeded certainly also had something to say of the masters who produced Ringhorn and the above-mentioned cars and feather garbs. That they were made by ancient artists and not by the highest gods is an idea of ancient Aryan birth. In Rigveda it was the Ribhus, the counterparts of the Ivalde sons, who smithied the wonderful car-ship of the Asvinians and Indra's horses.

The appellations *Rögnir* and *Regin* also occur outside of Haustlaung in connection with each other, and this even as late as in the *Skida-Rima,* composed between 1400 and 1450, where Regin is represented as a smith (*Rögnir kallar Regin til sín*: *rammliga skaltu smida*—str. 102). In Forspjallsljod (10) we read: *Galdr gólo, gaundom ritho Rögnir ok Regin at ranni heimis*—"Rogner and Regin sang magic songs at the edge of the earth and constructed magic implements." They who do this are artists, smiths. In strophe 8 they are called *viggiar,* and *viggi* is a synonym of *smidr* (Younger Edda, i. 587). While they do this Idun is absent from Asgard (Forspjallsljod, str. 6), and a terrible cold threatens to destroy the earth. The words in Völuspa, with which the terrible fimbul-winter of antiquity is characterised, *loptr lævi blandinn,* are adopted by Forspjallsljod (str. 6—*lopti med lævi*), thus showing that the same mythic event is there described. The existence of the order of the world is threatened, the earth and the source of light are attacked by evil influences, the life of nature is dying, from the north (east), from the Elivagar rivers come piercing, rime-cold arrows of frost, which kill men and destroy the vegetation of the earth. The southern source of the lower world, whose function it is to furnish warming saps to the world-tree, was not able to prevent the devastations of the frost. "It was so ordained," it is said in Forspjallsljod, str. 2, "that Urd's *Odrærir* (Urd's fountain) did not have sufficient power to supply protection against the terrible cold."* The destruction is caused by Rogner and Regin. Their magic songs are heard even in Asgard. Odin listens in Lidskjalf and perceives that the song comes from the uttermost end of the world. The gods are seized by the thought that the end of the world is approaching, and send their messengers to the lower world in order to obtain there from the wise norn a solution of the problem of the world and to get the impending fate of the world proclaimed.

In the dictionaries and in the mythological text-books *Rögnir* is said to be one of Odin's epithets. In his excellent commentary on Vellekla, Freudenthal has expressed a doubt as to the correctness of this view. I have myself made a list of all the passages in the Old Norse literature where the name occurs, and I have thereby reached the conclusion that the statement in the dictionaries and in the text-books has no other foundation than the name-list in *Eddubrott* and the above-cited *Skidarima*, composed in the fifteenth century. The conceptions of the latter in regard to heathen mythology are of such a nature that it should

---

*The editions have changed *Urdar* to *Urdr*, and thereby converted the above-cited passage into nonsense, for which in turn the author of Forspjallsljod was blamed, and it was presented as an argument to prove that the poem is spurious.

never in earnest be regarded as an authority anent this question. In the Old Norse records there cannot be found a single passage where *Rögnir* is used as an epithet of Odin. It is everywhere used in reference to a mythic being who was a smith and a singer of magic songs, and regularly, and without exception, refers to Thjasse. While Thjodolf designates Thjasse as the Rogner of the wing-cars, his descendant Hakon Jarl gets the same epithet in Einar Skalaglam's paraphrases. He is *hjörs brak-Rögnir*, "the Rogner of the sword-din," and *Geirrásar-gard-Rögnir*, "the Rogner of the wall of the sword-flight (the shield)." The Thjasse descendant, Sigurd Hladejarl, is, in harmony herewith, called *fens furs Rögnir*. *Thrym-Rögnir* (Eg., 58) alludes to Thjasse as ruler in Thrymheim. A parallel phrase to *thrym-Rögnir* is *thrym-Regin* (Younger Edda, i. 436). Thus, while Thjasse is characterised as *Rögnir*, Saxo has preserved the fact that Volund's brother, Orvandel-Egil, bore the epithet Regin. Saxo Latinises Regin into Regnerus, and gives this name to Ericus-Svipdag's father (*Hist.*, 192). The epithet *Rögnir* confines itself exclusively to a certain group—to Thjasse and his supposed descendants. Among them it is, as it were, an inheritance.

The paraphrases in Vellekla are of great mythological importance. While other mythic records relate that Thjasse carried away Idun, the goddess of vegetation, the goddess who controls the regenerating forces in nature, and that he thus assisted in bringing about the great winter of antiquity, we learn from Vellekla that it was he who directly, and by separate magic acts, produced this winter, and that he, accordingly, acted the same part in this respect as Rogner and Regin do in Forspjallsljod.

Thus, for example, the poem on Hakon Jarl, when the latter fought against the sons of Gunhild, says: *Hjörs brak-Rögnir skók bogna hagl or Hlakkar seglum,* "the Rogner of the sword-din shook the hail of the bows from the sails of the valkyrie." The mythic kernel of the paraphrase is: *Rögnir skók hagl ur seglum,* "Rogner shook hails from the sails." The idea is still to be found in the sagas that men endowed with magic powers could produce a hailstorm by shaking napkins or bags, filling the air with ashes, or by untying knots. And in Christian records it is particularly stated of Hakon Jarl that he held in honour two mythic beings—Thorgerd and Irpa—who, when requested, could produce storms, rain, and hail. No doubt this tradition is connected with Hakon's supposed descent from Thjasse, the cause of hailstorms and of the fimbulwinter. By making Rogner the "Rogner of the sword-din," and the hail sent by him "the hail of the bows," and the sails or napkins shook by him "the sails of the valkyrie"—that is to say, the shields—the skald makes the mythological kernel pointed out develop into figures applicable to the warrior to the battle.

In other paraphrases Vellekla says that the descendant of Thjasse, Hakon, made "the death-cold sword-storm grow against the life of udal men in Odin's storm," and that he was "an elf of the earth of the wood-land" coming from the north, who, with "murder-frost," received the warriors of the south (Emperor Otto's army) at Dannevirke. Upon the whole Vellekla chooses the figures used in describing the achievements of Hakon from the domain of cold and storm, and there can be no doubt that it does so in imitation of the Thjasse-myth.

In another poem to Hakon Jarl, of which poem there is only a fragment extant, the skald Einar speaks of Hakon's generosity, and says: *Verk Rögnis mer hogna*, "Rogner's works please me." We know that Hakon Jarl once gave Einar two gilt silver goblets, to which belonged two scales in the form of statuettes, the one of gold, the other of silver, which scales were thought to possess magic qualities, and that Hakon on another occasion gave him an exceedingly precious engraved shield, inlaid between the engraved parts with gold and studded with precious stones. It was customary for the skalds to make songs on such gifts. It follows, therefore, that the "works of Rogner," with which Einar says he was pleased, are the presents which Hakon, the supposed descendant of Rogner-Thjasse, gave him; and I find this interpretation the more necessary for the reason that we have already found several unanimous evidences of Thjasse's position in the mythology as an artist of the olden time.

Forspjallsljod's Rogner "sings magic songs" and "concocts witchcraft" in order to encourage and strengthen by these means of magic the attack of the powers of frost on the world protected by the gods. Haustlaung calls Thjasse *ramman reimud Jötunheima*, "the powerful *reimud* of Jotunheim." The word *reimud* occurs nowhere else. It is thought to be connected with *reimt* and *reimleikar*, words which in the writings of Christian times refer to ghosts, supernatural phenomena, and *reimudr*

THOR, HYMIR, AND THE MIDGARD SERPENT.

(From an etching by Lorenz Frölich.)

HYMIR, a giant and ruler of the winter sea, was the owner of a great kettle that brewed any quantity desired of the finest ale. The gods, eager to possess the kettle, sent Thor to obtain it. Proceeding to the borders of heaven, where Hymir lived, Thor assumed the form of a young man and appearing before the giant, asked permission to accompany him on a fishing excursion. The giant objected that so small a youth could not endure the hardships of such a journey, but finally consented. Thor secured necessary bait by tearing the head from a bull, and the two then set off to row far out to sea. Thor insisted upon going further until they came near the borders of the world, and the two began to fish. Hymir soon hooked and drew up two whales, which he boastfully showed as proof of his strength, but soon after Thor hooked the Midgard Serpent, which rose spouting floods of venom that greatly terrified Hymir. Thor pulled with so much strength on the line that he broke through the bottom of the boat, but his feet stood upon the bottom of the sea and he raised his hammer to strike the serpent; Hymir was so alarmed, however, that he cut the line and let the serpent escape. Thor then rowed back with Hymir to his castle, where he slew Hymir and several other giants and secured the kettle.

See page 855.

In describing the achievements of Hakon from
of cold and storm, and there can be no doubt that it does
so in imitation of the Thjasse-myth.

In another poem to Hakon Jarl, of which there is
only a fragment extant, the skald Einar speaks of Hakon's
generosity, and says. *"Verk Rognis mer ...
ner's* works please me." We know that Hakon Jarl
gave Einar two gilt silver goblets, to which belonged two
scales in the form of statuettes, the one of gold, the other
of silver, which scales were thought to possess magic
qualities...

my... ... and the hammer together...

Hymir was so alarmed, however, that he cut
the serpent escaped. Thor then rowed back with
cocts witchcraft ... courage and strength by
these means of ... the attack of the powers of frost on
the world ... by the gods. Haustlaung calls
Thjasse *ramman ... Jötunheima,* "the powerful *reimud* of Jotunheim." The word *reimud* occurs nowhere
else. It is thought to be connected with *reimt* and *reimleikar,* words which ... the writings of Christian
fer to ghosts, supernatural phenomena, and *reimudr*

914

Jötunheima has therefore been interpreted as "the one who made Jotunheim the scene of his magic arts and ghost-like appearances." From what has been stated above, it is manifest that this interpretation is correct.

A passage in Thorsdrapa (str. 3), to which I shall recur below, informs us that at the time when Thor made his famous journey to the fire-giant Geirrod, Rogner had not yet come to an agreement with Loke in regard to the plan of bringing ruin on the gods. Rogner was, therefore, during a certain period of his life, the foe of the gods, but during a preceding period he was not an enemy. The same is true of Thjasse. He was for a time *hapta snytrir,* "the one giving the gods treasures." At another time he carried away Idun, and appeared as one changed into *dólgr ballastr vallar,* "the most powerful foe of the earth" (Haustl., 6), an expression which characterises him as the cause of the fimbul-winter.

There still remain one or two important passages in regard to the correct interpretation of the epithet Rogner. In Atlakvida (33) it is said of Gudrun when she goes to meet her husband Atle, who has returned home, carrying in her hand a golden goblet, that she goes to *reifa gjöld Rögnis,* "to present that requital or that revenge which Rogner gave." To avenge her brothers, Gudrun slew in Atle's absence the two young sons she had with him and made goblets of their skulls. Into one of these she poured the drink of welcome for Atle. A similar revenge is told about Volund. The latter secretly kills *Nidadr's* two young sons and makes goblets out of their skulls for their father. In the passage it is stated that the revenge of Gudrun against Atle was of the same kind as Rogner's revenge against some one whom he owed a grudge. So far as our records contain any information, Volund is the only one to whom the epithet Rogner is applicable in this case. Of no one else is it reported that he took a revenge of such a kind that Gudrun's could be compared therewith. In all other passages the epithet Rogner refers to "the father of the swords," to the ancient artist Thjasse, the son of Alvalde. Here it refers to the father of the most excellent sword, to the ancient artist Volund, the son of Ivalde.

The strophe in Vellekla, which compares the Thjasse descendant Hakon Jarl with the hail-producing Rogner, also alludes to another point in the myth concerning him by a paraphrase the kernel of which is: *Varat svanglý-jadi at frýja ofbyrjar nè drifu,* "it was impossible to defy the swan-pleaser in the matter of storm and bad weather." The paraphrase is made applicable to Hakon by making the "swan-pleaser" into the "pleaser of the swan of the sword's high-billowing fjord"—that is to say, the one who pleases the bird of the battlefield, that is, the raven. The storm is changed into "the storm of arrows," and the bad weather into the "bad weather of the goddess of the battle." The mythological kernel of this paraphrase, and that which sheds light on our theme, is the fact that Rogner in the mythology was "one who pleased the swans." In the heroic poem three swan-maids are devoted in their love to Volund and his brothers. Volundarkvida says that the third one lays her arms around Volund-Anund's white neck.

We will now combine the results of this investigation concerning Rogner, and in so doing we will first consider what is said of him when the name occurs independently, and not connected with paraphrases, and then what is said of him in paraphrases in which his name constitutes the kernel.

Forspjallsljod describes Rogner as dwelling on the northern-most edge of the earth at the time when Idun was absent from Asgard. There he sings magic songs and concocts witchcraft, by which means he sends a destructive winter out upon the world. He is a "smith," and in his company is found one or more than one mythic person called Regin. (Regin may be singular or plural.)

Einar Skalaglam, who received costly treasures from Hakon Jarl, speaks in his song of praise to the latter of the "works of Rogner," which please him, and which must be the treasures he received from the Jarl.

In Thorsdrapa, Eilif Gudrunson relates that Rogner had not yet "associated himself" with Loke when Thor made his expedition to Geirrod.

Atlakvida states that he revenged himself on some one, with which revenge the song compares Gudrun's when she hands to Atle the goblets made of the skulls of the two young sons of the latter.

All the facts presented in these passages are rediscovered in the myth concerning Ivalde's sons—Volund, Egil, and Slagfin. There was a time when they were the friends of the gods and smithied for them costly treasures, and there was another time when they had the same plans as Loke tried to carry out in a secret manner—

that is, to dethrone the gods and destroy what they had created. They deliver their foster-son Frey, the young god of harvests, to the giants (see Nos. 109, 112)—an event which, like Idun's disappearance from Asgard, refers to the coming of the fimbul-winter—and they depart to the most northern edge of the lower world where they dwell with swan-maids, dises of growth, who, like Idun in Forspjallsljod (str. 8), must have changed character and joined the world-hostile plots of their lovers. (Of Idun it is said, in the strophe mentioned, that she clothed herself in a wolf-skin given her by the smiths, and *lyndi breytti, lek at lævisi, litom skipti.*) The revenge which Volund, during his imprisonment by Nidad, takes against the latter explains why Atlakvida characterises Gudrun's terrible deed as "Rogner's revenge." In regard to the witchcraft (*gand*) concocted by Rogner and Regin, it is to be said that the sword of victory made by Volund is a *gandr* in the original sense of this word—an implement endowed with magic powers, and it was made during his sojourn in the Wolfdales.

One passage in Volundarkvida (str. 5), which hitherto has defied every effort at interpretation, shows that his skill was occupied with other magic things while he dwelt there. The passage reads: *Lucthi hann alla lindbauga vel.* The "lind"-rings in question, smithied of "red gold" (see the preceding lines in strophe 5), are, according to the prefix, *lind, linnr,* serpent-formed rings, which again are gand- (witchcraft) rings on account of the mysterious qualities ascribed to the serpent. *Lindbaugi* is another form for *linnbaugi,* just as *lindból* is another form for *linnból.* The part played by the serpent in the magic arts made it, when under the influence or in the possession of the magician, a *gand,* whence *linnr,* a serpent, could be used as a paraphrase of *gandr,* and *gandr* could in turn, in the compound *Jörmungandr,* be used as an epithet for the Midgard-serpent. The rings which Volund "closed well together" are gand-rings. The very rope (*bast, böstr*—Volundarkvida, 7, 12) on which he hangs the seven hundred gand-rings he has finished seems to be a gand, an object of witchcraft, with which Volund can bind and from which he can release the wind. When Nidad's men surprised Volund in his sleep and bound him with this rope, he asks ambiguously who "had bound the wind" with it (str. 12). In two passages in Volundarkvida (str. 4, 8) he is called *vedreygr,* "the storm-observer," or "the storm-terrible." The word may have either meaning. That Volund for his purposes, like Rogner, made use of magic songs is manifest from Saxo (*Hist.,* 323, 324). According to Saxo it was by means of Volund-Haquinus' magic song that the Volund-sword, wielded by Svipdag-Ericus, was able to conquer Thor's hammer and Halfdan's club.

Passing now to the passages where the name Rogner occurs in paraphrases, I would particularly emphasize what I have already demonstrated: that Haustlaung with this name refers to Thjasse; that poems of a more recent date than Haustlaung, and connected with the same celebrated song, apply it to the supposed descendants of Thjasse, Hakon Jarl and his kinsmen; that all of these paraphrases represent Rogner as a producer of storm, snow, and hail; and that Rogner made "wind-cars," was a "Regin of the motion of the feather-leaf" (the wing), and "one who pleased the swans." Therefore (*a*) Rogner is an epithet of Thjasse, and at the same time it designates Volund; (*b*) all that is said of Rogner, when the name in the paraphrases is a Thjasse-epithet, applies to Volund; (*c*) all that is said of Rogner, independently of paraphrases, applies to Volund

(18) A usage in the Old Norse poetry is to designate a person by the name of his opponent, when, by means of an additional characterisation, it can be made evident that the former and not the latter is meant. Thus, a giant can be called *berg-thórr* or *grjót-Módi,* because he once had Thor or Thor's son Mode as an opponent, and these epithets particularly apply to giants who actually fought with Thor or Mode in the mythology. In contrast with their successors in Christian times, the heathen skalds took great pains to give their paraphrases special justification and support in some mythological event. For the same reason that a giant who had fought with Mode could be called *grjót-Módi,* Volund, as Nidad's foe, could be called *grjót-Nidudr.* This epithet also occurs a single time in the Old Norse poetry, namely, in Haustlaung, and there it is applied to Thjasse. The paraphrase shows that the skald had in his mind a corresponding (antithetic) circumstance between Thjasse and *Nidadr* (*Nidudr*). What we are able to gather from our sources is, that Volund and *Nidadr* had had an encounter, and that one of so decisive a character, that the epithet *grjót-Nidudr* naturally would make the hearers think of Volund.

(19) When Loke had struck Thjasse, who was in eagle guise, with the magic pole, Thjasse flew up; and as Loke's hand was glued fast to one end of the pole and the eagle held fast to the other end, Loke had to accompany the eagle on its flight. Haustlaung says that Thjasse, pleased with his prey, bore him a long distance (*of veg lángan*) through the air. He directed his course in such a manner that Loke's body fared badly, probably being dragged over trees and rocks (*svá at slitna sundr úlfs födor mundi*). Then follows in the poem the lines given below, which I quote from Codex Regius, with the exception of a single word (*midjungs,* instead of *mildings*), which I cite from Codex Wormianus. Here, as elsewhere, I base nothing on text emendations, because even such, for which the best of reasons may be given, do not furnish sufficient foundation for mythological investigation, when the changes are not supported by some manuscript, or are in and of themselves absolutely necessary.

> thá vard thórs ofrunni,
> thúngr var Loptr, of sprúnginn;
> málunautr hvats mátti
> midjungs fridar bidja.

The contents of these lines, in the light of what has now been stated, are as follows:

Thjasse's pleasure in dragging Loke with him, and making his limbs come in disagreeable contact with objects on their way, was so great that he did not abstain therefrom, before he felt that he had over-exerted himself. Strong as he was, this could not but happen, for he had been flying with his burden very far from the place where he captured Loke in the ambush he had laid; and, besides, Loke was heavy. The badly-hurt Loke had during the whole time desired to beg for mercy, but during the flight he was unable to do so. When Thjasse finally sank to the ground, Loke obtained a breathing space, so that he could sue for mercy.

In the four lines there are four paraphrases. Thjasse is called *thórs ofrunni* or *thórs ofrúni,* "he who made Thor run," or "he who was Thor's friend," and *"midjungr,"* a word the meaning of which it is of no importance to investigate in connection with the question under consideration. Loke is called *Loptr,* a surname which is applied to him many times, and *málunautr hvats midjungs,* "he who had journeyed with the female companion of the powerful Midjung (Thjasse)." The female companion (*mála*) of Thjasse is Idun, and the paraphrase refers to the myth telling how Loke carried Idun away from Thjasse's halls, and flew with her to Asgard.

With these preparatory remarks I am ready to present a literal translation of the passage:

(Thjasse flew a long way with Loke, so that the latter came near being torn into pieces), ". . . thereupon (*thá=deinde*) became he who caused Thor to run (*vard Ihórs ofrunni*)—or who became Thor's friend (*Ihórs ofrúni*)—tired out (*ofsprúnginn*), (for) Lopt was heavy (*thúngr var Loptr*). He (Loke) who had made a journey with the powerful Midjung's (Thjasse's) female companion (*málunautr hvats midjungs*) could (now finally) sue for peace (*mátti fridar bidja*)."

In the lines—

922

thá vard thórs ofrunni
thúngr var Loptr, ofsprúnginn— .

thúngr var Loptr clearly stands as an intermediate sentence, which, in connection with what has been stated
above, namely, that Thjasse had been flying a long way
with his burden, will justify and explain why Thjasse,
though exceedingly strong, stronger than *Hrungnir* (the
Grotte-song), still was at the point of succumbing from
over-exertion. The skald has thus given the reason why
Thjasse, "rejoicing in what he had caught," sank to the
earth with his victim, before Loke became more used up
than was the case. To understand the connection, the
word *mátti* in the third line is of importance. Hitherto
the words *málunautr hvats mátti midjungs fridar bidja*
have been interpreted as if they meant that Loke "was
compelled" to ask Thjasse for peace. *Mátti* has been
understood to mean *coactus est*. Finnur Jonsson (*Krit.
Stud.*, p. 48) has pointed out that not a single passage can
with certainty or probability be found where the verb
mega, mátti, means "to be compelled." Everywhere it
can be translated "to be able." Thus the words *mátti
fridar bidja* mean that Loke *could*, was able to, ask
Thjasse for peace. The reason why he was able is stated
above, where it is said that Thjasse got tired of flying
with his heavy burden. Before that, and during the flight
and the disagreeable collisions between Loke's body and
objects with which he came in contact, he was not able to
treat with his capturer; but when the latter had settled on
the ground, Loke got a breathing space, and could beg to

923

be spared. The half strophe thus interpreted gives the most logical connection, and gives three causes and three results: (1) Loke was able to use his eloquent tongue in speaking to Thjasse, since the latter ceased to fly before Loke was torn into pieces; (2) Thor's *ofrunni* or *ofrúni* ended his air-journey, because he, though a very powerful person, felt that he had over-exerted himself; (3) he felt wearied because Loke, with whom he had been flying, was heavy. But from this it follows with absolute certainty that the skald, with Thor's *ofrunni* or *ofrúni*, meant Thjasse and not Loke, as has hitherto been supposed. The epithet Thor's *ofrunni*, "he who made Thor run," must accordingly be explained by some mythic event, which shows that Thor at one time had to take flight on account of Thjasse. A single circumstance has come to our knowledge, where Thor retreats before an opponent, and it is hardly credible that the mythology should allow its favourite to retreat conquered more than once. On that occasion it is Volund's sword, wielded by Svipdag, which cleaves Thor's hammer and compels him to retire. Thus Volund was at one time Thor's *ofrunni*. In Haustlaung it is Thjasse. Here, too, we therefore meet the fact which has so frequently come to the surface in these investigations, namely, that the same thing is told of Volund and of Thjasse.

But by the side of *ofrunni* we have another reading which must be considered. Codex Wormianus has *ofrúni* instead of *ofrunni*, and, as Wisén has pointed out, this *runni* must, for the sake of the metre, be read *rúni*. According to this reading Thjasse must at some time have been Thor's *ofrúni,* that is, Thor's confidential friend. This reading also finds its support in the mythology, as shall be demonstrated further on. I may here be allowed to repeat what I have remarked before, that of two readings only the one can be the original, while both may be justified by the mythology.

(20) In the mythology are found characters that form a group by themselves, and whose characteristic peculiarity is that they practise skee-running in connection with the use of the bow and arrow. This group consists of the brothers Volund, Egil, Slagfin, Egil's son Ull, and Thjasse's daughter Skade. In the introduction to Volundarkvida it is said of the three brothers that they ran on skees in the Wolfdales and hunted. We have already referred to Egil's wonderful skees, that could be used on the water as well as on the snow. Of Ull we read in Gylfaginning (Younger Edda, i. 102): "He is so excellent an archer and skee-runner that no one is his equal;" and Saxo tells about his Ollerus that he could enchant a bone (the ice-shoe formed of a bone, the pendant of the skee), so that it became changed into a ship. Ull's skees accordingly have the same qualities as those of his father Egil, namely, that they can also be used on the sea. Ull's skees seem furthermore to have had another very remarkable character, namely, that when their possessor did not need them for locomotion on land or on sea, they could be transformed into a shield and be used in war. In this way we explain that the skalds could employ *skip Ullar, Ullar far, knörr Örva áss,* as paraphrases for shields, and that, according to one statement in the Edda Lovasina,

Ullr átti skip that, er Skjöldr hét. So far as his accomplishments are concerned, Ull is in fact the counterpart of his father Egil, and the same may be said of Skade. While Ull is called "the god of the skees," Skade is called "the goddess of the skees," "the dis of the skees," and "the dis of the sea-bone," *sævar beins dis,* a paraphrase which manifestly has the same origin as Saxo's account of the bone enchanted by Ull. Thus Thjasse's daughter has an attribute belonging to the circle of Volund's kinsmen.

The names also connect those whom we find to be kinsmen of Volund with Thjasse's. Alvalde is Thjasse's father; Ivalde is Volund's. *Ívaldi* is another form for *Idvaldi.* The long prefixed *Í* in *Ívaldi* is explained by the disappearance of *d* from *Idvaldi.* *Id* reappears in the name of Ivalde's daughter *Idunn* and Thjasse's brother *Idi,* and these are the only mythological names in which *Id* appears. Furthermore, it has already been pointed out, that of Alvalde's (*Ölvaldi's*) three sons there is one who has the epithet Wildboar (*Aurnir, Urnir*); and that among Ivalde's three sons there is one—namely, Orvandel-Egil—who has the same epithet (*Ibor, Ebur, Ebbo*); and that among Alvalde's sons one—namely, Thjasse—has the epithet *Fjallgyldir,* "mountain-wolf" (Haustlaung); while among Ivalde-Olmod's sons there is one—namely, Volund—who has the epithet *Ásólfr,* which also means "mountain-wolf."

In this connection it must not be forgotten that tradition has attached the qualities of giants, not only to Thjasse, but also to Volund. That this does not appear in the Elder Edda depends simply on the fact that Volund is not mentioned by this name in the genuine mythic songs, but only in the heroic fragment which we have in Volundarkvida. The memory that Volund, though an elf-prince in the mythology, and certainly not a full-blooded giant on his father's side, was regarded and celebrated in song as an *iötunn*,—the memory of this not only survives in Vilkinasaga, but appears there in an exaggeration fostered by later traditions, to the effect that his father Vade (see No. 110) is there called a giant, while his father's mother is said to have been a mermaid. In another respect, too, there survives in Vilkinasaga the memory of a relationship between Volund and the most famous giant-being. He and the giants Etgeir (*Eggther*) and Vidolf are cousins, according to chapter 175. If we examine the Norse sources, we find Vidolf mentioned in Hyndluljod (53) as progenitor of all the mythological valas, and Aurboda, the most notorious of the valas of mythology, mentioned in strophe 30 as a kinswoman of Thjasse. Thus while Hyndluljod makes Thjasse, the Vilkinasaga makes Volund, a kinsman of the giant Vidolf.

Though in a form greatly changed, the Vilkinasaga has also preserved the memory of the manner in which Volund's father closed his career. With some smiths ("dwarfs") who lived in a remote mountain, Vade had made an agreement, according to which, in return for a certain compensation, his son Volund should learn their wonderful art as smiths. When, toward the close of the time agreed upon, Vade appeared outside of the mountain, he was, before entering, killed by an avalanche in accordance with the treacherous arrangement of these smiths.

In the mythology Thjasse's father is the great drink-champion who, among his many names and epithets, as we have seen, also has some that refer to his position in the mythology in regard to fermented beverage: *Svigdir* (the great drinker) *Ölvaldi, Ölmódr, Sumbl Finnakonungr.* In regard to *Svigdir's* death, it has already been shown (see No. 89) that, on his complete disappearance from the mythology, he is outside of a mountain in which Suttung and Suttung's sons, descendants of Surt-Durinn, with Mimer the most ancient smith (see No. 89), have their halls; that on his arrival a treacherous dwarf, the doorkeeper of Suttung's sons, goes to meet him, and that he is "betrayed" by the dwarf, never enters the rocky halls, and consequently must have died outside.

Vilkinasaga's very late statements (probably taken from German traditions), in regard to the death of Volund's father, thus correspond in the main features with what is related in the Norse records as to how Thjasse's father disappeared from the scene of mythology.

In regard to the birth and rank of Thjasse's father among the mythic powers, the following statements in poems from the heathen time are to be observed. When Haustlaung tells how Thjasse falls into the vaferflames kindled around Asgard, it makes use of the words *Greipar bidils son svidnar,* "the son of Greip's wooer is scorched." Thus Thjasse's mother is the giantess Greip, who, according to a stanza cited in the Younger Edda, i. 288, is a daughter of the giant *Geirrödr* and a sister of Gjalp. One of these sisters, and, so far as we can see, Greip, is, in Thorsdrapa, called *meinsvarans hapts arma farmr,* "the embrace of the arms of the perjurous *hapt*." *Höpt,* sing *hapt,* is like *bönd,* meaning the same, an appellation of lower and higher powers, *numina* of various ranks. If by the perjurous mistress of the *hapt* Greip, and not the sister Gjalp, is meant, then Thjasse's father is a being who belonged to the number of the *numina* of the mythology, and who, with a giantess whose *bidill* he had been, begat the son Thjasse, and probably also the latter's brothers *Idi* and *Gángr* (*Aurnir*). What rank this perjurous *hapt* held among the powers is indicated in Vellekla, strophe 9, which, like the foregoing strophe 8, and the succeeding strophes 10, 11, treats of Hakon Jarl's conflicts at Dannevirke, whither he was summoned, in the capacity of a vassal under the Danish king, Harald Blue-tooth, to defend the heathen North against Emperor Otto II.'s effort to convert Denmark to Christianity by arms. The strophe, which here, too, in its paraphrases presents parallels between Hakon Jarl and his mythic progenitor Thjasse, says that the Danish king (*fémildr konungr*) desired that the Morkwood's Hlodyn's (Mork-wood's earth's, that is to say, the woody Norway's) elf, he who came from the North (*myrkmarkar Hlodynjar alfs, thess er kom nordan*), was to be tested in "murder-frost," that is to say, in war (*vid mord-frost freista*), when he (Denmark's king) angrily bade the cold-hard storm-watcher (*stirdan vedrhirdi,* Hakon Jarl) of the Hordaland dwellers (of the Norsemen) defend Dannevirke (*Virki varda*) against the southland Njords of the shield-din (*fyr serkja-hlym-val-Njördum,* "the princes of the south-land warriors").

Here, too, the myth about Thjasse and of the fimbul-winter forms the kernel out of which the paraphrases adapted to Hakon Jarl have grown. Hakon is clothed with the mask of the cold-hard storm-watcher who comes from the North and can let loose the winter-winds. Emperor Otto and the chiefs who led the southern troops under him are compared with Njord and his kinsmen, who, in the mythology, fought with Volund and the powers of frost, and the battle between the warriors of the South and the North is compared with a "murder-frost," in which Hakon coming from the North meets the Christian continental Teutons at Dannevirke.

Thus the mythical kernel of the strophe is as follows: The elf of the Morkwood of Hloydn, the cold-hard storm-watcher, tested his power with frost-weather when he fought with Njord and his kinsmen.

The Hlodyn of the Morkwood—that is to say, the goddess of the Jotunheim woods—is in this connection Thjasse's daughter Skade, who, in Haleygjatal, is called *Járnvidja* of *Járnvidr,* the Ironwood, which is identical with the Morkwood (Darkwood). Thjasse himself, whose father is called "a perjurous *hapt*" in Thorsdrapa, is here called an elf. Alone, this passage would not be sufficient to decide the question as to which class of mythical beings Thjasse and his father belonged, the less so as *álfr,* applied in a paraphrase, might allude to any sort of being according to the characterisation added. But "perjurous *hapt*" cannot possibly be a paraphrase for a giant. Every divinity that has violated its oath is "a perjurous *hapt*," and the mythology speaks of such perjuries. If a god has committed perjury, this is no reason why he should be called a giant. If a giant has committed perjury, this is no reason why he should be called a *hapt*, for it is nothing specially characteristic of the giant nature that it commits perjury or violates its oath. In fact, it seems to me that there should be the gravest doubts about Thjasse's being a giant in the strictest and completest sense of the word, from the circumstances that he is a star-hero; that distinguished persons considered it an honour to be descended from him; that Hakon Jarl's skalds never tired of clothing him with the appearance of his supposed progenitor, and of comparing the historical achievements of the one with the mythical exploits of the other; and that he, Thjasse, not only robbed Idun, which indeed a genuine giant might do, but that he also lived with her many long years, and, so far as we can see, begat with her the daughter Skade. It should be remembered, from the foregoing pages, what pains the mythology takes to get the other asynje, Freyja, who had fallen into the hands of giants, back pure and undefiled to Asgard, and it is therefore difficult to believe that Idun should be humiliated and made to live for many years in intimacy with a real giant. It follows from this that when Thjasse, in the above-cited mythological kernel of the strophe of Vellekla, is called an *álfr*, and when his father in Thorsdrapa is called a *hapt*, a being of higher or lower divine rank, then *álfr* is a further definition of the idea *hapt*, and informs us to which class of *numina*

Thjasse belonged—namely, the lower class of gods called elves. Thus, on his father's side, Thjasse is an elf. So is Volund. In Volundarkvida he is called a prince of elves. Furthermore, it should be observed that, in the strophe-kernel presented above, Thjasse is represented as one who has fought with Njord and his allies. In Saxo it is Anund-Volund and his brother the archer who fight with Njord-Fridlevus and his companions; and as Njord in Saxo marries Anund-Volund's daughter, while in the mythology he marries Thjasse's daughter, then this is another recurrence of the fact which continually comes to the surface in this investigation, namely, that whatever is told of Volund is also told of Thjasse.

114.

PROOFS THAT IVALDE'S SONS ARE OLVALDE'S (*continued*).
A REVIEW OF THORSDRAPA.

(21) We now come to a mythic record in which Thjasse's brothers *Idi* and *Gángr,* and he too, in a paraphrase, are mentioned under circumstances well suited to throw light on the subject before us, which is very important in regard to the epic connection of the mythology.

Of Thor's expedition to Geirrod, we have two very different accounts. One is recorded by the author of Skaldskaparmal; the other is found in Eilif Gundrunson's Thorsdrapa.

In Skaldskaparmal (Younger Edda, i. 284) we read:

Only for pleasure Loke made an expedition in Freyja's feather guise, and was led by his curiosity to seat himself in an opening in the wall of Geirrod's house and peep in. There he was captured by one of Geirrod's servants, and the giant, who noticed from his eyes that it was not a real falcon, did not release him before he had agreed so to arrange matters that Thor should come to Geirrod's hall without bringing with him his hammer and belt of strength. This Loke was able to bring about. Thor went to Geirrod without taking any of these implements—not even his steel gloves—with him. Loke accompanied him. On the way thither Loke visited the giantess whose name was *Grídr,* and who was Vidar the Silent's mother. From her Thor learned the facts about Geirrod—namely, that the latter was a cunning giant and difficult to get on with. She lent Thor her own belt of strength, her own iron gloves, and her staff, *Gridarvölr.* Then Thor proceeded to the river which is called Vimur, and which is the greatest of all rivers. There he buckled on his belt of strength, and supported himself in the stream on the *Gridarvölr.* Loke held himself fast to the belt of strength. When Thor reached the middle of the stream, the water rose to his shoulders. Thor then perceived that up in a mountain chasm below which the river flowed stood Gjalp, Geirrod's daughter, with one foot on each side of the river, and it was she who caused the rising of the tide. Then Thor picked up a stone and threw it at the giantess, saying: "At its mouth the river is to be stopped." He did not miss his mark. Having reached the other bank of the river, he took hold of a rowan, and thus gained the land. Hence the proverb: "Thor's salvation, the rowan." And when Thor came to Geirrod a goat-house

933

was first given to him and Loke (according to Codex Regius; according to the Upsala Codex a guest-house) as their lodgings. Then are related the adventures Thor had with Geirrod's daughters Gjalp and Greip, and how he, invited to perform games in Geirrod's hall, was met by a glowing iron which Geirrod threw against him with a pair of tongs, but which he caught with the iron gloves and threw back with so great force that the iron passed through a post, behind which Geirrod had concealed himself, and through Geirrod himself and his house wall, and then penetrated into the earth.

This narrative, composed freely from mythical and pseudo-mythical elements, is related to Thorsdrapa, composed in heathen times, about in the same manner as Bragaraedur's account of Odin and Suttung is related to that of Havamál. Just as in Bragaraedur *punctum saliens* lies in the coarse jest about how poor poetry originated, so here a crude anecdote built on the proverb, "A stream is to be stemmed at its mouth," seems to be the basis of the story. In Christian times the mythology had to furnish the theme not only for ancient history, heroic poems, and popular traditions, but also for comic songs.

Now, a few words in regard to Thorsdrapa. This song, excellent from the standpoint of poetry and important from a mythological point of view, has, in my opinion, hitherto been entirely misunderstood, not so much on account of the difficulties found in the text—for these disappear, when they are considered without any preconceived opinion in regard to the contents—as on account of the undeserved faith in Skaldskaparmal's account of

Thor's visit to Geïrrod, and on account of the efforts made under the influence of this misleading authority to rediscover the statements of the latter in the heathen poem. In these efforts the poetics of the Christian period in Iceland have been applied to the poem, and in this way all mythological names, whose real meaning was forgotten in later times, have received a general faded signification, which on a more careful examination is proved to be incorrect. With a collection of names as an armoury, in which the names of real or supposed "dwarfs," "giants," "sea-kings," &c., are brought together and arranged as synonyms, this system of poetics teaches that from such lists we may take whatever dwarf name, giant name, &c., we please to designate whichever "dwarf," "giant," &c., we please. If, therefore, Thorsdrapa mentions "*Idi's* chalet" and "*Gángr's* war-vans," then, according to this system of poetics, *Idi* and *Gángr's*—though they in heathen times designated particular mythic persons who had their own history, their own personal careers— have no other meaning than the general one of "a giant," for the reason that *Idi* and *Gángr* are incorporated in the above-named lists of giant names. Such a system of poetics could not arise before the most of the mythological names had become mere empty sounds, the personalities to whom they belonged being forgotten. The fact that they have been adapted, and still continue to be adapted, to the poems of the heathen skalds, is one of the reasons why the important contributions which names and paraphrases in the heathen poetry are able to furnish in mythological investigations have remained an unused treasure.

935

While Skaldskaparmal makes Loke and no one else accompany Thor to Geirrod, and represents the whole matter as a visit to the giant by Thor, we learn from Thorsdrapa that this journey to Jotunheim is an expedition of war, which Thor makes at the head of his warriors against the much-dreaded chief of giants, and that on the way thither he had to fight a real battle with Geirrod's giants before he is able to penetrate to the destination of his expedition, Geirrod's hall, where the giants put to flight in the battle just mentioned gather, and where another battle is fought. Thorsdrapa does not mention with a single word that Loke accompanied Thor on this warlike expedition. Instead of this, we learn that he had a secret understanding with one of Geirrod's daughters, that he encouraged Thor to go, and gave him untruthful accounts of the character of the road, so that, if not Thor himself, then at least the allies who went with him, might perish by the ambush laid in wait for them. That Loke, under such circumstances, should accompany Thor is highly incredible, since his misrepresentations in regard to the character of the way would be discovered on the journey, and reveal him as a traitor. But since Skaldskaparmal states that Loke was Thor's companion, the interpreters of Thorsdrapa have allowed him so to remain, and have attributed to him—the traitor and secret ally of the giants—and to Thjalfe (who is not mentioned in the Skaldskaparmal account) the exploits which Thor's companions perform against the giants. That the poem, for instance, in the expression *Thjáfi med ýta sinni,* "Thjalfe with his companions," in the most distinct manner emphasises the fact that a whole host of warriors had Thor as their leader on this expedition, was passed over as one of the obscure passages in which the poem was supposed to abound, and the obscurity of which simply consists in their contradicting the story in Skaldskaparmal. Thorsdrapa does not mention with a single word that Thor, on his journey to Geirrod, stopped at the home of a giantess *Gridr,* and borrowed from her a staff, a belt of strength, and iron gloves; and I regard it as probable that this whole episode in Skaldskaparmal has no other foundation than that the staff which Thor uses as his support on wading across the rapid stream is in Thorsdrapa now called *grídarvölr,* "the safety staff," and again, *brautar lids tollr,* "the way-helping tree." The name *grídarvölr,* and such proverbs as *at ósi skall á stemma* and *reynir er björg thórs,* appear to be the staple wares by the aid of which the story in Skaldskaparmal was framed. The explanation given in Skaldskaparmal of the proverb *reynir er björg thórs,* that, by seizing hold of a rowan growing on the river bank, Thor succeeded in getting out of the river, is, no doubt, an invention by the author of the story. The statement cannot possibly have had any support in the mythology. In it Thor is endowed with ability to grow equal to any stream he may have to cross. The rowan mentioned in the proverb is probably none other than the "way-helping tree," the "safety staff," on which he supports himself while wading, and which, according to Thorsdrapa (19), is a *brotningr skógar,* a tree broken or pulled up in the woods.

I now pass to the consideration of the contents of Thorsdrapa:

937

Strophe 1. The deceitful Loke encourages Thor to go from home and visit Geirrod, "the master of the temple of the steep altars." The great liar assures him that green paths would take him to Geirrod's halls, that is to say, they were accessible to travellers on foot, and not obstructed by rivers.

NOTE.—For Thor himself the condition of the roads might be of less importance. He who wades across the Elivagar rivers and subterranean streams did not need to be very anxious about finding water-courses crossing his paths. But from the continuation of the poem we learn that this expedition to Jotunheim was not a visit as a guest, or a meeting to fight a duel, as when Thor went to find Hrungner, but this time he is to press into Jotunheim with a whole army, and thus the character of the road he was to travel was of some importance. The ambush laid in his way does not concern Thor himself, but the giant-foes who constitute his army. If the latter perish in the ambush, then Geirrod and his giants will have Thor alone to fight against, and may then have some hope of victory.

Strophe 2. Thor did not require much urging to undertake the expedition. He leaves Asgard to visit Jotunheim. Of what happened on the way between Asgard and the Elivagar rivers, before Thor penetrated into Jotunheim, the strophe says:

thá er gjardvenjodr	When the belt-wearer (Thor the possessor of the belt of strength)

938

endr (=iterum, rursus)	now, as on former occasions,
rikri Idja Gandvikr-setrs sko-tum	strengthened by the men of Ide's chalet situated near Gandvik,
gördist frá thridia til Ymsa kindar,	was on his way from Odin to Ymse's (Ymer's) race,
fystust their (Cod. Worm.) fýrstuz (Cod. Reg.)	it was to them (to Thor and to the men of Ide's chalet) a joy (or they rushed thither)
at thrysta thorns nidjum	to conquer Thorn's (Bol-thorn-Ymer's) kinsmen.

Note.—The common understanding of this passage is (1) that *endr* has nothing to do with the contents, but is a complementary word which may be translated with "once upon a time," a part which *endr* has to play only too often in the interpretation of the old poems; (2) that Ide is merely a general giant name, applicable, like every other giant name, in a paraphrase *Idja setr,* which is supposed to mean Jotunheim; (3) that *rikri Idja setrs skotum* or *rikri Gandvikr skotum* was to give the hearers or readers of Thorsdrapa the (utterly unnecessary) information that Thor was stronger than the giants; and (4) that they who longed to subdue Ymer's kismen were Thor and Loke —the same Loke who, in secret understanding with the giant-chief and with one of his daughters (see below), has the purpose of enticing Thor and his companions in arms into a trap!

Rikri . . . skotum is to be regarded as an elliptical sentence in which the instrumental preposition, as is often the case, is to be understood. When Thor came from

939

Asgard to the chalet of Ide, situated near Gandvik, he there gets companions in arms, and through them he becomes *rikri,* through them he gets an addition to his own powers in the impending conflicts. The fact that when Thor invades Jotunheim he is at the head of an army is perfectly evident from certain expressions in the poem, and from the poem as a whole. Whence could all these warriors come all of a sudden? They are not dwellers in Asgard, and he has not brought them with him in his lightning chariot. They live near Gandvik, which means "the magic bay," the Elivagar. Gandvik was a purely mythological-geographical name before it became the name of the White Sea in a late Christian time, when the sea between Greenland and America got the mythic name Ginungagap. Their being the inhabitants on the coast of a bay gives the author of Thorsdrapa an occasion further on to designate them as vikings, bayings. We have already seen that it is a day's journey between Asgard and the Elivagar (see No. 108), and that on the southern coast Thor has an inn, where he stops, and where his precious team and chariot are taken care of while he makes expeditions into Jotunheim. The continuation of the poem shows that this time, too, he stopped at this inn, and that he got his warriors there. Now, as always before, he proceeds on foot, after having reached Jotunheim.

Strophe 3 first makes a mythic chronological statement, namely, that the daughter of Geirrod, "skilled in magic," had come to an understanding with Loke, before Rogner became the ally of the latter. This mythic chronological statement shows (1) that there was a time when Rogner did not share Loke's plans, which were inimical to the gods; (2) that the events recounted in Thorsdrapa took place before Rogner became a foe of the gods. Why Thorsdrapa thinks it necessary to give this information becomes apparent already in the fourth strophe.

Then the departure from Ide's chalet is mentioned. The host hostile to the giants proceeds to Jotunheim, but before it gets thither it must traverse an intermediate region which is called Endil's meadow.

We might expect that instead of speaking of a meadow as the boundary territory which had to be traversed before getting into Jotunheim, the poem would have spoken of the body of water behind which Jotunheim lies, and mentioned it by one of its names—Elivagar, Gandvik, or Hraun. But on a more careful examination it appears that Endil's meadow is only a paraphrase for a body of water. The proof of this is found in the fact that "Endil's skees," *Endils andrar, Endils itrskid,* is a common paraphrase for ship. So is *Endils eykr,* "Endil's horse." The meadow which Endil crosses on such skees and on such a horse must therefore be a body of water. And no other water can be meant than that which lies between Endil's chalet and Jotunheim, that is, Elivagar, Gandvik.

The name *Endill* may be the same as *Vendill, Vandill* (Younger Edda, i. 548), and abbreviation of *Örvandill.* The initial *V* was originally a semi-vowel, and as such it alliterated with other semi-vowels and with vowels (compare the rhymes on an Oland runic stone, *Vandils jörmungrundar urgrandari*). This easily-disappearing semi-vowel may have been thrown out in later times where it seemed to obscure the alliteration, and thus the form Endil may have arisen from Vendil, Vandil. "Örvandel's meadow" is accordingly in poetic language synonymous with Elivagar, and the paraphrase is a fitting one, since Orvandel-Egil had skees which bore him over land and sea, and since Elivagar was the scene of his adventures.

Strophe 4 tells that after crossing "Endil's meadow" the host of warriors invaded Jotunheim on foot, and that information about their invasion into the land of the giants came to the witches there.

Two important facts are here given in regard to these warriors: they are called *Gángs gunn-vanir* and *Vargs fridar,* "Gang's warrior-vans," and "Varg's defenders of the land." Thus, in the first strophes of Thorsdrapa, we meet with the names of Olvalde's three sons: *Rögnir* (Thjasse), *Idi,* and *Gángr.* The poem mentions Rogner's name in stating that the expedition occurred before Rogner became the foe of the gods; it names Ide's name when it tells that it was at his (Ide's) chalet near Gandvik that Thor gathered these warriors around him; and it names *Gángr's* name, and in connection therewith *Vargr's* name, when it is to state who the leaders were of those champions who accompanied Thor against Geirrod. Under such circumstances it is manifest that Thorsdrapa relates an episode in which Ide, Gang, and Thjasse appear as friends of Thor and foes of the giants, and that the poem locates their original country in the regions on the south coast of Elivagar, and makes *Idja setr* to be situated near the same strand, and play in Thor's expeditions the same part as Orvandel-Egil's abode near the Elivagar, which is also called chalet, *Geirvandil's setr,* and *Ýsetr.* The *Vargr* who is mentioned is, therefore, so far as can be seen, Rogner-Thjasse himself, who in Haustlaung, as we know, is called *fjallgyldir,* that is to say, wolf.

All the warriors accompanying Thor were eager to fight Ymer's descendants, as we have seen in the second strophe. But the last lines of strophe 4 represent one in particular as longing to contend with one of the warlike and terrible giantesses of giant-land. This champion is not mentioned by name, but he is characterised as *bragd-mildr,* "quick to conceive and quick to move;" as *brædi-vændr,* "he who is wont to offer food to eat;" and as *bölkveitir* or *bölkvetir Loka,* "he who compensated Loke's evil deed." The characterisations fit Orvandel-Egil, the nimble archer and skee-runner, who, at his chalet, receives Thor as his guest, when the latter is on his way to Jotunheim, and who gave Thor Thjalfe and Roskva as a compensation, when Loke had deceitfully induced Thjalfe to break a bone belonging to one of Thor's slaughtered goats for the purpose of getting at the marrow. If Thorsdrapa had added that the champion thus designated also was the best archer of mythology, there could be no doubt that Egil was meant. This addition is made further on in the poem, and of itself confirms the fact that Egil took part in the expedition.

Strophe 5, compared with strophes 6 and 7, informs us that Thor, with his troop of champions, in the course of his march came into one of the wild mountain-regions of Jotunheim. The weather is bad and hail-showers fall.

And here Thor finds out that Loke has deceived him in the most insolent manner. By his directions Thor has led his forces to the place where they now are, and here rushes forth from between the mountains a river into which great streams, swelling with hail-showers, roll down from the mountains with seething ice-water. To find in such a river a ford by which his companions can cross was for Thor a difficult matter.

Strophe 6. Meanwhile the men from Ide's chalet had confidently descended into the river. A comparison with strophes 7 and 8 shows that they cautiously kept near Thor, and waded a little farther up the river than he. They used their spears as staffs, which they put down into the stony bottom of the river. The din of the spears, when their metallic points came in contact with the stones of the bottom blended with the noise of the eddies roaring around the rocks of the river (*Knátti hreggi höggvinn hlymthel vid möl glymja, enn fjalla fellihryn thaut med Fedju stedja*).

Strophe 7. In the meantime the river constantly rises and increases in violence, and its ocean-like billows are already breaking against Thor's powerful shoulders. If this is to continue, Thor will have to resort to the power inherent in him of rising equally with the increase of the waves.

NOTE.—But the warriors from Ide's sæter, who do not possess this power, what are they to do? The plan laid between Loke and the witches of Jotunheim is manifestly to drown them. And the succeeding strophes show that they are in the most imminent danger.

944

Strophes 8 and 9. These bold warriors waded with firm steps; but the billowing masses of water increased in swiftness every moment. While Thor's powerful hands hold fast to the staff of safety, the current is altogether too strong for the spears, which the Gandvik champions have to support themselves on. On the mountains stood giantesses increasing the strength of the current. Then it happened that "the god of the bow, driven by the violence of the billows, rushed upon Thor's shoulders (*kykva naudar áss, blasinn hrönnjardar skafls hvetvidri, thurdi haudrs runn of herdi*), while Thjalfe with his comrades came, as if they had been automatically lifted up, and seized hold of the belt of the celestial prince" (Thor) (*unnz thjálfi med ýta sinni kom sjálflopta á himinsjóla skaunar-seil*).

NOTE.—Thus the plan laid by Loke and the giantesses to drown the men hostile to the giants, the men dwelling on the south coast of the Elivagar, came near succeeding. They were saved by their prudence in wading higher up the stream than Thor, so that, if they lost their foothold, they could be hurled by the eddies against him. One of the Gandvik champions, and, as the continuation of the poems shows, the foremost one among them, here characterised as "the god of the bow," is tossed by a storm-billow against Thor's shoulders, and there saves himself. Thjalfe and the whole remaining host of the warriors of Ide's sæter have at the same time been carried by the waves down against *Hlodyn's* powerful son, and save themselves by seizing hold of his belt of strength. With "the god of the bow" on his shoulders, and with a whole host of warriors clinging to his waist, Thor continues his wading across the stream.

In strophe 8, the Gandvik champions are designated by two paraphrases. We have already seen them described as "Gang's warrior-vans" and as "Varg's land-defenders." Here they are called "the clever warriors of the viking-sæter" (*vikinga setrs snotrir gunnar runnar*) and "Odin's land-defenders, bound by oaths" (*Gauta eidsvara fridar*). That Ide's sæter is called "the vikings' sæter" is explained by the fact that it is situated near Gand*vik,* and that these *bayings* had the Elivagar as the scene of their conflicts with the powers of frost. That they are Odin's land-defenders, bound by oaths, means that they are mythical beings, who in rank are lower than the Asas, and are pledged by oaths to serve Odin and defend his territory against the giants. Their sæter (chalet) near Gandvik is therefore an outpost against the powers of frost. It follows that Ide, Gang, and Thjasse originally are *numina,* though of a lower, serving rank; that their relation to the higher world of gods was of such a character that they could not by their very nature be regarded as foes of the giants, but are bound to the cause of the gods by oaths; but on the other hand they could not be full-blooded giants of the race produced from Ymer's feet (see No. 86). Their original home is not Jotunheim itself, but a land bordering on the home of the giants, and this mytho-geographical locality must correspond with their mytho-genealogical position. The last strophe in Thorsdrapa calls the giants slain by the Gandvik champions "Alfheim's calves," Alfheim's cattle to be slaughtered, and this seems to indicate that these champions belong to the third and lowest of those clans into which the divinities of the Teutonic mythology are divided, that is, the elves.

The Gandvik champion who rescues himself on Thor's shoulders, while the rest of them hold fast to his girdle, is a celebrated archer, and so well known to the hearers of Thorsdrapa, that it was not necessary to mention him by name in order to make it clear who he was. In fact, the epithet applied to him, "the god of the bow" (*áss kykva naudar,* and in strophe 18, *tvívidar Týr*), is quite sufficient to designate him as the foremost archer of mythology, that is, Orvandel-Egil, who is here carried on Thor's shoulders through the raging waves, just as on another occasion he was carried by Thor in his basket across the Elivagar. Already in strophe 4 he is referred to as the hero nimble in thought and body, who is known for his hospitality, and who made compensation for Loke's evil deed. The foremost one next after him among the Gandvik champions is Thjalfe, Egil's foster-son. The others are designated as Thjalfe's *ýta sinni,* his body of men.

Thus we find that the two foremost among "Gang's warrior-vans," who with Thor marched forth from "Ide's sæter," before Rogner (Thjasse) became Loke's ally, are Volund's and Slagfin's brother Egil and Egil's foster-son Thjalfe. We find that Egil and Thjalfe belong to the inhabitants of Ide's sæter, where Thor on this occasion had stopped, and where he had left his chariot and goats, for now, as on other occasions, he goes on foot to Jotunheim.

947

And as in other sources Egil is mentioned as the one who on such occasions gives lodgings to Thor and his goats, and as Thorsdrapa also indicates that he is the hospitable host who had received Thor in his house, and had paid him a ransom for the damage caused by Loke to one of his goats, then this must be a most satisfactory proof that Ide's sæter is the same place as the *Geirvadils* setr inhabited by Egil and his brothers, and that Orvandel-Egil is identical either with Ide or Gang, from which it follows, again, that Alvalde's (Olvalde's) sons, Ide, Gang, and Thjasse, are identical with Ivalde's sons, Slagfin, Egil, and Volund.

That Egil is identical with Gang and not with Ide is apparent from a comparison with the Grotte-song. There Olvalde's sons are called *Idi, Aurnir,* and *Thjazi,* while in the Younger Edda they are called *Idi, Gángr,* and *Thjazi.* Thus Aurnir is identical with *Gángr,* and as *Aurnir* means "wild boar," and as "wild boar" (Ebur, Ibor, Ebbo) is an epithet of Egil, Orvandel-Egil must be identical with Gang.

In regard to the rest of Thorsdrapa I may be brief, since it is of less interest to the subject under discussion.

Strophe 10. In spite of the perilous adventure described above, the hearts of Thjalfe and the Gandvik champions were no more terrified than Thor's. Here they are designated as *eids fiardar*, "the men pledged by oath," with which is to be compared *eidsvara fridar* in strophe 8.

Strophe's 11, 12, show that Thor landed safely with his burden. Scarcely had he and his companions got a firm foothold on the other strand before Geirrod's giant-clan, "the world-tree-destroying folk of the sea-belt," came to the spot, and a conflict arose, in which the attacks of the giants were firmly repulsed, and the latter were finally forced to retreat.

Strophe 13. After the victory Thor's terrible hosts pressed farther into Jotenheim to open Geirrod's hall, and they arrived there amid the din and noise of cave-dwellers.

The following strophes mention that Thor broke the backs of Geirrod's daughters, and pressed with his warriors into Geirrod's hall, where he was received with a piece of red-hot iron hurled by the latter, which, hurled back by Thor, caused the death of the giant-chief. Thor had given the glowing javelin such a force that some one who stood near him, probably Egil, "drank so that he reeled in the air-current of the piece of iron the air-drink of Hrimner's daughter" (*svalg hrapmunum á siu lopti Hrimnis drósar lyptisylg*). Hrimner's daughter is Gulveig-Heid (Hyndluljod, 32), and her "air-drink" is the fire, over which the gods held her lifted on their spears (Völuspa, 21).

As we see from the context, Geirrod's halls were filled with the men who had fled from the battle near the river, and within the mountain there arose another conflict, which is described in the last three strophes of the poem. Geirrod's hall shook with the din of battle. Thor swung his bloody hammer. "The staff of safety," "the help-tree of the way," the staff on which Thor supported himself in crossing the river, fell into Egil's hands (*kom at tvívidar Tývi brautar lids tollr*), who did not here have room to use his bow, but who, with this "convenient tree jerked (or broken) from the forest," gave death-blows to "the calves of Alfheim." The arrows from his quiver could not be used in this crowded place against the men of the mountain-chief.

The fact that the giants in Thorsdrapa use the sling is of interest to the question concerning the position of the various weapons of mythology. Geirrod is called *vegtaugar thrjótr,* "the industrious applier of the sling" (str. 17), and *álmtaugar 'Ægir,* "the Ægir of the sling made of elm-bast."

In the last strophe Egil is said to be *helblótinn* and *hneitir, undirfjálfs bliku,* expressions to which I shall recur further on.

Like the relation between Volund and his swan-maids in Volundarkvida, the relation between Rogner-Thjasse and Idun in Forspjallsljod is not that of the robber to his unwilling victim, but one of mutual harmony. This is confirmed by a poem which I shall analyse when the investigation reaches a point that demands it, and according to which Idun was from her childhood tied by bonds of love and by oath to the highly-gifted but unhappy son of Ivalde, to the great artist who, by his irreconcilable thirst for revenge, became the Lucifer of Teutonic mythology, while Loke is its Mefisto. I presume that the means of rejuvenation, the divine remedy against age (*ellilyf ása* —Haustlaung), which Idun alone in Asgard knows and possesses, was a product of Thjasse-Volund's art. The middle age also remembered Volund (Wieland) as a physician, and this trait seems to be from the oldest time, for in Rigveda, too, the counterparts of the Ivalde sons, that is, the Ribhus, at the request of the gods, invent means of rejuvenation. It may be presumed that the mythology described his exterior personality in a clear manner. From his mother he must have inherited his giant strength, which, according to the Grotte-song, surpassed Hrungner's and that of the father of the latter (*Hard var Hrungnir ok hans fadir, thó var Thjazi theim auflgari*—str. 9). With his strength beauty was doubtless united. Otherwise, Volundarkvida's author would scarcely have said that his swan-maid laid her arms around Anund's (Volund's) "white" neck. That his eyes were conceived as glittering may be concluded from the fact that they distinguish him on the starry canopy as a star-hero, and that in Volundarkvida Nidhad's queen speaks of the threatening glow in the gaze of the fettered artist (*amon ero augu ormi theim enom fråna*—str. 17).

Ivalde's sons—Thjasse-Volund, Aurnir-Egil, and Ide-Slagfin—are, as we have seen, bastards of an elf and a giantess (Greip, Gambara). Ivalde's daughters, on the other hand (see No. 113), have as mother a sun-dis, daughter of the ruler of the atmosphere, Nokver. In other sources the statement in Forspjallsljod (6) is confirmed, that Ivalde had two groups of children, and that she who "among the races of elves was called Idun" belonged to one of them. Thus, while Idun and her sisters are half-sisters to Ivalde's sons, these are in turn half-brothers to pure giants, sons of Greip, and these giants are, according to the Grotte-song (str. 9), the fathers of Fenja and Menja. The relationship of the Ivalde sons

to the gods on the one hand and to the giants on the other
may be illustrated by the following scheme:

Ivalde begets (1) with a sun-dis	(2) with the giantess Greip—	Greip bears with a giant	
Idun and her sisters.	Thjasse-Volund and his brothers.	giant Fenja.	giant Menja.

115.

REVIEW OF THE PROOFS OF VOLUND'S IDENTITY WITH
THJASSE.

The circumstances which first drew my attention to
the necessity of investigating whether Thjasse and
Volund were not different names of the same mythic personality, which the mythology particularly called Thjasse,
and which the heroic saga springing from the mythology
in Christian times particularly called Volund, were the
following: (1) In the study of Saxo I found in no less
than three passages that Njord, under different historical
masks, marries a daughter of Volund, while in the mythology he marries a daughter of Thjasse. (2) In investigating the statements anent Volund's father in Volundarkvida's text and prose appendix I found that these led
to the result that Volund was a son of Sumbl, the Finn
king—that is to say, of Olvalde, Thjasse's father. (3)
My researches in regard to the myth about the mead produced the result that Svigder-Olvalde perished by the
treachery of a dwarf outside of a mountain, where one of
the smith-races of the mythology, Suttung's sons, had
their abode. In Vilkinasaga's account of the death of

Volund's father I discovered the main outlines of the same mythic episode.

The correspondence of so different sources in so unexpected a matter was altogether too remarkable to permit it to be overlooked in my mythological researches. The fact that the name-variation itself, Alvalde (for Olvalde), as Thjasse's father is called in Harbardsljod, was in meaning and form a complete synonym of Ivalde I had already observed, but without attaching any importance thereto.

The next step was to examine whether a similar proof of the identity of Thjasse's and Volund's mother was to be found. In one Norse mythological source Thjasse's mother is called Greip. Volund's and Egil's (Ayo's and Ibor's, Aggo's and Ebbo's) mother is in Paulus Diaconus and in Origo Longobardorum called Gambara, in Saxo Gambaruc. The Norse stem in the Latinised name Gambara is *Gammr,* which is a synonym of Greip, the name of Thjasse's mother. Thus I found a reference to the identity of Thjasse's mother and Volund's mother.

From the parents I went to the brothers. One of Volund's brothers bore the epithet Aurnir, "wild boar." Aurnir's wife is remembered in the Christian traditions as one who forebodes the future. Ebur's wife is a mythological seeress. One of Thjasse's brothers, Ide, is the only one in the mythology whose name points to an original connection with Ivalde (Idvalde), Volund's father, and with Idun, Volund's half-sister. Volund himself bears the epithet Brunne, and Thjasse's home is Brunnsacre. One of Thjasse's sons is slain at the instigation of Loke, and Loke, who in Lokasenna takes pleasure in stating this, boasts in the same poem that he has caused the slaying of Thjasse.

In regard to bonds of relationship in general, I found that on the one side Volund, like Thjasse, was regarded as a giant, and had relations among the giants, among whom Vidolf is mentioned both as Volund's and Thjasse's relative, and that on the other hand Volund is called an elf-prince, and that Thjasse's father belonged to the clan of elves, and that Thjasse's daughter is characterised, like Volund and his nearest relatives, as a skee-runner and hunter, and in this respect has the same epithet as Volund's nephew Ull. I found, furthermore, that so far as tradition has preserved the memory of star-heroes, every mythic person who belonged to their number was called a son of Ivalde or a son of Olvalde. Orvandel-Egil is a star-hero and a son of Ivalde. The Watlings, after whom the Milky Way is named, are descendants of Vate-Vade, Volund's father. Thjasse is a star-hero and the son of Olvalde. Ide, too, Thjasse's brother, "the torch-bearer," may have been a star-hero, and, as we shall show later, the memory of Volund's brother Slagfin was partly connected with the Milky Way and partly with the spots on the moon; while, according to another tradition, it is Volund's father whose image is seen in these spots (see Nos. 121, 123).

I found that Rogner is a Thjasse-epithet, and that all that is stated of Rogner is also told of Volund. Rogner was, like the latter, first the friend of the gods and then their foe. He was a "swan-gladdener," and Volund the lover of a swan-maid. Like Volund he fought against

Njord. Like Volund he proceeded to the northernmost edge of the world, and there he worked with magic implements through the powers of frost for the destruction of the gods and of the world. And from some one he has taken the same ransom as Volund did, when the latter killed Nidhad's young sons and made goblets of their skulls.

I found that while Olvalde's sons, Ide, Aurner (Gang), and Thjasse, still were friends of the gods, they had their abode on the south coast of the Elivagar, where Ivalde had his home, called after him *Geirvadils setr,* and where his son Orvandel-Egil afterwards dwelt; that Thor on his way to Jotunheim visits Ide's *setr,* and that he is a guest in Egil's dwelling; that the mythological warriors who dwell around Ide's *setr* are called "warrior-vans," and that these "Gang's warrior-vans" have these very persons, Egil and his foster-son Thjalfe, as their leaders when they accompany Thor to fight the giants, wherefore the *setr* of the Olvalde sons Ide and Gang must be identical with that of the Ivalde sons, and Ide, Gang, and Thjasse identical with Slagfin, Egil, and Volund.

On these foundations the identity of Olvalde's sons with Ivalde's sons is sufficiently supported, even though our mythic records had preserved no evidence that Thjasse, like Volund, was the most celebrated artist of mythology. But such evidence is not wanting. As the real meaning of *Regin* is "shaper," "workman," and as this has been retained as a smith-name in Christian times, there is every reason to assume that Thjasse, who is called *fjadrar-blads leik-Regin* and *vingvagna Rögnir,* did himself make, like

955

Volund, the eagle guise which he, like Volund, wears. The son of Ivalde, Volund, made the most precious treasures for the gods while he still was their friend, and the Olvalde son Thjasse is called *hapta snytrir,* "the decorator of the gods," doubtless for the reason that he had smithied treasures for the gods during a time when he was their friend and Thor's *ofrúni* (Thor's confidential friend). Volund is the most famous and, so far as we can see, also the first sword-smith, which seems to appear from the fact that his father Ivalde, though a valiant champion, does not use the sword but the spear as a weapon, and is therefore called *Geirvandill.* Thjasse was the first sword-smith, otherwise he would not have been called *fadir mörna,* "the father of the swords." Splendid implements are called *verk Rögnis* and *Thjaza thingskil, Idja glýsmál, Idja ord*—expressions which do not find their adequate explanation in the Younger Edda's account of the division of Olvalde's estate, but in the myth about the judgment which the gods once proclaimed in the contest concerning the skill of Sindre and the sons of Ivalde, when the treasures of the latter presented in court had to plead their own cause.

116.

A LOOK AT THE MYTH CONCERNING THJASSE-VOLUND. HIS EPITHET HLEBARDR. HIS WORST DEED OF RE-VENGE.

What our mythic records tell us about the sons of Olvalde and the sons of Ivalde is under such circumstances to be regarded as fragments which come to us from one and the same original myth. When combined, the fragments are found to dovetail together and form one whole. Volundarkvida (28) indicates that something terrible, something that in the highest degree aroused his indignation and awakened his deep and satanic thirst for revenge, had happened to Volund ere he, accompanied by his brothers, betook himself to the wintry wilderness, where he smithied the sword of revenge and the gand rings; and the poem makes Volund add that this injustice remained to be avenged when he left the Wolf-dales. It lies in the nature of the case that the saga about Volund did not end where the fragment of the Volundarkvida which we possess is interrupted. The balance of the saga must have related what Volund did to accomplish the revenge which he still had to take, and how the effort to take vengeance resulted. The continuation probably also had something to say about that swan-maid, that dis of vegetation, who by the name Hervor Alvitr spends nine years with Volund in the Wolfdales, and then, seized by longing, departs with the other swan-maids, but of whose faithful love Volund is perfectly convinced (Volundarkvida, 10). While Volund is Nidhad's prisoner, the hope he has built on the sword of revenge and victory smithied by him seems to be frustrated. The sword is in the power of Mimer-Nidhad, the friend of the gods. But the hope of the plan of revenge must have awakened again when Svipdag, Volund's nephew, succeeded in coming up from the lower world with the weapon in his possession. The conflict between the powers of frost and the kinsmen of

Ivalde, who had deserted the gods, on the one side, and the gods and their favourite Halfdan, the Teutonic patriarch, on the other side, was kindled anew (see No. 33). Halfdan is repulsed, and finally falls in the war in which Volund got satisfaction by the fact that his sword conquered Thor's Mjolner and made Thor retreat. But once more the hope based on the sword of revenge is frustrated, this time by the possessor of the sword itself, Volund's young kinsman, who—victor in the war, but conquered by the love he cherished for Freyja, rescued by him—becomes the husband of the fair asynje and gives the sword of Volund to Frey, the god of the harvests. That, in spite of this crossing of his plan of revenge, Volund still did not give it up may be taken for granted. He is described not only as the most revengeful, but also as the most persistent and patient person (see "Doer the Scald's Complaint"), when patience could promote his plans. To make war on the gods with the aid of the giants, when the sword of victory had fallen into the hands of the latter, could not give him the least hope of success. After the mythology has given Volund satisfaction for the despicable judgment passed on the products of his skill, it unites the chain of events in such a manner that the same weapon which refuted the judgment and was to cause the ruin of the gods became their palladium against its own maker. What was Volund able to do afterwards, and what did he do? The answer to this question is given in the myth about Thjasse. With Idun —the Hervor Alvitr of the heroic poem—he confined himself in a mountain, whose halls he presumably decorated with all the wonders which the sagas of the middle ages, describing splendid mountain-halls and parks within the mountains, inherited from the mythology. The mountain must have been situated in a region difficult of access to the gods—according to Bragaraedur in Jotunheim. At all events, Thjasse is there secure against every effort to disturb him, forcibly, in his retreat. The means against the depredations of time and years which Idun possesses have their virtue only when in her care. Without this means, even the gods of Asgard are subject to the influence of time, and are to grow old and die. And in the sense of a myth symbolising nature, the same means must have had its share in the rejuvenation of creation through the saps rising every year in trees and herbs. The destruction of the world—the approach of which Volund wished to precipitate with his sword of revenge— must come slowly, but surely, if Idun remains away from Asgard. This plan is frustrated by the gods through Loke, as an instrument compelled by necessity—compelled by necessity (Haustlaung, str. 11), although he delighted in the mischief of deceiving even his allies. Near Thjasse's mountain-halls is a body of water, on which he occasionally rows out to fish (Bragaraedur.) Once, when he rows out for this purpose, perhaps accompanied by Skade, Idun is at home alone. Loke, who seems to have studied his customs, flies in a borrowed feather guise into the mountain and steals Idun, who, changed into a nut, is carried in his claws through space to Asgard. But the robbing of Idun was not enough for Loke. He enticed Thjasse to pursue. In his inconsiderate zeal, the latter dons his eagle guise and hastens after the robber into Asgard's vaferflames, where he falls by the javelins of the gods and by Thor's hammer. Sindre's work, the one surpassed by Volund, causes his death, and is avenged. I have already pointed out that this event explains Loke's words to Idun in Lokasenna, where he speaks of the murder of one of the Ivalde sons, and insists that she, Idun, embraced the one who caused his death.

The fate of the great artist and his tragical death help to throw light on the character of Loke and on the part he played in the mythology. Ivalde's sons are, in the beginning, the zealous friends of the gods, and the decorators and protectors of their creation. They smithy ornaments, which are the symbols of vegetation; and at their outpost by the Elivagar they defend the domain of vegetation against Jotunheim's powers of frost. As I have already stated, they are, like the Ribhus, at the same time heroes, promoters of growth, and artists of antiquity. The mythology had also manifestly endowed the sons of Ivalde with pleasing qualities—profound knowledge of the mysteries of nature, intelligence, strength, beauty, and with faithfulness toward their beloved. We find that, in time of adversity, the brothers were firmly united, and that their swan-maids love them in joy and in distress. For the powers of evil it was, therefore, of the greatest moment to bring about strife between the gods and these their "sworn men." Loke, who is a *gedreynir* (Thorsdrapa), "a searcher of the qualities of the soul," a "tempter of the character," has discovered in the great artist of antiquity the false but hitherto unawakened qualities of his character—his ambition and irreconcilable thirst for revenge. These qualties, particularly the latter, burst forth fully developed suddenly after the injustice which, at Loke's instigation, the gods have done to the sons of Ivalde. The thirst for revenge breaks out in Thjasse-Volund in a despicable misdeed. There is reason for assuming that the terrible vengeance which, according to the heroic saga, he took against Nidhad, and which had its counterpart in the mythology itself, was not the worst crime which the epic of the Teutonic mythology had to blame him for. Harbardsljod (20) alludes to another and worse one. Speaking of Thjasse (str. 19), *Hárbardr*-Loke* there boasts that—

> hardan jotun
> ec bugda Hlebard vera,
> gaf han mer gambantein,
> en ec velta hann or viti.

Harbard-Loke here speaks of a giant who, in his mind, was a valiant one, but whose "senses he stole," that is, whom he "cunningly deprived of thought and reflection." There are two circumstances to which these words might apply. The one concerns the giant-builder who built the Asgard-wall, and, angry on account of the trick by which Loke cheated him out of the compensation agreed on, rushed against the gods and was slain by Thor. The

---

*Holtzmann and Bergmann have long since pointed out that Harbard is identical with Loke. The idea that Harbard, who in every trait is Loke in Lokasenna, and, like him, appears as a mocker of the gods and boasts of his evil deeds and of his success with the fair sex, should be Odin, is one of the proofs showing how an unmethodical symbolic interpretation could go astray. In the second part of this work I shall fully discuss Harbardsljod. Proofs are to be found from the last days of heathendom in Iceland that it was then well known that the Harbard who is mentioned in this poem was a foe of the gods.

other concerns Thjasse, who, seeing his beloved carried away by Loke and his plan about to be frustrated, recklessly rushed into his certain ruin. The real name of the giant alluded to is not given, but it is indicated by the epithet *Hlébardr,* which, according to the Younger Edda, (ii. 484), is a snyonym of *Vargr* and *Gyldir.* It has already been shown above that *Vargr* in Thorsdrapa and *Fjallgyldir* in Haustlaung are epithets of Thjasse. Loke says that this same giant, whose sense he cunningly robbed, had previously given him a *gambanteinn.* This word means a weapon made by Volund. His sword of revenge and victory is called *gambanteinn* in Skirnersmal. But *gambanteinn* is, at the same time, a synonym of *mistelteinn,* hence, in an Icelandic saga from the Christian time, Volund's sword of victory also reappears by the name *mistelteinn* (see No. 60). Thus the giant Hlebard gave Loke a weapon, which, according to its designation, is either Volund's sword of victory or the mistletoe. It cannot be the sword of victory. We know the hands to which this sword has gone and is to go: Volund's, Mimer-Nidhad's, the night-dis Sinmara's, Svipdag's, Frey's, Aurboda's and Eggther's, and finally Fjalar's and Surt's. The weapon which Thjasse's namesake Hlebard gives Loke must, accordingly, have been the mistletoe. In this connection we must bear in mind what is said of the mistletoe. Unfortunately, the few words of Völuspa are the only entirely reliable record we have on this subject; but certain features of Gylfaginning's account (Younger Edda, i. 172-174) may be mythologically correct. "Slender and fair"—not dangerous and fair to behold—grew, according to Völuspa, the mistletoe, "higher than the fields" (as a parasite on the trees); but from the shrub which seemed innocent became "a dangerous arrow of pain," which *Hödr* hurled. According to a poetic fragment united with Vegtams-kvida ("Balder's draumar"), and according to Gylfaginning, the gods had previously exacted an oath from all things not to harm Balder; but, according to Gylfaginning, they had omitted to exact an oath from one thing, namely, the mistletoe. By cunning Loke found this out. He went and pulled up the mistletoe, which he was afterwards able to put into Hoder's hand, while, according to Gylfaginning, the gods were amusing themselves by seeing how every weapon aimed at Balder hit him without harming him. But that Loke should hand Hoder this shrub in the form in which it had grown on the tree, and that Hoder should use it in this form to shoot Balder, is as improbable as that Hoder was blind.* We must take Völuspa's words to mean that the shrub became an arrow, and we must conceive that this arrow looked like every other arrow, and for this reason did not awaken suspicion. Otherwise the suspicion would at once have been awakened, for they who had exacted the oath of things, and Frigg who had sent the messengers to exact the oaths, knew that the mistletoe was the only thing in the whole world that had not been sworn. The heathen songs no-

---

*When I come to consider the Balder-myth in the second part of this work, I shall point out the source from which the author of Gylfaginning, misunderstandingly, has drawn the conclusion that the man of exploits, the warrior, the archer, and the hunter Hoder was blind. The misunderstanding gave welcome support to the symbolic interpretation, which, in the blind Hoder, found among other things a symbol of night (but night has "many eyes").

where betray such inconsistencies and such thoughtlessness as abound in the accounts of the Younger Edda. The former are always well conceived, at times incisive, but they always reveal a keen sense of everything that may give even to the miraculous the appearance of reality and logic. The mistletoe was made into an arrow by some one who knew how to turn it into a "dangerous arrow of pain" in an infallible manner. The unhappy shot depended on the magic qualities that were given to the mistletoe by the hands that changed it into an arrow. The event becomes comprehensible, and the statements found in the various sources dovetail together and bear the test of sound criticism, if Loke, availing himself of the only thing which had not been bound by oath not to harm Balder, goes with this shrub, which of itself was innocent and hardly fit for an arrow, to the artist who hated the gods, to the artist who had smithied the sword of revenge, and if the latter, with his magic skill as a smith, makes out of the *mistelteinn* a new *gambanteinn* dangerous to the gods, and gives the weapon to Loke in order that he might accomplish his evil purpose therewith. As Hlebard is a Thjasse-synonym, as this Thjasse-synonym is connected with the weapon-name *gambanteinn,* which indicates a Thjasse-work, and as Loke has treated Thjasse as he says he has treated Hlebard—by a cunning act he robbed him of his senses—then all accessible facts go to establish the theory that by Hlebard is meant the celebrated ancient artist deceived by Loke. And as Hlebard has given him a weapon which is designated by the name of the sword of revenge, but which is not the sword of revenge, while the latter, on the other hand and for corresponding reasons, also gets the name *mistelteinn,* then all the facts go to show that the weapon which Hlebard gave to Loke was the mistletoe fraught with woes and changed to an arrow. If Glyfaginning's unreliable account, based on fragmentary and partly misunderstood mythic records presented in a disjointed manner, had not been found, and if we had been referred exclusively to the few but reliable statements which are to be found in regard to the matter in the poetic songs, then a correct picture of this episode, though not so complete as to details, would have been the result of a compilation of the statements extant. The result would then have been: (1) Balder was slain by an arrow shot by Hoder (Völuspa, Vegtamskvida); (2) Hoder was not the real slayer, but Loke (Lokasenna, 28); (3) the material of which the arrow was made was a tender or slender (*mjór*) mistletoe (Völuspa); (4) previously all things had sworn not to harm Balder ("Balder's draumar"), but the mistletoe must, for some reason or other, have been overlooked by the messengers sent out to exact the oaths, since Balder was mortally wounded by it; (5) since it was Loke who arranged (*réd*) matters so that this happened, it must have been he who had charge of the mistletoe for the carrying out of his evil purpose; (6) the mistletoe fell into the hands of a giant-smith hostile to the gods, and mentioned under circumstances that refer to Thjasse (Harbardsljod); (7) by his skill as a smith he gave such qualities to the mistletoe as to change it into "a dangerous arrow of pain," and then gave the arrow to Loke (Harbardsljod); (8) from Loke's hands it passed into Hoder's, and was shot by the latter (Loka-senna, Völuspa).

It is dangerous to employ nature-symbolism as a means of mythological investigation. It is unserviceable for that purpose, so long as it cannot be subjected to the rules of severe methodics. On the other hand, it is admissible and justifiable to consider from a natural symbolic stand-point the results gained in a mythological investigation by the methodological system. If, as already indicated, Hlebard is identical with Thjasse-Volund, then he who was the cause of the fimbul-winter and sent the powers of frost out upon the earth, also had his hand in the death of the sun-god Balder and in his descent to the lower world. There is logic in this. And there is logic in the very fact that the weapon with which the sun-god is slain is made from the mistletoe, which blossoms and produces fruit in the winter, and is a plant which rather shuns than seeks the light of the sun. When we remember how the popular traditions have explained the appearance and qualities of various animals and plants by connecting them with the figures of mythology or of legendary lore, then I suppose it is possible that the popular fancy saw in the mistletoe's dread of light the effect of grief and shame at having been an instrument in evil hands for evil pur-poses. Various things indicate that the mistletoe orig-inally was a sacred plant, not only among the Celts, but also among the Teutons. The Hindooic Aryans also knew sacred parasitical plants.

The word *gamban* which forms a part of *gambanteinn*

means "compensation," "ransom," when used as a noun, and otherwise "retaliating." In the Anglo-Saxon poetry occurs (see Grein's Dictionary) the phrase *gamban gyldan,* "to compensate," "to pay dues." In the Norse sources *gamban* occurs only in the compounds *gambanteinn* (Skirnersmal, 32; Harbardsljod, 20), *gambanreidi* (Skirnersmal, 33), and *gambansumbl* (Lokasenna, 8). In the song of Skirner, the latter threatens Gerd, who refused Frey's offer of marriage, that she shall be struck by *gambanreidi goda,* the avenging wrath of the gods. In Lokasenna, Loke comes unbidden into the banquet of the gods in Ægir's hall to mix bitterness with their gladness, and he demands either a place at the banquet table or to be turned out of doors. Brage answers that the gods never will grant him a seat at a banquet, "since they well know for whom among beings they are to prepare *gambansumbl,*" a banquet of revenge or a drink of revenge. This he manifestly mentions as a threat, referring to the fate which soon afterwards happens to Loke, when he is captured and bound, and when a venom-spitting serpent is fastened above his mouth. For the common assumption that *gamban* means something "grand," "magnificent," "divine," there is not a single shadow of reason. *Gambanteinn* is accordingly "the twig of revenge," and thus we have the mythological reason why Thjasse-Volund's sword of revenge and the mistletoe arrow were so called. With them he desires to avenge the insult to which he refers in Volundarkvida, 28: *Nu heﬁ ec hefnt harma minna allra nema einna ivithgjarnra.*

117.

THE GUARD AT HVERGELMER AND THE ELIVAGAR.

It has already been shown (see Nos. 59, 93) that the Elivagar have their source in the subterranean fountain Hvergelmer, situated on a mountain, which separates the subterranean region of bliss (Hel) from Nifelhel. Here, near the source of the Elivagar, stands the great world-mill, which revolves the starry heavens, causes the ebb and flood of the ocean and regulates its currents, and grinds the bodies of the primeval giants into layers of mould on the rocky substrata (see Nos. 79, 80). From Hvergelmer, the mother of all waters, the northern root of the world-tree draws saps, which rise into its topmost branches, evaporate into *Eikthyrnir* above Asgard, and flow thence as vafer-laden clouds (see No. 36), which emit fructifying showers upon Midgard, and through the earth they return to their original source, the fountain Hvergelmer. The Hvergelmer mountain (the Nida-mountains, *Nidafjöll*) cannot have been left without care and protection, as it is of so vast importance in the economy of the world, and this the less since it at the same time forms the boundary between the lower world's realm of bliss and Nifelhel, the subterranean Jotunheim, whose frost-thurses sustain the same relation to the inhabitants on the evergreen fields of bliss as the powers of frost in the upper Jotunheim sustain to the gods of Asgard and to the inhabitants of Midgard. There is no reason for assuming that the guard of brave sworn warriors of the Asgard gods, those warriors whom we have already seen in array near the Elivagar, should have only a part of this body of water to keep watch over. The clan of the elves, under their chiefs, the three sons of Ivalde, even though direct evidence were wanting, must be regarded as having watched over the Elivagar along their whole extent, even to their source, and as having had the same important duty in reference to the giants of the lower world as in reference to those of the upper. As its name indicates, Nifelheim is shrouded in darkness and mist, against which the peaks of the Hvergelmer mountain form the natural rampart as a protection to the smiling fields of bliss. But gales and storms might lift themselves above these peaks and enshroud even Mimer's and Urd's realms in mist. The elves are endowed with power to hinder this. The last strophe in Thorsdrapa, so interesting from a mythological standpoint, confirms this view. Egil is there called *hneitir undir-fjálfs bliku,* and is said to be *helblótinn.* *Blika* is a name for clouds while they are still near the horizon and appear as pale vapours, which to those skilled in regard to the weather forbode an approaching storm (compare Vigfusson's Dict., 69). *Undir-fjálfr* is thought by Egilson to mean subterranean mountains, by Vigfusson "the deep," *abyssus.* *Hneitir undir-fjalfs bliku* is "he who conquers (or resolves, scatters) the clouds rising, storm-foreboding, from the abyss (or over the lower-world mountain)." As Egil can be thus characterised, it is easy to explain why he is called *helblótinn,*" "he who receives sacrifices in the subterranean realm of bliss." He guards the Teutonic elysian fields against the powers of frost and the mists of Nifelheim, and therefore receives tokens of gratitude from their pious inhabitants.

The vocation of the sons of Ivalde, as the keepers of the Hvergelmer fountain and of the Elivagar, has its counterpart in the vocation which, in the Iranian mythology, is attributed to Thjasse's prototype, the star-hero Tistrya (Tishya). The fountain Hvergelmer, the source of the ocean and of all waters, has in the Iranian mythology its counterpart in the immense body of water Vourukasha. Just as the Teutonic world-tree grows from its northern root out of Hvergelmer, the Iranian world-tree Gaokerena grows out of Vourukasha (Bundehesh, 18). Vourukasha is guarded by Tistrya, assisted by two heroes belonging to the class of mythological beings that are called Yazatas (Izads; in the Veda literature Yajata), "they who deserve offerings," and in the Iranian mythology they form the third rank of divine beings, and thus correspond to the elves of the Teutonic mythology. Assisted by these two heroes and by the "fevers of the just," Tistrya defends Vourukasha, and occasionally fights against the demon Apaosha, who desires to destroy the world (Bundehesh, 7). Tistrya, as such, appears in three forms: as a youth with bright and glistening eyes, as a wild boar, and as a horse. Can it be an accident that these forms have their counterparts in the Teutonic mythology in the fact that one of Thjasse's brothers (Egil-Orvandel-Ebur) has the epithet "wild boar," and that, as shall be shown below, his other brother (Slagfin) bears the epithet Hengest, and that Thjasse-Volund himself, who for years was possessor of, and

presumably invented, the "remedy against aging," which
Idun, his beloved, has charge of—that Thjasse-Volund
himself was regarded as a youth with a "white neck"
(Volundarkvida, 2) and with glittering eyes (Volundarkvida, 17), which after his death were placed in the beav-
ens as stars?

118.

I now come to the third Ivalde son, Slagfin. The name
Slagfin (*Slagfidr*) occurs nowhere else than in Volundarkvida, and in the prose introduction to the same.
All that we learn of him is that, like Egil, he accompanied his brother Volund to the Wolfdales; that, like
them, he runs on skees and is a hunter; and that, when
the swan-maids, in the ninth year of their abode in the
Wolfdales, are overcome by longing and return to the
south, he goes away to find his beloved, just as Egil goes
to find his. We learn, furthermore, that Slagfin's swan-
maid is a sister of Volund's and a kinswoman of Egil's,
and that she, accordingly, is Slagfin's sister (half-sister).
She is called *Hladgudr Svanhvit,* likewise a name which
occurs nowhere else. Her (and accordingly also that of
Volund's swan-maid) mother is called Swan-feather,
Svanfjödr (Slagfin's beloved is *Svanfjadrar drós*—str.
2). The name Svan-feather reminds us of the Svanhild
Gold-feather mentioned in Fornm., ii. 7, wife of one
Finalf. If Svanfeather is identical with Svanhild Gold-

feather, then Finalf must originally be identical with Ivalde, who also is an elf and bears the name *Finnakon-ungr, Sumblus Phinnorum rex.* But this then simply confirms what we already know, namely, that the Ivalde sons and two of the swan-maids are brothers and sisters. It, however, gives us no clue by which we can trace Slagfin in other sources, and rediscover him bearing other names, and restore the myth concerning him which seems to be lost. That he, however, played an important part in the mythology may be assumed already from the fact that his brothers hold places so central in the great epic of the mythology. It is, therefore, highly probable that he is mentioned in our mythic fragments, though concealed under some other name. One of these names, viz., Ide, we have already found (see No. 114); and thereby we have learned that he, with his brother Egil, had a citadel near the Elivagar, and guarded their coasts against the powers of frost. But of his fate in general we are ignorant. No extensive researches are required, however, before we find circumstances which, compared with each other, give us the result that Slagfin is Gjuke, and therewith the way is open for a nearer acquaintance with his position in the heroic saga, and before that in the mythology. His identity with Gjuke is manifest from the following circumstances:

The Gjukungs, famous in the heroic saga, are, according to the saga itself, the first ones who bear this name. Their father is Gjuke, from whom this patronymic is derived. Through their father they belong to a race that is called Hniflungs, Niflungs, Nebelungs. The Gjukungs form a branch of the Niflung race, hence all Gjukungs are Niflungs, but not all Niflungs Gjukungs. The Younger Edda says correctly, *Af Niflunga ætt var Gjuki* (Younger Edda, i. 522), and Atlakvida (17) shows that the Gjukungs constitute only a part of the Niflungs. The identity of the Gjukungs in this relative sense with the Niflungs is known and pointed out in Atlamal (47, 52, 88), in Brot Sigurdarkvida (16), in Atlakvida (11, 17, 27), and in "Drap Niflunga."

Who the Niflung race are in the widest sense of the word, or what known heroes the race embraced besides Gjuke and his sons—to this question the saga of Helge Hundingsbane (i. 48) gives important information, inasmuch as the passage informs us that the hostile race which Helge Hundingsbane—that is to say, Halfdan Borgarson (see No. 29)—combats are the Niflungs. Foremost among the Niflungs Hodbrod is mentioned in this poem, whose betrothed Helge (Halfdan Borgarson) gets into his power. It has already been shown that, in this heroic poem, Hodbrod is the copy of the mythological Orvandel-Egil (see Nos. 29, 32, 101). It follows that Volund, Orvandel-Egil, and Slagfin are Niflungs, and that Gjuke either is identical with one of them or that he at all events is descended from the same progenitor as they.

The great treasure of works smithied from gold and other precious things which the Gjukungs owned, according to the heroic traditions, are designated in the different sources in the same manner as inherited. In Atlakvida (11) the Gjukung treasure is called *arf Ni-*

flunga; so also in Atlakvida (27). In Gudrunarkvida
(ii. 25) the queen of the deceased Gjuke promises her
and Gjuke's daughter, Gudrun, that she is to have the
control of all the treasures "after (*at*) her dead father
(*fjöld allz fjar at thin faudur daudan*), and we are told
that those treasures, together with the halls in which they
were kept and the precious carpets, are an inheritance
after (*at*) *Hlaudver,* "the fallen prince" (*hringa rauda
Hlaudves sali, arsal allan at jofur fallin*). From Volundarkvida we gather that Volund's and Slagfin's swan-
maids are daughters of Hlaudver and sisters of their
lovers. Thus Hlaudver is identical with Ivalde, Volund's, Egil's, and Slagfin's father (see No. 123). Ivalde's
splendidly decorated halls, together with at least one
son's share of his golden treasures, have thus passed as
an inheritance to Gjuke, and from Gjuke to his sons, the
Gjukungs. While the first song about Helge Hundingsbane tells us that Volund, Egil, and Slagfin were, like
Gjuke, Niflungs, we here learn that Gjuke was the heir
of Volund's, Egil's, and Slagfin's father. And while
Thorsdrapa, compared with other sources, has already
informed us that Ide-Slagfin and Gang-Egil inhabited
that citadel near the Elivagar which is called "Ide's
chalet" and Geirvadel's (Geirvandel's) chalet, and while
Geirvandel is demonstrably an epithet of Ivalde,* and as
Ivalde's citadel accordingly passed into the possession of
Slagfin and Egil, we here find that Ivalde's citadel was
inherited by Gjuke. Finally, we must compare here-

.. *In Saxo Gervandillus (*Geirvandill*) is the father of Horvandillus
(*Örvandill*). Orvandel has been proved to be identical with Egil. And as
Egil is the son of Ivalde, Geirvandel is identical with Ivalde.

with Bragaraedur (ch. 2), where it is said that Ivalde (there called Olvalde) was survived by his sons, who harmoniously divided his great treasures. Thus Gjuke is one of the sons of Ivalde, and inherited halls and treasures after Ivalde; and as he can be neither Volund nor Egil, whose fates we already know, he must be Slagfin— a result confirmed by the evidence which we shall gradnally present below.

119.

THE NIFLUNG HOARD IS THE TREASURE LEFT BY VOLUND
AND HIS BROTHERS.

When Volund and Egil, angry at the gods, abandoned Frey to the power of the giants and set out for the Wolf-dales, they were unable to take with them their immense treasures inherited from their father and augmented by themselves. Nor did they need them for their purposes. Volund carried with him a golden fountain in his wealth-bringing arm-ring (see Nos. 87, 98, 101) from which the seven hundred rings, that Nidhad to his astonishment discovered in his smithy, must have come. But the riches left by these brothers ought not to fall into the hands of the gods, who were their enemies. Consequently they were concealed. Saxo (*Hist.*, 193) says of the father of Svipdag-Ericus, that is to say, of Orvan-del-Egil, that he long had had great treasures concealed in earth caves (*gazæ, quas diu clausæ telluris antra condiderant*). The same is true of Gjuke-Slagfin, who went with his brothers to the Wolfdales. Vilkinasaga (see

975

below), has rescued an account of a treasure which was preserved in the interior of a mountain, and which he owned. The same is still more and particularly applicable to Volund, as he was the most famous smith of the mythology and of the heroic saga. The popular fancy conceived these treasures left and concealed by Volund as being kept in earth caves, or in mountain halls, guarded and brooded over by dragons. Or it conceived them as lying on the bottom of the sea, or in the bottom of deep rivers, guarded by some dwarf inhabiting a rocky island near by. Many of the songs and sagas of heathendom and of the older days of Christianity were connected with the refinding and acquisition of the Niblung hoard by some hero or other as the Volsung Sigmund, the Borgar descendant Hadding-Dieterich, and Siegfried-Sigurd-Fafnersbane. The Niflung treasure, *hodd Niflunga* (Atlakvida, 26), *Nibelunge Hort,* is in its more limited sense these Volund treasures, and in its most general signification the golden wealth left by the three brothers. This wealth the saga represents as gathered again largely in the hands of the Gjukungs, after Sigurd, upon the victory over Fafner, has reunited the most important one of Volund's concealed treasures with that of the Gjukung's, and has married the Gjukung sister Gudrun. The German tradition, preserved in middle-age poems, shows that the continental Teutons long remembered that the *Nibelunge Hort* originally was owned by Volund, Egil, and Slagfin-Gjuke. In *Lied von Siegfried* the treasure is owned by three brothers who are "Niblungs." Only one of them is named, and he is called King Englin, a name which, with its variation Eugel, manifestly is a variation of Eigel, as he is called in the Orentel saga and in Vilkinasaga, and of Egil as he is called in the Norse records. King Euglin is, according to *Lied von Siegfried,* an interpreter of stars. Siegfried bids him *Lasz mich deyner kunst geniessen, Astronomey genannt.* This peculiar statement is explained by the myth according to which Orvandel-Egil is a star-hero. Egil becomes, like Atlas of the antique mythology, a king versed in astronomy in the historical interpretation of mythology. In *Nibelunge Noth* the treasure is owned by "the valiant" Niblungs, Schilbunc and Niblunc. Schilbunc is the Norse *Skilfingr,* and I have already shown above that Ivalde-Svigder is the progenitor of the Skilfings. The poem Biterolf knows that the treasure originally belonged to *Nibelót, der machet himele guldin; selber wolt er got sîn.* These remarkable words have their only explanation in the myths concerning the Niflung Volund, who first ornamented Asgard with golden works of art, and subsequently wished to destroy the inhabitants of Asgard in order to be god himself. The Norse heroic saga makes the treasures brooded over by Fafner to have been previously guarded by the dwarf Andvare, and makes the latter (Sigurdarkvida Fafn., ii. 3) refer to the first owner. The saga characterises the treasure guarded by him as *that gull, er Gustr átti.* In the very nature of the case the first maker and possessor of these works must have been one of the most celebrated artists of the mythology; and as *Gustr* means "wind," "breath of wind;" as, again, Volund in the mythology is the only artist who is designated by a synonym of *Gustr,* that is, by *Byrr,* "wind" (Volundarkvda, 12), and by *Loptr,* "the airy one" (Fjölsvinnsmal, 26); as, furthermore, the song cycle concerning Sigurd Fafnersbane is connected with the children of Gjuke Volund's brother, and in several other respects strikes roots down into the myth concerning Ivalde's sons; and as, finally, the German tradition shows an original connection between *Nibelunge Hort* and the treasures of the Ivalde sons, then every fact goes to show that in *Gustr* we have an epithet of Volund, and that the Niflung hoard, both in the Norse and in the German Sigurd-Siegfried saga was the inheritance and the works of Volund and his brothers. Vigfusson assumes that the first part of the compound Slagfin is *slagr,* "a tone," "a melody," played on a stringed instrument. The correctness of this opinion is corroborated by the fact that Slagfin-Gjuke's son, Gunnar, is the greatest player on stringed instruments in the heroic literature. In the den of serpents he still plays his harp, so that the crawling venomous creatures are enchanted by the tones. This wonderful art of his is explained by the fact that his father is "the stringed instrument's" Finn, that is, Slagfin. The horse Grane, who carries Sigurd and the hoard taken from Fafner, probably at one time bore Volund himself, when he proceeded to the Wolfdales. Grane at all events had a place in the Volund-myth. The way traversed by Volund from his own golden realm to the Wolfdales, and which in part was through the northern regions of the lower world (*fyr mágrindr nedan*—Fjölsvinnsmal, 26) is in Volundarkvida (14) called Grane's way. Finally, it must here be stated that Sigurdrifva, to whom Sigurd proceeds after he has gotten possession of Fafner's treasure, (Griperssaga, 13-15), is a mythic character transferred to the heroic saga, who, as shall be shown in the second part of this work, held a conspicuous position in the myths concerning the Ivalde sons and their swan-maids. She is, in fact, the heroic copy of Idun, and originally she had nothing to do with Budle's daughter Brynhild. The cycle of the Sigurd songs thus attaches itself as the last ring or circle in the powerful epic to the myth concerning the Ivalde sons. The Sigurd songs arch themselves over the fateful treasures which were smithied and left by the fallen Lucifer of the Teutonic mythology, and which, like his sword of revenge and his arrow of revenge, are filled with curses and coming woe. In the heroic poems the Ivalde sons are their owners. The son's son Svipdag wields the sword of revenge. The son's sons Gunnar and Hogne go as the possessors of the Niblung treasure to meet their ruin. The myth concerning their fathers, the Ivalde sons, arches itself over the enmity caused by Loke between the gods on the one hand, and the great artists, the elf-princes, the protectors of growth, the personified forces of the life of nature, on the other hand. In connection herewith the myth about Ivalde himself revolves mainly around "the mead," the *soma,* the strength-giving saps in nature. He too, like his sons afterwards, gets into conflict with the gods and rebels against them, seeks to deprive them of the *soma* sap which he had discovered, allies himself with Suttung's sons, in whose keeping the precious liquid is rediscovered, and is slain outside of their door, while Odin is within and carries out the plan by which the mead becomes accessible to gods and to men (see No. 89). This chain of events thus continues through three generations. And interwoven with it is the chain of events opposed to it, which develops through the generations of the other great mythic race of heroes: that of the Heimdal son Borgar, of the Borgar son Halfdan, and of the Halfdan sons Hadding and Guthorm (Dieterich and Ermenrich). Borgar fights and must yield to the assault of Ivalde, and subsequently of his sons from the North in alliance with the powers of frost (see Nos. 22, 28). Halfdan contends with Ivalde's sons, recaptures for vegetation the Teutonic country as far as to "Svarin's mound," but is slain by Ivalde's grandson Svipdag, armed with the Volund sword (see Nos. 32, 33, 102, 103). In the conflict between Svipdag and Guthorm-Ermenrich on the one side, and Hadding on the other, we see the champions divided into two camps according to the mythological antecedents of their families: Amalians and Hildings on Hadding's side, the descendants of Ivalde on the other (see Nos. 42, 43). Accordingly, the Gjukungs, "the kings on the Rhine," are in the German tradition on Ermenrich's side. Accordingly, Vidga Volundson, in spite of his bond of friendship with Hadding-Dieterich, also fights under Ermenrich's banner. Accordingly, Vildebur-Egil is again called to life in the heroic saga, and there appears as the protector and helper of the Volund son, his own nephew. And accordingly, Vate-Walther, too (see No. 123), identical with Ivalde, Volund's father, is reproduced in the heroic saga to bear the banner of Ermenrich in the battles (cp. No. 43).

120.

SLAGFIN-GJUKE'S SYNONYMS DANKRAT (THAKK-RÁDR), IRUNG, ALDRIAN. SLAGFIN A STAR-HERO LIKE HIS BROTHERS. ALDRIAN'S IDENTITY WITH CHELDRICUS-GELDERUS.

Slagfin-Gjuke has many names in the German traditions, as in the Norse. Along with the name Gibich, Gibche (Gjuke), occur the synonyms Dankrat, Irung, and Aldrian. In the latter part of Nibelunge Noth Gibich is called Dankrat (cp. "Klage;" Biterolf also has the name Dankrat, and speaks of it in a manner which shows that in some of the sources used by the author Dankrat was a synonym of Gibich). In Vilkinasaga Gjuke appears now as Irung, now as Aldrian. Aldrian is (Vilkinasaga, 150) king of Niflungaland, and has the sons Hogne, Gunnar, Gernoz, and Gilzer. Irung (Vilkin., 15) is also king of Niflungaland, and has the sons Hogne, Gunnar, Gudzorm, Gernoz, and Gisler. As Gjuke also is a Niflung, and has the sons Hogne, Gunnar, and Guthorm, there can be no doubt that Gjuke, Gibche, Dankrat, Irung, and Aldrian are synonyms, designating one and the same person, namely, Volundarkvida's Slagfin, the Ide of the mythology. Nibelunge Noth, too, speaks of Aldrian as the father of Hagen (Hogne). Aldrian's wife is called Oda, Gibich's "Frau Uote," Dankrat's "Frau Ute."

The Norse form for Dankrat (Tancred) is *thakkrádr,* Thakkrad. This name appears a single time in the Norse records, and then in connection with Volund and Nidhad. In Volundarkvida (39) Thakkrad is mentioned as Nidhad's chief servant, who still remains in his service when Volund, his revenge accomplished, flies in an eagle's guise away from his prison. That this servant bears a name that belongs to Slagfin-Gjuke, Volund's brother, cannot be an accident. We must compare an account in Vilkinasaga, according to which Volund's other brother Egil was in Nidhad's service when Volund flew away. It follows that the heroic saga made not only Volund, but also Slagfin and Egil, fall into Nidhad's hands. Both in Volundarkvida itself and in its prose introduction we read that when the home-sick swan-maids had left the Wolfdales, Egil and Slagfin betook themselves thence, Egil going to the east to look for his swan-maid Olrun, Slagfin going south to find his Svanhvit (Volundarkvida, 4), and that Nidhad thereupon learned—the song does not say how—that Volund was alone in the Wolfdales (Volundarkvida, 6). The assumption here lies near at hand, that Nidhad found it out from the fact that Slagfin and Egil, though going away in different directions, fell into his power while they were looking for their beloved. Whether this feature belonged to the myth or not cannot be determined. At all events it is remarkable that we refind in Volundarkvida the Gjuke name Thakkrad, as in Vilkinasaga we find Volund's brother Egil in Nidhad's environment.

The name Irung, Iring, as a synonym of Gjuke, is of

more importance from a mythological point of view. Widukind of Corvei (about the year 950) tells us in ch. 13 of his Saxon Chronicle that "the Milky Way is designated by Iring's name even to this day." Just previously he has mentioned a Saxon warrior by this name, whom he believes to have been the cause of this appellation (. . . *Iringi nomine, quem ita vocitant, lacteus cœli circulus sit vocatus;* and in the Aursberg Chronicle, according to J. Grimm,. .*lacteus cœli circulus Iringis, nomine Iringesstraza sit vocatus*). According to Anglo-Saxon glossaries, the Milky Way is called *Iringes uueg.* With this we should compare the statements made above, that the Milky Way among the Teutonic population of England was called the way of the Watlings (that is, the descendants of Vate, *i. e.,* Ivalde). Both the statements harmonize. In the one it is the descendants of Ivalde in general, in the other it is Slagfin-Iring whose name is connected with the Milky Way. Thus Slagfin, like Volund and Orvandel-Egil, was a star-hero. In "Klage" it is said of Iring and two other heroes, in whose company he appears in two other poems, that they committed grave mistakes and were declared banished, and that they, in spite of efforts at reconciliation, remained under the penalty to the end of their lives. Biterolf says that they were exiles and threatened by their foes. Here we have a reverberation of the myth concerning the conflict between the gods and the Ivalde sons, of Frey's unsuccessful effort to reconcile the enemies, and of their flight to the extreme north of the earth. In the German poems they take flight to Attila.

The Gjuke synonym Aldrian is a name formed in analogy with **Albrian,** which is a variation of Elberich. In analogy herewith Aldrian should be a variation of Elderich, Helderich. In Galfrid of Monmouth's British History there is a Saxon saga-hero Cheldricus, who, in alliance with a Saxon chief Baldulf, fights with King Artus' general Cador, and is slain by him. How far the name-forms Aldrian-Elderich have any connection with the Latinised Cheldricus I think best to leave undetermined; but there are other reasons which, independently of a real or apparent name-identity, indicate that this Cheldricus is the same person as Aldrian-Gjuke. Bugge has already pointed out that Baldrian corresponds to Balder, Cador to *Hödr;* that Galfrid's account has points of contact with Saxo's about the war between Balder and Hoder, and that Galfrid's Cheldricus corresponds to Saxo's King Gelderus, *Geldr,* who fights with Hoder and falls in conflict with him.

That which at once strikes us in Saxo's account of Gelderus (see No. 101) is that he takes arms against Hotherus, when he learns that the latter has got possession of the sword of victory and the wealth-producing ring—treasures that were smithied by Volund, and in that sense belonged to the Niblung hoard. That Saxo in this manner gave a reason for the appearance of Gelderus can only be explained by the fact that Gelderus had been in some way connected with the Niblung hoard, and looked upon himself as more entitled to it than Hotherus. This right could hardly be based on any other reason than the fact that Gelderus was a Niflung, a kinsman of the maker and owner of the treasures. In the Vilkinasaga the keeper and protector of the Niblung hoard, the one who has the key to the rocky chambers where the hoard is kept bears the very name Aldrian, consequently the very surname of Slagfin-Gjuke, Volund's and Egil's brother. This of itself indicates that Gelderus is Slagfin-Aldrian.

121.

SLAGFIN'S IDENTITY WITH HJUKE. HIS APPEARANCE IN THE MOON-MYTH AND IN THE BALDER-MYTH. BIL'S IDENTITY WITH IDUN.

From Slagfin-Gelderus' part in the war between the two divine brothers Balder and Hoder, as described both by Saxo and by Galfrid, we must draw the conclusion that he is a mythic person historified, and one who had taken an important part in the Balder-myth as Balder's friend, and also as Hoder's though he bore weapons against the latter. According to Saxo, Hoder honours the dust of his slain opponent Gelderus in a manner which indicates a previous friendly relation between them. He first gives Gelderus a most splendid funeral (*pulcherrimum funeris obsequium*), then he builds a magnificent grave-mound for him, and decorates it with tokens of his respect (*veneratio*) for the dead one.

The position of Slagfin-Gelderus to the two contending divine brothers, his brothership-in-arms with Balder, the respect and devotion he receives from his opponent Hoder, can only be explained by the fact that he had very intimate relations with the two brothers and with the mythical persons who play a part in the Balder-myth. According to Saxo, Hoder was fostered by *Gevarr,* the moon-god, Nanna's father. As Nanna's foster-brother, he falls in love with her who becomes the wife of his brother, Balder. Now the mythology actually mentions an individual who was adopted by the moon-god, and accordingly was Hoder's foster-brother, but does not in fact belong to the number of the real gods. This foster-son inherits in the old Norse records one of the names with which the moon-god is designated in the Anglo-Saxon poems—that is, *Hoce,* a name identical with the Norse *Hjúke.* Hnaf (*Hnæfr, Næfr,* Nanna's father) is also, as already shown, called Hoce in the Beowulf poem (see Nos. 90, 91). From the story about Bil and Hjuke, belonging to the myth about the mead and preserved in the Younger Edda, we know that the moon-god took these children to himself, when they were to carry to their father *Vidfinnr,* the precious burden which they had dipped out of the mead-fountain, Byrger (see Nos, 90, 91).

That this taking up was equivalent to an adoption of these children by the moon-god is manifest from the position Bil afterwards got in the circle of gods. She becomes an asynje (Younger Edda, i. 118, 556) and distributes the Teutonic mythological *soma,* the creative sap of nature and inspiration, the same liquid as she carried when she was taken up by the moon-god. The skalds of earth pray to her (*ef unna itr vildi Bil skáldi!*) and Asgard's skald-god, Brage, refreshes himself with her in Gevarr-Nokver's silver-ship (see Sonatorrek; cp. Nos. 90,

91). Odin came to her every day and got a drink from the mead of the moon-ship, when the latter was sinking toward the horizon in the west. The ship is in Grimnersmal called *Sökkvabekkr,* "the setting or sinking ship," in which Odin and *Saga* "daily drink from golden goblets," while "cool billows in soughing sound flow over" the place where they sit. The cool billows that roar over Sokvabek are the waves of the atmospheric sea, in which Nokver's ship sails, and they are the waves of the ocean when the silver-ship sinks into the sea. The epithet *Saga* is used in the same manner as *Bil,* and it probably has the same reason for its origin as that which led the skalds to call the bucket which Bil and Hjuke carried *Sægr.* *Bil,* again, is merely a synonym of Idun. In Haustlaung, Idun is called *Byrgis ár-Gefn,* "Byrger's harvest-giving dis;" Thjasse is called *Byrgis ár-Gefnar bjarga-Tyr,* "Byrger's harvest-giving dis, mountain-Tyr." Idun is thus named partly after the fountain from which Bil and Hjuke fetched the mead, partly after the bucket in which it was carried.

That Hjuke, like Bil-Idun, was regarded by the moon-god as a foster-child, should not be doubted, the less so as we have already seen that he, in the Norse sources, bears his foster-father's name. As an adopted son of the moon-god, he is a foster-brother of Hoder and Nanna. Hjuke must therefore have occupied a position in the mythology similar to that in which we find Gelderus as a brother-in-arms of Nanna's husband, and as one who was held in friendship even by his opponent, Hoder. As a brother of the Ivalde daughter, Bil-Idun, he too must be an Ivalde son, and consequently one of the three brothers, either Slagfin, or Orvandel-Egil, or Volund. The mythic context does not permit his identification with Volund or Egil. Consequently he must be Slagfin. That Gelderus is Slagfin has already been shown.

This also explains how, in Christian times, when the myths were told as history, the Niflungs-Gjukungs were said to be descended from *Næfr, Nefir,* (*Nefir er Niflunger eru, frá komnir*—Younger Edda, i. 520.) It is connected with the fact that Slagfin, like his brothers, is a Niflung (see No. 118) and an adopted son of the moon-god, whose name he bore.

Bil's and Hjuke's father is called *Vidfinnr.* We have already seen that Slagfin's and his brothers' father, Ivalde, is called *Finnr, Finnakonungr* (Introduction to Volundarkvida), and that he is identical with *Sumbl Finnakonungr, and Finnálfr.* In fact the name *Finnr* never occurs in the mythic records, either alone or in compounds or in paraphrases, except where it alludes to Ivalde or his son, Slagfin. Thus, for instance, the byrnie, *Finnzleif,* in Ynglingasaga, is borne by a historified mythic person, by whose name Saxo called a foster-son of Gevarr, the moon-god. The reason why Ivalde got the name *Finnr* shall be given below (see No. 123). And as Ivalde (*Sumbl Finnakonungr*—Olvalde) plays an important part in the mead-myth, and as the same is true of Vidfin, who is robbed of Byrger's liquid, then there is every reason for the conclusion that Vidfin's, Hjuke's, and Bil-Idun's father is identical with *Finnakonungr,* **the** father of Slagfin and of his sister.

Gjuke and Hjuke are therefore names borne by one and the same person—by Slagfin, the Niflung, who is the progenitor of the Gjukungs. They also look like analogous formations from different roots. This also gives us the explanation of the name of the Asgard bridge, *Bilröst*, "Bil's way." The Milky Way is Bil-Idun's way, just as it is her brother Hjuke's; for we have already seen that the Milky Way is called Irung's way, and that Irung is a synonym of Slagfin-Gjuke. Bil travelled the shining way when she was taken up to Asgard as an asynje. Slagfin travelled it as Balder's and Hoder's foster-brother. If we now add that the same way was travelled by Svipdag when he sought and found Freyja in Asgard, and by Thjasse-Volund's daughter, Skade, when she demanded from the gods a ransom for the slaying of her father, then we find here no less than four descendants of Ivalde who have travelled over the Milky Way to Asgard; and as Volund's father among his numerous names also bore that of Vate, Vade (see Vilkinasaga), then this explains how the Milky Way came to be called Watling Street in the Old English literature.*

In the mythology there was a circle of a few individuals who were celebrated players on stringed instruments. They are Balder, Hoder, Slagfin, and Brage. In the heroic poems the group is increased with Slagfin-Gjuke's son, Gunnar, and with Hjarrandi, the Horund of the German poem "Gudrun," to whom I shall recur in my

---

*Thus Vigfusson's opinion that the Asgard bridge is identical with the Milky Way is correct. That the rainbow should be regarded as the Bilrost with its bridge-heads is an invention by the author of Gylfaginning.

treatise on the heroic sagas. Balder's playing is remembered by Galfrid of Monmouth. Hoder's is mentioned in Saxo, and perhaps also in the Edda's *Hadarlag*, a special kind of metre or manner of singing. Slagfin's quality as a musician is apparent from his name, and is inherited by his son, Gunnar. Hjarrandi-Horund appears in the Gudrun epic by the side of Vate (Ivalde), and there is reason for identifying him with Gevarr himself. All these names and persons are connected with the myth concerning the *soma* preserved in the moon. While the first drink of the liquid of inspiration and of creative force is handed to Odin by Mimer, we afterwards find a supply of the liquid preserved by the moon-god; and those mythic persons who are connected with him are the very ones who appear as the great harp-players. Balder is the son-in-law of the moon-god, Hoder and Slagfin are his foster-sons, Gunnar is Slagfin's son, Brage becomes the husband of Bil-Idun, and Hjarrandi is no doubt the moon-god himself, who sings so that the birds in the woods, the beasts on the ground, and the fishes in the sea listen and are charmed ("Gudrun," 1415-1418, 1523-1525, 1555-1558).

Both in Saxo and in Galfrid Hoder meets Slagfin with the bow in his conflict with him (Cheldricus in Galfrid; Gelderus in Saxo). The bow plays a chief part in the relation between the gods and the sons of Ivalde. Hoder also met Egil in conflict with the bow (see No. 112), and was then defeated, but Egil's noble-mindedness forbade his harming Slagfin's foster-brother. Hoder, as an archer, gets satisfaction for the defeat in Saxo, when with his favourite weapon he conquers Egil's brother, Slagfin (Gelderus), who also is an archer. And finally, with an arrow treacherously laid on Hoder's bow, Volund, in demoniac thirst for revenge and at Loke's instigation, takes the life of Balder, Hoder's brother.

122.

REVIEW OF THE SYNONYMS OF THE SONS OF IVALDE.

The names by which Slagfin is found in our records are accordingly *Idi, Gjúki,* Dankrat (*thakkrádr*), Irung, Aldrian, Cheldricus, Gelderus, *Hjúki.* We have yet to mention one more, Hengest (*Hengist*), to which I shall return below. Of these names, Gelderus (*Geldr*), Cheldricus, and Aldrian form a group by themselves, and they are possibly simply variations of the same word. The meaning of the name Hengest, "a gelding," is connected with the same group, and particularly to the variation *Geldr.* The most important Slagfin epithets, from a mythological standpoint, are Ide, Gjuke, Hjuke, and Irung.

The names of Volund (Wieland, Veland) in the various records are, as we have seen, *thjazi,* Ajo (Aggo), Anund (*Önundr*), *Rögnir, Brunni, Ásólfr, Vargr, Fjallgyldir, Hlébardr, Byrr, Gustr, Loptr.,* Haquinus (Aki, Ecke). Of these names and epithets *Ásólfr, Vargr, Fjallgyldir,* and *Hlébardr* form a group by themselves, and refer to his animal-symbol, the wolf. The other brothers also have animal-symbols. Egil is sym-

bolised as a wild boar and a bear by the names *Aurnir,
Ebur, Isólfr.* Slagfin is symbolised as a horse in Hengest, and also in the paraphrase *öndr-Jálkr,* "the gelding of the skees." Like his brothers, he is a runner on
skees. The Volund epithet, *Brunni,* also alludes to
skee-running. *Rögnir* and *Regin* are names of Volund
and his brothers in their capacity of artists. The names
Ajo, Anund, and Thjasse (the sparkling) may have
their origin in ancient Aryan times.

The names of the third brother, Egil, are *Gangr, Örvandill, Egill,* Agelmund, Eigel, Euglin, *Hödbroddr,* Toko,
and Avo, the archer; Ebur (Ibor, Wild-Ebur, Villefer,
Ebbo), *Aurnir Isólfr.* Of these names *Egill,* Agelmund,
Egil, and Englin form a separate group; *Örvandill Hödbroddr,* Toko, and Avo sagittarius form another group,
referring to his fame as an archer; Ebur, Aurnir, and
Isolfr a third, referring to his animal-symbols.

123.

IVALDE.

In the course taken by our investigation we have already met with and pointed out several names and epithets by which Ivalde occurs in the mythology and in
the heroic poems. Such are *Geirvandill,* with the variation *Geirvadill; Vadi* (Vate), *Allvaldi, Audvaldi, Olvaldi, Svigdir (Svegdir), Ölmódr, Sumbl Finnakonungr*
(Sumblus Phinnorum rex), *Finnakonungr, Vidfinnr,
Finnálfr, Fin Folcvalding, Hlaudverr.*

Of these names *Ívaldi, Allvaldi, Audvaldi,* and *Ölvaldi*

form a group by themselves, inasmuch as they all have the, part, *valdi, valdr,* "mighty," an epithet preserved from the mythology in those heroic sagas which have treated distinct portions of the Ivalde-myth, where the hero reappears as Walther, Valthari, Valdere, Valtarius Manufortis.

Another group is formed by *Ölvaldi, Ölmodr, Svidir, Sumbl Finnakonungr. Svigdir* means, as already shown, "the great drinker," and *Sumbl* is a synonym of "ale," "mead." All the names in this group refer to the quality of their bearer as a person belonging to the myth about the mead.

The name *Sumbl Finnakonungr* is at the same time connected with a third group of names—*Finnakonungr, Finnr, Vidfinnr, Finnálfr, Fin Folcvalding.* With this group the epithets *Vadi* and *Vadill* (in *Geirvadill*) have a real mythological connection, which shall be pointed out below.

Finally, *Geirvadill* is connected with the epithet *Geirvandill* from the fact that both belong to Ivalde on account of his place in the weapon-myth.

As has been shown above, Geirvandill means "the one occupied with the spear," or, more accurately, "the one who exhibits great care and skill in regard to the spear" (from *geir,* spear, and *vanda,* to apply care to something in order that it may serve its purpose). In Saxo, Gervandillus-Geirvandel is the father of Horvendillus-Orvandel; the spear-hero is the father of the archer. It is evident that the epithets of the son and father are parallel formations, and that as the one designates the foremost archer in mythology, the other must refer to a prominent spear-champion. It is of no slight importance to our knowledge of the Teutonic weapon-myth that the foremost representatives of the spear, the bow, and the sword among the heroes are grandfather, father, and son. Svipdag, Ivalde's grandson, the son of Orvandel-Egil, is above all others the sword-champion, "the sword-elf" (*sverdálfr*—see Olaf Trygv., 43, where Svipdag-Erik's namesake and supposed descendant, Erik, Jarl Hakonson, is called by this epithet). It is he who from the lower world fetches the best and most terrible sword, which was also probably regarded as the first of its kind in that age, as his uncle, who had made it, was called "the father of swords" (see Nos. 113, 114, 115). Svipdag's father is the most excellent archer whose memory still survives in the story about William Tell. The grandfather, Ivalde, must have been the most excellent marksman with the spear. The memory of this survives not only in the epithets, *Geirvandill* and *Geirvadill,* but also in the heroic poem, "Valtarius Manufortis," written before the year 950 by Eckehard in St. Gallen, and in Vilkinasaga, which has preserved certain features of the Ivalde-myth.

Clad in an armour smithied by Volund (*Vuelandia fabrica*), Valtarius appears as the great spear-champion, who despises all other weapons of attack—

Vualtarius erat vir maximus undique telis
Suspectamque habuit cuncto sibi tempori pugnam (v. 366-7).

With the spear he meets a sword-champion—

Hic gladio fidens hic acer et arduus hasta (v. 822);

and he has developed the use of the spear into an art, all of whose secrets were originally known by him alone, then also by Hagano, who learned them from the former (v. 336, 367). Vilkinasaga speaks of Valthari as an excellent spear-champion. Sure of success, he wagers his head in a competitive contest with this weapon.

It has already been shown above (see No. 89) that *Svigdir*-Ivalde in the mythic saga concerning the race-heroes was the first ruler of the Swedes, just as his sons, Volund and Egil, became those of the Longobardians and Slagfin that of the Burgundians, and, as shall be shown below, also that of the Saxons. Even in the Ynglingasaga, compiled in the twelfth century, he remains, by the name *Svegdir* among the first kings of the Yngling race, and in reality as the first hero; for his forerunners, *Fjölnir, Freyr,* and *Odinn,* are prehuman gods (in regard to *Fjölnir,* see Völuspa). That *Svidir* was made the race-hero of the Swedes is explained by the fact that Ivalde, before his sons, before he had yet become the foe of the gods and a "perjured *hapt,*" was the guardian of the northern Teutonic world against the, powers of frost, and that the Sviones were the northernmost race of the Teutonic domain. The elf-citadel on the southern coast of the Elivagar was *Geirvadill*-Ivalde's *setr* before it became that of his sons (see Nos. 109, 113-115, 117, 118). The continental Teutons, like their kinsmen on the Scandian peninsula, knew that north of the Swedes and in the uttermost north lived a non-Teutonic people who ran on skees and practised hunting—the Finns. And as the realm that was subject to the race-hero of the Swedes in the mythology extended to the Elivagar, where his *setr* was situated, even the Finns must have been subject to his sceptre. This explains his surname, *Finnakonungr, Finnr, Vidfinnr,* Fin Folcvalding, and also the fact that his descendants form a group of skee-runners. To the location of the *setr* near the Elivagar, at the point where Thor was wont to wade across this body of water (see Nos. 109, 114), we have a reference in the Ivalde epithets, *Vadill Vadi.* They indicate his occupation as the keeper of the ford. Vilkinasaga makes him a wader of the same kind as Thor, and makes him bear his son, Volund, across a sound while the latter was still a lad. Reasons which I may yet have an opportunity to present indicate that Ivalde's mother was the mightiest amazon of Teutonic mythology, whose memory survives in Saxo's account of Queen Rusila, Rusla (*Hist.,* 178, 365, 394-396), and in the German heroic-saga's Rütze. This queen of the elves, dwelling south of the Elivagar, is also remembered by Tactitus' informer. In *Germania* (45) we read: *Svionibus Sitonum gentes continuantur. Cetera similes uno different quod femina dominatur. . . .Hic Suebiæ fines*— "The Sviones are bounded by the Sitones. While they are like each other in other things they differ in the one respect, that a woman rules over the Sitones. Here the confines of Suebia end." The name Sitones does not occur elsewhere, and it would be vain to seek it in the domain of reality. Beyond the domain of the Sviones extended at that time that of the mythic geography. The Sitones, who were governed by a queen, belonged

to the Teutonic mythology, like the Hellusians and Ox-
ionians, mentioned elsewhere in *Germania.* It is not
impossible that the name *Sitones,* of which the stem is
sit, is connected with the Norse mythological name of the
chief citadel in their country—*setr* (*Geirvadill's setr, Ide's
setr;* cp. *setr-verjendr* as a designation in Ynglingasaga
[17] of the descendants of *Svigdir*-Ivalde). The word
setr is derived from *setja,* a causative form of *sitja,* the
Gothic *sitan.*

I now pass to the name *Hlaudverr,* in Volundarkvida.
This poem does not state directly who Volund's, Egil's,
and Slagfin's father was, but it does so indirectly by
mentioning the name of the father of Volund's and
Slagfin's swan-maids, and by stating that these swan-
maids were sisters of the brothers. Volund's swan-maid
is called *theirra systir* in str. 2. Among the many un-
called-for "emendations" made in the text of the Elder
Edda is also the change of *theirra* to *theirrar,* made for
the reason that the student, forgetting that Volundarkvida was a poem born of mythology, regarded it as impossible for a brother and sister to be husband and wife,
and for the reason that it was observed in the prose introduction to Volundarkvida that the father of the three
brothers was *Finnakonungr.* *Hlaudverr* is also found
in a German source, "Biterolf," as King Liutwar. There
he appears in the war between Hadding-Dieterich and
Gudhorm-Ermenrich, and the poem makes him a champion on the side where all who in the mythology were
foes of the Asas generally got their place, that is, on Ermenrich's. There he occupied the most conspicuous

997

place as Ermenrich's standard-bearer, and, with Sabene, leads his forces. The same position as Ermenrich's standard-bearer occupies is held in "Dieterich's Flucht" by Vate, that is to say, *Vadi*-Ivalde, and in Vilkinasaga by Valthari, that is to say again, Ivalde. Liutwar, Vate, and Valthari are originally one and the same person in these German records, just as Hlaudver (corresponding to Liutwar), Vade (corresponding to Vate), and Ivalde (corresponding to Valthari) are identical in the Scandinavian Volundarkvida's statement, that Volund's and Slagfin's swan-maids are their sisters (half-sisters, as we shall see), and, like them, daughters of Ivalde, is thus found to be correct by the comparison of widely-separated sources.

While the father of these two swan-maids is called *Hlaudverr* in Volundarkvida, the father of the third swan-maid, Egil's beloved, is called King *Kiarr* in Valland. As Egil was first married to the dis of vegetation, Groa, whose father is Sigtryg in the heroic saga, and then to Sif, his swan-maid must be one of these two. In Volundarkvida, where none of the swan-maids have their common mythological names, she is called Olrun, and is said to be not a sister, but a kinswoman (*kunn*—str. 15) of both the others. *Hlaudverr* (Ivalde) and *Kiarr* are therefore kinsmen. Who *Kiarr* was in the mythology I cannot now consider. Both these kings of mythological descent reappear in the cycle of the Sigurd songs. It has already been shown above (No. 118) that the Gjukungs appear in the Sigurd saga as heirs and possessors of *Hlauddverrs halls* and treasures; it is added

that "they possess the whitest shield from *Kiarr's* hall
(Gudrunarkvida, ii. 25; Atlakvida, 7). Here we accordingly once more find the connection already pointed
out between the persons appearing in Volundarkvida and
those in the Gjukungsaga. The fathers of the swan-
maids who love Volund and his brothers reappear in
the Sigurd songs as heroes who had already left the
scene of action, and who had owned immense treasures,
which after their death have passed by inheritance into
the possession of the Gjukungs. This also follows from
the fact that the Gjukungs are descendants of Gjuke-
Slagfin, and that Slagfin and his brothers are Niflungs,
heirs of Hlaudver-Ivalde, who was *gullaudigr mjök*
(Younger Edda).

Like his sons, Ivalde originally stood in a friendly relation to the higher reigning gods; he was their sworn
man, and from his citadel near the Elivagar, *Geirvadills
setr*, he protected the creation of the gods from the powers of frost. But, like his sons, and before them, he
fell into enmity with the gods and became "a perjured
hapt." The features of the Ivalde-myth, which have
been preserved in the heroic poems and shed light on the
relation between the moon-god and him, are told partly in
the account of Gevarus, Nanna's father, in Saxo, and
partly in the poems about Walther (Valtarius, Walthari)
and Fin Folcvalding. From these accounts it appears that
Ivalde abducted a daughter of the moon-god; that enmity arose between them; that, after the defeat of Ivalde,
Sunna's and Nanna's father offered him peace, and that
the peace was confirmed by oath; that Ivalde broke the

oath, attacked Gevar-Nokver and burnt him; that, during the hostilities between them, Slagfin-Gjuke, though
a son of Ivalde, did not take the side of his natural father, but that of his foster-father; and that Ivalde had
to pay for his own deeds with ruin and death.

Concerning the point that Ivalde abducted a daughter
of Gevar-Nokver and married her, the Latin poems Val-
tarins Manufortis, Nibelunge Noth, Biterolf, Vilkinasaga, and Boguphalus (Chronicon Poloniæ) relate that
Walther fled with a princess named Hildigund. On the
flight he was attacked by Gjukungs, according to Valtarius Manufortis. The chief one of these (in the poem
Gunthari, Gjuke's son) received in the battle a wound
"clean to the hip-bone." The statement anent the wound,
which Walther gave to the chief one among the Gjukungs,
has its roots in the mythology where the chief Gjukung,
that is, Gjuke himself, appears with surnames (Hengest,
Geldr, *öndr-Jálkr*) alluding to the wound inflicted. In
the Anglo-Saxon heroic poem Fin Folcvalding is married
to Hildeburh, a daughter of Hnæf-Hoce, and in Hyndluljod (cp. str. 17 with str. 15) *Hildigunnr* is the mother
of Halfdan's wife Almveig, and consequently the wife of
Sumbl Finnakonungr, that is, Ivalde. *Hildigunn's* father
is called *Sækonungr* in Hyndluljod, a synonym of
Nökkver ("the ship-captain," the moon-god), and Hildigun's mother is called *Sváfa,* the same name as that by
which Nanna is introduced in the poem concerning Helge
Hjorvardson. Hildeburh, Hnæf-Hoce's daughter, is
identical with Hildigun, daughter of *Sækonungr.* Compare furthermore str. 20 in Hyndluljod, which speaks of

Nanna as Nokver's daughter, and thus refers back to str. 17, where Hildigun is mentioned as the daughter of *Sækonungr*. The phrase *Nanna var næst thar Nauckva dottir* shows that *Nŏkkver* and another elder daughter of his were named in one of the immediately preceding strophes. But in these no man's name or epithet occurs except *Sækonungr*, "the sea-king," which can refer to *Nŏkkver*, "the ship-owner," or "ship-captain," and the "daughter" last mentioned in the poem is *Hildigunnr*.

Of the names of Ivalde's wife the various records contain the following statements:

Hlaudver-Ivalde is married to Svanfeather (*Svanfjödr*, Volundarkvida).

Finnalf-Ivalde is married to Svanhild Gold-feather, daughter of Sol (Fornal. saga).

Fin Folcvalding-Ivalde is married to Hildeburh, daughter of Hnæf-Hoce (Beowulf poem).

Walther-Ivalde is married to Hildigunt (German poems).

Sumbl-Finnakonungr is married to Hildigun, daughter of Sækonungr Nokver, the same as *Hnæfr, Hnefr*, Nanna's father (Hyndluljod, compared with Saxo and other sources).

She who is called Svanfeather, the sun-daughter Svanhild Gold-feather, Hildeburh, Hildigunt, and Hildigun is accordingly a sister of the moon-dis Nanna, and a daughter of the ruler of the atmosphere and of the moon. She is herself a sun-dis. In regard to the composition of the name, we must compare Hildigun, *Hiltigunt*, with Nanna's surname *Sinhtgunt*. The Teutonic, or at all events the Norse, mythology knew two divinities of the sun, mother and daughter. Grimnersmal (47) tells us that the older one, *Alfraudull,* has a daughter, who, not at the present time, but in the future, is to drive the car of the sun (*eina dottur berr Alfraudull . . .*). The elder is the wife of the moon-god. The younger one is the Sunna mentioned in the Merseburg formula (see No. 92), Sinhtgunt-Nanna's sister. As a surname, Sunna also occurs in the Norse literature (Alvissmal, 17; Younger Edda, i. 472, and elsewhere).

In the Beowulf poem and in "Battle of Furnesburg," we find Fin Folcvalding, Hildeburh's husband, as the foe of his father-in-law Hnæf, and conquered by him and Hengest. After a war ending unluckily for him, he makes peace with his victors, breaks the peace, attacks the citadel in the night, and cremates the slain and wounded in an immense funeral pyre. Hnæf is among those fallen, and Hildeburh weeps at his funeral pyre; Hengest escapes and afterwards avenges Hnæf's death. Saxo confirms the fact, that the historified person who in the mythology is the moon-god is attacked and burnt by one of his "satraps," and afterwards avenged. This he tells of his Gevarus, Nanna's father (*Hist.,* 131). The correspondence on this point shows that the episode has its root in the mythology, though it would be vain to try to find out the symbolic significance from a standpoint of physical nature of the fact that the moon-god was attacked and burnt by the husband of his daughter, the sun-dis.

Meanwhile we obtain from these scattered mythic frag-

KING SVAFRLAME SECURES THE SWORD TYRFING.

(From a painting by Lorenz Frölich.)

IN the Icelandic Hervar's Saga is an account of the mythical sword called Tyrfing, which Odin commanded the dwarfs Durin and Dvalin to forge for his grandson, King Svafrlame. When, against their will, they were compelled to deliver the sword to the king, the dwarfs pronounced a curse upon it, declaring that it should never be drawn from its sheath without causing the death of some one. Soon after Svafrlame was killed by Arngrim and the sword passed to Angantyr, who, in turn, was slain by Hjalmar and, to abate the curse, Tyrfing was buried with him. Angantyr's daughter, Hervor, however, by a spell, exorcised the spirit of her father and obtained the sword, after which it had many owners in succession, but the curse remained, for it brought death as before to every one who unsheathed it.

events the Norse mythology knew two divinities of the
sun, mother and daughter.   us
that the older one, *Alfrauđull*, has a daughter, who,
at the present time, but in the future, is to drive the car
of the sun (*eina dottur berr Alfrauđull* . . .).
elder is the wife of the moon-god. The younger
is the Sunna mentioned in the Merseburg formula
No. 92), Sinhtgunt-Nanna's sister. As a surname,
Sunna also occurs in the Norse literature (Alvissmal,
17; Younger Edda, i. 472, and elsewhere).

Beowulf poem and in "Battle of Fürnesburg,"
we find Fin Folcvalding, Hildeburh's husband, as the foe
of Hnaefo and conquered by him and
he
breaks, the peace attacks
and
is among
pyre;
Hengest

Saxo   in
the mythology
one of his
he tells of his Gevarus.   father (*Hist.*, 131). The
correspondence on this point shows that the episode has
its root in the mythology, though it would be vain to
try to find out the significance from a standpoint of physical nature the fact that the moon-god
was attacked and   by the husband of his daughter,
the sun-dis.
Meanwhile we   from these

1002

ments preserved in the heroic poems, when compared with the statements found in the mythology itself, the following connected story as the myth about the mead:

Originally, the mead, the *soma,* belongs to Mimer alone. From an unknown depth it rises in the lower world directly under the world-tree, whose middle root is watered by the well of the precious liquid. Only by self-sacrifice, after prayers and tears, is Odin permitted to take a drink from this fountain. The drink increases his strength and wisdom, and enables him to give order to the world situated above the lower regions. From its middle root the world-tree draws liquids from the mead-fountain, which bless the einherjes of Asgard as a beverage, and bless the people of Midgard as a fructifying honey-dew. Still this mead is not pure; it is mixed with the liquids from Urd's and Hvergelmer's fountains. But somewhere in the Jotunheims, the genuine mead was discovered in the fountain Byrger. This discovery was kept secret. The keeper of the secret was Ivalde, the sworn watchman near the Elivagar. In the night he sent his son Slagfin (afterwards called after his adopted father Hjuke) and his daughter Bil (Idun) to dip liquid from the fountain Byrger and bring it to him. But the children never returned. The moon-god had taken them and Byrger's liquids unto himself, and thus the gods of Asgard were able to partake of this drink. Without the consent of the moon-god, Ivalde on his part secured his daughter the sun-dis, and doubtless she bears to him the daughters Idun, Almveig, and other dises of growth and rejuvenation, after he had begotten Slagfin, Egil, and Volund with the giantess Greip. The moon-god and Ivalde have accordingly taken children from each other. The circumstance that the mead, which gives the gods their creative power and wisdom, was robbed from Ivalde—this find which he kept secret and wished to keep for himself alone—makes him the irreconcilable foe of the moon-god, is the cause of the war between them, and leads him to violate the oath which he had taken to him. He attacks Gevar in the night, kills and burns him, and recaptures the mead preserved in the ship of the moon. He is henceforth for ever a foe of the gods, and allies himself with the worst enemies of their world, the powers of frost and fire. Deep down in Hades there has long dwelt another foe of the gods, Surt-Durin, the clan-chief of Suttung's sons, the father of Fjalar. In the oldest time he too was the friend of the gods, and co-operated with Mimer in the first creation (see No. 89). But this bond of friendship had now long been broken. Down into the deep and dark dales in which this clan hostile to the gods dwells, Ivalde brings his mead-treasure into safety. He apparently gives it as the price of Fjalar's daughter Gunlad, and as a pledge of his alliance with the world of giants. On the day of the wedding, Odin comes before him, and clad in his guise, into Surt's halls, marries Gunlad, robs the liquids of Byrger, and flies in eagle guise with them to Asgard. On the wedding day Ivalde comes outside of Surt's mountain-abode, but never enters. A dwarf, the keeper of the halls, entices him into his ruin. It has already been stated that he was probably buried beneath an avalanche.

The myth concerning the carrying of the mead to the moon, and concerning its fate there, has left various traces in the traditions of the Teutonic people. In the North, Hjuke and Bil with their mead-burden were the objects seen in the spots on the moon. In southern Sweden, according to Ling, it was still known in the beginning of this century, that the bucket carried by the figures in the moon was a "brewing kettle," consequently containing or having contained a brewed liquid. According to English traditions, not the two children of Vidfin, but a drunken criminal (Ritson's *Ancient Songs;* cp. J. Grimm, *Deut. Myth.,* 681), dwelt in the full·moon, and that of which he is charged in widely circulated traditions is that he was gathering fagots for the purpose of crime, or in an improper time (on the Sabbath). Both the statements that he is drunk and that his crime consists in the gathering of fagots—lead us to suppose that this "man in the moon" originally was Ivalde, the drink-champion and the mead-robber, who attacked and burnt the moon-god. His punishment is that he will never get to heaven, but will remain in the moon, and there he is for ever to carry a bundle of thorn-fagots (thus according to a German tradition, and also according to a tradition told by Chaucer). Most probably, he has to carry the thorn-rod of the moon-god burnt by him. The moon-god (see Nos. 75, 91) ruled over the Teutonic Erynnies armed with rods (*limar*), and in this capacity he bore the epithet *Eylimi*. A Dutch poem from the fourteenth century says that the culprit *in duitshe heet Ludergheer*. A variation which J. Grimm (*Deut. Myth.,* 683) quotes is Lodeger. The name refers, as Grimm has pointed out, to the Old High German Liutker, the Lüdiger of the German middle-age poem. In "Nibelunge Noth," Lüdiger contends with the Gjukungs; in "Dieterichs Flucht," he abandons Dieterich's cause and allies himself with the evil Ermenrich. Like Liutwar, Lüdiger is a pendant to the Norse Hlaudver, in whom we have already rediscovered Ivalde. While, according to the Younger Edda, both the Ivalde children Hjuke and Bil appear in the moon, according to the English and German traditions it is their criminal father who appears on the scene of the fire he kindled, drunk with the mead he robbed, and punished with the rod kept by his victim.

The statement in Forspjallsljod, that Ivalde had two groups of children, corresponds with the result at which we have arrived. By the giantess Greip he is the father of Slagfin, Egil, and Volund; by the sun-dis Gevar, Nokver's daughter and Nanna's sister, he is the father of dises of growth, among whom are Idun, who first is Volund's beloved or wife, and thereupon is married to Brage. Another daughter of Ivalde is the beloved of Slagfin-Gjuke, Auda, the "frau Ute" of the German heroic saga. A third is Signe-Alveig, in Saxo the daughter of *Sumblus Phinnorum* (Ivalde). At his wedding with her, Egil is attacked and slain by Halfdan. Hadding is Halfdan's and her son.

Several things indicate that, when their father became a foe of the gods, Ivalde's sons were still their friends, and that Slagfin particularly was on the side of his foster-father in the conflict with Ivalde. With this corresponds also the conduct of the Gjukungs toward Valtarius, when he takes flight with Hildigun. In the Anglo-Saxon heroic poetry, the name Hengest is borne by the person who there takes Slagfin's place as Hnæf-Gevar's nearest man. The introduction to the Younger Edda has from its English authorities the statement that *Heingestr* (Hengest) was a son of Vitta and a near kinsman of Svipdag. If, as previous investigators have assumed, Vitta is Vade, then Hengest is a son of Ivalde, and this harmonises with the statement anent his kinship with Svipdag, who is a grandson of Ivalde. The meaning of the word Hengest refers of itself to Slagfin-*Geldr*. The name *Geldr* is a participle of *gelda,* and means *castratus.* The original meaning of Hengest is "a gelding," *equus castratus* (in the modern German the word got for the first time its present meaning). That the adjective idea *castratus* was transferred to the substantive *equus castratus* is explained by the fact that *Gils, Gisl,* a mythic name for a horse (Younger Edda, i. 70, 482), was also a Gjukung name. One of Hengest's ancestors in his genealogy in Beda and in the Anglo-Saxon Chronicle is called Vict-gils; one of Slagfin-Gjuke's sons is named *Gilser.* A neither mythic nor historic brother of Hengest added in later times is named Horsa. The Ravenna geography says that when the Saxons left their old abodes on the continent, they marched *cum principe suo Anschis,* and with their chief *Ans-gisl,* who therefore here appears in the place of Hengest. Synonymous with Hengest is the Norse *Jálkr, equus castratus,* and that some member of the mythological group of skee-runners, that is, some one of the male members of the Ivalde race, in the Norse version ,of the Teutonic mythology, bore this epithet is proved by the paraphrase *ŏndr-Jálkr,* "the *equus castratus* of the skee-runners." The cause of the designation is found in the event described above, which has been handed down by the poem "Valtarius Manufortis." The chief one of the Gjukungs, originally Gjuke himself, there fights with Valtarius, who in the mythology was his father, and receives in the conflict a wound "clean to the thigh-bone." This wound may have symbolic significance from the fact that the fight is between father and son. According to the English chronicler Nennius, Hengest had two brothers, Ochta and Ebissa. In spite of their corruption these names remind us of Slagfin's brothers, Aggo-Ajo (Volund) and Ibor-Ebbo (Egil).

According to the historified saga, Hengest was the leader of the first Saxon army which landed in Britain. All scholars have long since agreed that this Hengest is a mythical character. The migration saga of the Teutonic mythology was transferred by the heathen Saxons to England, and survived there until Christian times. After the names of the real leaders of the Saxon immigration were forgotten, Hengest was permitted to take their place, because in the mythology he had been a leader of the Saxon emigrants from their original country, the Scandian peninsula (see No. 16), and because this immigration was blended in Christian times with the memory of the emigration from Germany to Britain. Thus, while the Longobardians made Volund and Egil (Ajo and Ibor) the leaders of their emigration, the Saxons made Volund's and Egil's brother Slagfin (Hengest-Gjuke) their leader. The Burgundians also regarded Slagfin (Gjuke) as their emigration hero and royal progenitor. Of this there is evidence partly in *Lex Burgundionum,* the preface of which enumerates Burgundian kings who have Gjukung names; partly in a Middle High German poem, which makes the Gjukungs Burgundian kings. The Saxon migration saga and the Burgundian are therefore, like those of the other Teutonic races, connected with the Ivalde race and with the fimbul-winter.

THE END.

DICTIONARY

OF

PRINCIPAL PROPER NAMES
IN TEUTONIC MYTHOLOGY,

*with Explanations of the Character, Attributes
and Significance of the Gods, Goddesses,
Giants, Dwarfs and associated
creatures and places.*

DICTIONARY

OF

GODS AND GODDESSES.

A

ÆGIR. [Anglo-Sax, *eagor*, the sea]. The god who presides over the stormy sea. He entertains the gods every harvest, and brews ale for them. *Æger.*

AGNAR. A son of King Hraudung and foster-son of Frigg. *Agnar.*

AGNAR. A son of King Geirrod. He serves drink to Grimner (Odin). *Agnar.*

ALFR. An elf, fairy; a class of beings like the dwarfs, between gods and men. They were of two kinds: elves of light (*Ljosalfar*) and elves of darkness (*Dokkalfar*). The abode of the elves is *Alfheimr*, fairy-land, and their king is the god Frey. *Elf.*

ALFODR or ALFADIR [Father of all]. The name of Odin as the supreme god. *Allfather.*

ALFHEIMR. Elf-land, fairy-land. Frey's dwelling. *Alfheim.*

ALSVIDR. The all-wise. One of the horses of the sun. *Alsvid.*

ALVISS. The dwarf who answers Thor's questions in the lay of Alvis. *Alvis.*

AMSVARTNIR. The name of the sea, in which the island was situated where the wolf Fenrer was chained. *Amsvartner.*

ANNARR or ONARR. Husband of night and father of Jord (*the earth*). *Annar.*

ANDHRIMNIR. The cook in Valhal. *Andhrimner.*

ANDVARI. The name of a pike-shaped dwarf; the owner of the fatal ring called *Andvaranautr. Andvare.*

ANDVARAFORS. The force or waterfall in which the dwarf Andvare kept himself in the form of a pike fish. *Andvare-Force.*

ANDVARANAUTR. The fatal ring given Andvare (the wary spirit). *Andvarenaut.*

ANGANTYR. He has a legal dispute with Ottar Heimske, who is favored by Freyja. *Angantyr.*

ANGEYJA. One of Heimdal's nine mothers. The Elder Edda says in the Lay of Hyndla: Nine giant maids gave birth to the gracious god, at the world's margin. These are: Gjalp, Greip, Eistla, Angeyja, Ulfrun, Eyrgjafa, Imd, Atla, and Jarnsaxa. *Angeyja.*

ANGRBODA [Anguish-creating]. A giantess; mother of the Fenris-wolf by Loke. *Angerboda.*

ARVAKR [Early awake]. The name of one of the horses of the sun. *Aarvak.*

ASS or AS; plural ÆSIR. The *asas*, gods. The word appears in such English names as *Os*born, *Os*wald, etc. With an *n* it is found in the Germ. *Ans*gar (Anglo-Sax. *Os*car). The term *aesir* is used to distinguish Odin, Thor, etc., from the *vanir* (vans). *Asa.*

ASA-LOKI. Loke, so called to distinguish him from Utgard-Loke, who is a giant. *Asa-Loke.*

ASA-THORR. A common name for Thor. *Asa-Thor.*

ASGARDR. The residence of the gods (*asas*). *Asgard.*

ASKR. The name of the first man created by Odin, Hœner and Loder. *Ask.*

ASYNJA; plural ASYNJUR. A goddess; feminine of *Ass. Asynje.*

ATLA. One of Heimdal's nine mothers. *Atla.*

AUDHUMLA; also written AUDHUMBLA. The cow formed from the frozen vapors resolved into drops. She nourished the giant Ymer. *Audhumbla.*

AURBODA. Gymer's wife and Gerd's mother. *Aurboda.*

AURGELMIR. A giant; grandfather of Bergelmer; called also Ymer. *Aurgelmer.*

AUSTRI. A dwarf presiding over the east region. *Austre. East.*

B

BALDR. God of the summer-sunlight. He was son of Odin and Frigg; slain by Hoder, at the instigation of Loke. He returns after Ragnarok. His dwelling is Breidablik. *Balder.*

BARREY. A pleasant grove in which Gerd agreed with Skirner to meet Frey. *Barey.*

BAUGI. A brother of Suttung, for whom (Baugi) Odin worked one summer in order to get his help in obtaining Suttung's mead of poetry. *Bauge.*

BELI. A giant, brother of Gerd, who was slain by Frey. *Bele.*

BERGELMIR. A giant; son of Thrudgelmer and grandson of Aurgelmer. *Bergelmer.*

BESTLA. Wife of Bur and mother of Odin. *Bestla.*

BEYLA. Frey's attendant; wife of Bygver. *Beyla.*

BIFROST. [To tremble; the trembling way]. The rainbow. *Bifrost.*

BILSKIRNIR. The heavenly abode of Thor, from the flashing of light in the lightning. *Bilskirner.*

BOLTHORN. A giant; father of Bestla, Odin's mother. *Bolthorn.*

BOLVERKR [Working terrible things]. An assumed name of Odin, when he went to get Suttung's mead. *Bolverk.*

BODN. One of the three vessels in which the poetical mead was kept. Hence poetry is called the wave of the *bodn.* *Bodn.*

BORR [*burr,* a son; Scotch *bairn*]. A son of Bure and father of Odin, Vile and Ve. *Bor.*

BRAGI. The god of poetry. A son of Odin. He is the best of skalds. *Brage.*

BREIDABLIK. [Literally to gleam, twinkle]. Balder's dwelling. *Breidablik.*

BRISINGAMEN. Freyja's necklace or ornament. *Brisingamen.*

BURI. The father of Bor. He was produced by the cow's licking the stones covered with rime, frost. *Bure.*

BYGGVIR. Frey's attendant; Beyla's husband. *Bygver.*

BYLEIPTR [Flame of the dwelling]. The brother of Loke. *Byleipt.*

D

DAGR [Day]. Son of Delling. *Dag.*

DAINN. A hart that gnaws the branches of Ygdrasil. *Daain.*

DELLINGR [Dayspring]. The father of Day. *Delling.*

DIS; plural DISIR. Attendant spirit or guardian angel. Any female mythic being may be called Dis. *Dis.*

DRAUPNIR. Odin's ring. It was put on Balder's funeral-pile. Skirner offered it to Gerd. *Draupner.*

DROMI. One of the fetters by which the Fenris-wolf was chained. *Drome.*

DUNEYRR, ⎤ Harts that gnaw the branches of Ygdrasil.
DURAPROP. ⎦ *Durathror.*

DURINN. A dwarf, second in degree. *Durin.*

DVALINN. A dwarf. *Dvalin.*

DVERGR. A dwarf. In modern Icelandic lore dwarfs disappear, but remain in local names, as Dverga-steinn, and in several words and phrases. From the belief that dwarfs lived in rocks an echo is called *dwerg-mal* (dwarf talk), and *dwerg-mala* means to echo. The dwarfs were skilled in metal-working.

E

EDDA. The literal meaning of the word is great-grandmother, but the term is usually applied to the mythological collection of poems discovered by Brynjolf Sveinsson in the year 1643. He, led by a fanciful and erroneous suggestion, gave to the book which he found the name Sæmundar Edda, Edda of Sæmund. This is the so-called *Elder Edda.* The *Younger Edda,* is a name applied to a work written by Snorre Sturleson, and contains old mythological lore and the old artificial rules for verse-making. The ancients applied the name *Edda* only to this work of Snorre. The *Elder Edda* was never so called. And it is also uncertain whether Snorre himself knew his work by the name of Edda. In the Rigsmal (Lay of Rig) Edda is the progenitrix of the race of thralls.

EGDIR. An eagle that appears at Ragnarok. *Egder.*

EGILL. The father of Thjalfe; a giant dwelling near the sea. Thor left his goats with him when on his way to the giant Hymer to get a vessel in which to brew ale.

EIKTHYRNIR. A hart that stands over Odin's hall (Valhal). From his antlers drops water from which rivers flow. *Eikthyrner.*

EINHERI; plural EINHERJAR. The only (*ein*) or great champions; the heroes who have fallen in battle and been admitted into Valhal. *Einherje.*

EIR. [The word signifies *peace, clemency*]. An attendant of Menglod, and the most skillful of all in the healing art. *Eir.*

EISTLA. One of Heimdal's nine mothers. *Eistla.*

ELDHRIMNIR. The kettle in which the boar Sæhrimner is cooked in Valhal. *Eldhrimner.*

ELDIR. The fire-producer; a servant of Æger. *Elder.*

ELIVAGAR. The ice-waves; poisonous cold streams that flow out of Niflheim. *Elivagar.*

EMBLA. The first woman. The gods found two lifeless trees, the *ask* (ash) and the *embla;* of the ash they made *man,* of the embla, *woman.*

EYRGJAFA. One of Heimdal's nine mothers. *Eyrgjafa.*

F

FAFNIR. Son of Hreidmar. He kills his father to get possession of the Andvarenaut. He afterwards changes himself into a dragon and guards the treasure on Gnita-heath. He is slain by Sigurd, and his heart is roasted and eaten. *Fafner.*

FALHOFNIR [Hollow-hoof]. One of the horses of the gods. *Falhofner.*

FARBAUTI [Ship-destroyer]. The father of Loke. *Farbaute.*

FENRIR or FENRISULFR. The monster-wolf. He is the son of Loke, who bites the hand of Tyr. The gods put him in chains, where he remains until Ragnarok. In Ragnarok he gets loose, swallows the sun and conquers Odin, but is killed by Vidar. *Fenrer* or *Fenris-wolf.*

FENSALIR. The abode of Frigg. *Fensal.*

FJALAR. A misnomer for Skrymer, in whose glove Thor took shelter. *Fjalar.*

FJALAR. A dwarf, who slew Kvaser, and composed from his blood the poetic mead. *Fjalar.*

FJALAR. A cock that crows at Ragnarok. *Fjalar.*

FIMAFENGR. The nimble servant of Æger. He was slain by the jealous Loke. *Fimafeng.*

FIMBUL. It means *mighty great.* In the mythology it appears as:

FIMBULFAMBI. A might fool. *Fimbulfambe.*

FIMBULTYR. The mighty god, great helper (Odin). *Fimbultyr.*

FIMBULVETR [*vetr,* winter]. The great and awful winter of three years' duration preceding the end of the world. *Fimbul-winter.*

FIMBULTHUL. A heavenly river. *Fimbulthul.*

FIMBULTHULR. The great wise man. *Fimbulthuler.*

FJOLNIR. One of Odin's many names. *Fjolner.*

FJORGYN. A personification of the earth; mother of Thor. *Fjorgyn.*

FOLKVANGR. [Paradise, a field]. The folk-field. Freyja's dwelling. *Folkvang.*

FORNJOTR. The most ancient giant. He was father of Æger, or Hler, the god of the ocean; of Loge, flame or fire, and of Kaare, wind. His wife was Ran. These divinities are generally regarded as belonging to an earlier mythology, probably to that of the Fins or Celts. *Fornjot.*

FORSETI [The fore-sitter, president, chairman]. Son of Balder and Nanna. His dwelling is Glitner, and his office is that of a peacemaker. *Forsete.*

FRANANGRS-FORS. The force or waterfall into which Loke, in the likeness of a salmon, cast himself, and where the gods caught him and bound him. *Fraananger-Force.*

FREKI. One of Odin's wolves. *Freke.*

FREYJA [Feminine of Freyr]. The daughter of Njord and sister of Frey. She dwells in Folkvang. Half the fallen in battle belong to her, the other half to Odin. She lends her feather disguise to Loke. She is the goddess of love. Her husband is Oder. Her necklace is Brisingamen. She has a boar with golden bristles. *Freyja.*

FREYR. He is son of Njord, husband of Skade, slayer of Bele, and falls in conflict with Surt in Ragnarok. Alfheim was given him as a tooth-gift. The ship Skidbladner was built for him. He falls in love with Gerd, Gymer's fair daughter. He gives his trusty sword to Skirner. *Frey.*

FRIGG. [Love]. She is the wife of Odin, and mother of Balder and queen of the gods, and reigns with Odin in Hlidskjalf. She exacts an oath from all things that they shall not harm Balder. *Frigg.*

FULLA [Fullness]. Frigg's attendant. She takes care of Frigg's toilette, clothes and slippers. Nanna sent her a finger-ring from Helheim. She is represented as wearing her hair flowing over her shoulders. *Fulla.*

G

GALAR. One of two dwarfs who killed Kvaser. Fjalar ' was the other. *Galar.*

GAGNRADE. A name assumed by Odin when he went to visit Vafthrudner. *Gagnraad.*

GANGLERI. One of Odin's names in Grimner's Lay. *Ganglere.*

GANGLERI. A name assumed by King Gylfe when he came to Asgard. *Ganglere.*

GARDROFA. The goddess Gnaa has a horse by name Hofvarpner. The sire of this horse is Hamskerper, and its mother is Gardrofa. *Gardrofa.*

GARMR. A dog that barks at Ragnarok. He is called the largest and best among dogs. *Garm.*

GEFJUN or GEFJON. A goddess. She is a maid, and all those who die maids become her maid-servants. She is present at Æger's feast. Odin says she knows men's destinies as well as he does himself. *Gefjun.*

GEIRRODR. A son of King Hraudung and foster-son of Odin; he becomes king and is visited by Odin, who calls himself Grimner. He is killed by his own sword. There is also a giant by name Geirrod, who was once visited by Thor. *Geirrod.*

GEIRSKOGUL. A valkyrie. *Geirskogul.*

GEIRVIMUL. A heavenly river. *Geirvimul.*

GERDR. Daughter of Gymer, a beautiful young giantess; beloved by Frey. *Gerd.*

GERI. [*gerr,* greedy]. One of Odin's wolves. *Gere.*

GERSEMI. One of Freyja's daughters. *Gerseme.*

GJALLARBRU [*gjalla,* to yell, to resound]. The bridge across the river Gjol, near Helheim. The bridge between the land of the living and the dead. *Gjallarbridge.*

GJALLARHORN. Heimdal's horn, which he will blow at Ragnarok. *Gjallar horn.*

GILLING. Father of Suttung, who possessed the poetic mead. He was slain by Fjalar and Galar. *Gilling.*

GIMLI [Heaven]. The abode of the righteous after Ragnarok. *Gimle.*

GJALP. One of Heimdal's nine mothers. *Gjalp.*

GINNUNGA-GAP. The great yawning gap, the premundane abyss, the chaos or formless void, in which dwelt the supreme powers before the creation. In the eleventh century the sea between Greenland and Vinland (America) was called Ginnunga-gap. *Ginungagap.*

GJOLL. One of the rivers Elivagar that flowed nearest the gate of Hel's abode. *Gjol.*

GISL [Sunbeam]. One of the horses of the gods. *Gisl.*

GLADR [Clear, bright]. One of the horses of the gods. *Glad.*

GLADSHEIMR [Home of brightness or gladness]. Odin's dwelling. *Gladsheim.*

GLASIR. A grove in Asgard. *Glaser.*

GLEIPNIR. The last fetter with which the wolf Fenrer was bound. *Gleipner.*

GLER [The glassy]. One of the horses of the gods. *Gler.*

GLITNIR [The glittering]. Forsete's golden hall. *Glitner.*

GNA. She is the messenger that Frigg sends into the various worlds on her errands. She has a horse called Hofvarpenr, that can run through air and water. *Gnaa.*

GNIPAHELLIR. The cave before which the dog Garm barks. *The Gnipa-cave.*

GNITAHEIDR. Fafner's abode, where he kept the treasure called Andvarenaut. *Gnita-heath.*

GOINN. A serpent under Ygdrasil. *Goin.*

GOLL. A valkyrie. *Gol.*

GOMUL. A heavenly river. *Gomul.*

GONDUL. A valkyrie. *Gondul.*

GOPUL. A heavenly river. *Gopul.*

GRABAKR. One of the serpents under Ygdrasil. *Graabak.*

GRAD. A heavenly river. *Graad.*

GRAFVITNIR. } Serpents under Ygdrasil. *Grafvitner;*
GRAFVOLLUDR. } *Grafvollud.*

GREIP. [Eng. *grip*]. One of Heimdal's nine giant mothers. *Greip.*

GRIMNIR. A kind of hood or cowl covering the upper part of the face. Grimner is a name of Odin from his traveling in disguise. *Grimner.*

GROA. The giantess mother of Orvandel. Thor went to her to have her charm the flint-stone out of his forehead. *Groa.*

GULLFAXI [Gold-mane]. The giant Hrungner's horse. *Goldfax.*

GULLINKAMBI [Gold-comb]. A cock that crows at Ragnarok. *Gullinkambe* or *Goldcomb.*

GULLTOPPR [Gold-top]. Heimdal's horse. *Goldtop.*

GULLVEIG [Gold-thirst]. A personification of gold. Though pierced and thrice burnt, she yet lives. *Gulveig.*

GULLINBURSTI [Golden bristles]. The name of Frey's hog. *Gullinburste.*

GUNGNIR [To tremble violently]. Odin's spear. *Gungner.*

GUNNLOD [To invite]. One who invites war. She was daughter of the giant Suttung, and had charge of the poetic mead. Odin got it from her. *Gunlad.*

GYLFI. A king of Svithod, who visited Asgard under the name of Ganglere. The first part of the Younger Edda is called Gylfaginning, which means the Delusion of Gylfe. *Gylfe.*

GYLLIR [Golden]. One of the horses of the gods. *Gyller.*

GYMIR. A giant; the father of Gerd, the beloved of Frey. *Gymer.*

GYMIR. Another name of the ocean divinity Æger. *Gymer.*

H

HALLINSKIDI. Another name of the god Heimdal. The possessor of the leaning (*halla*) way. *Hallinskid.*

HAMSKERPIR [Hide-hardener]. A horse; the sire of Hofvarpner, which was Gnaa's horse. *Hamskerper.*

HAR. The High One, applied to Odin. *Haar.*

HARBARDR. The name assumed by Odin in the Lay of Harbard. *Harbard.*

HEIDRUNR [Bright-running]. A goat that stands over Valhal. *Heidrun.*

HEIMDALR. He was the heavenly watchman in the old mythology, answering to St. Peter in the medieval. According to the Lay of Rig (Heimdal), he was the father and founder of the different classes of men, nobles, churls and thralls. He has a horn called Gjallar-horn, which he blows at Ragnarok. His dwelling is Himinbjorg. He is the keeper of Bifrost (the rainbow). Nine giantesses are his mothers. *Heimdal.*

HEL. [Anglo-Sax. and Eng. *hell;* to kill]. The goddess of death, born of Loke and Angerboda. She corresponds to Proserpina. Her habitation is Helheim, under one of the roots of Ygdrasil. *Hel.*

HELBLINDI. A name of Odin. *Helblinde.*

HELGRINDR. The gates of Hel. *Helgrind* or *Helgate.*

HELHEIM. The abode of Hel. *Helheim.*

HERFODR,   } [The father of hosts]. A name of Odin.
HERJAFODR. }   *Herfather.*

HERMODR [Courage of hosts]. Son of Odin, who gives him a helmet and a corselet. He rode on Sleipner to Hel to bring Balder back. *Hermod.*

HILDISVINI [Means war]. Freyja's hog. *Hilde-svine.*

HIMINBJORG [Heaven, help, defense; hence heaven defender]. Heimdal's dwelling. *Himinbjorg.*

HIMINBRJOTR [Heaven-breaker]. One of the giant Hymer's oxen. *Himinbrjoter.*

HLESEY. The abode of Æger. *Hlesey.*

HLIDSKJALF. The seat of Odin, whence he looked out over all the worlds. *Hlidskjalf.*

HLIN. One of the attendants of Frigg; but Frigg herself is sometimes called by this name. *Hlin.*

HLODYN. A goddess; a name of the earth; Thor's mother. *Hlodyn.*

HLORIDI [Eng. *low,* to bellow, roar, and *reid,* thunder] One of the names of Thor; the bellowing thunderer. *Hloride.*

HNIKARR, HNIKUDR. } Names of Odin, Hnikar and Hnikuder.

HNOSS [Anglo-Sax. to hammer]. A costly thing; the name of one of Freyja's daughters. *Hnos.*

HODDMIMISHOLT. Hodmimer's holt or grove, where the two human beings Lif and Lifthraser were preserved during Ragnarok. *Hodmimer's forest.*

HODR. The slayer of Balder. He is blind, returns to life in the regenerated world. The Cain of the Norse mythology. *Hoder.*

HOENIR. One of the three creating gods. With Odin and Loder Hœner creates Ask and Embla, the first human pair. *Hoener.*

HOFVARPNIR [Hoof-thrower]. Gnaa's horse. His father is Hamskerper and mother Gardrofa. *Hofvarpner.*

HRAESVELGR [Corpse-swallower]. A giant in an eagle's plumage, who produces the wind. *Hraesvelger.*

HRAUDUNGR. Geirrod's father. *Hraudung.*

HREIDMARR. Father of Regin and Fafner. He exacts the blood-fine from the gods for slaying Otter. He is slain by Fafner. *Hreidmar.*

HRIMFAXI [Rime-mane]. The horse of night. *Rimefax.*

HRIMTHURSAR [Eng. *rime,* hoar-frost]. Rime-giants or frost-giants, who dwell under one of Ygdrasil's roots. *Giants.*

HRODVITNIR. A wolf; father of the wolf Hate. *Hrodvitner.*

HROPTR. One of Odin's names. *Hropt.*

HRUNGNIR. A giant; friend of Hymer. Thor fought with him and slew him. *Hrungner.*

HRINGHORNI. The ship upon which Balder's body was burned. *Hringhorn.*

HROSSTHJOFR [Horse-thief]. A giant. *Hrosthjof.*

HUGINN [Mind]. One of Odin's ravens. *Hugin.*

HVERGELMIR [The old kettle]. The spring in the middle of Niflheim, whence flowed the rivers Elivagar. The Northern Tartaros. *Hvergelmer.*

HYMIR. A giant with whom Thor went fishing when he caught the Midgard-serpent. His wife was the mother of Tyr. Tyr and Thor went to him to procure a kettle for Æger in which to brew ale for the gods. *Hymer.*

HYNDLA. A vala visited by Freyja, who comes to her to learn the genealogy of her favorite, Ottar. *Hyndla.*

I

IDAVOLLR. A plain where the gods first assemble, where they establish their heavenly abodes, and where they assemble again after Ragnarok. The plains of Ida. *Idavold.*

IDUNN. Daughter of the dwarf Ivald; she was wife of Brage, and the goddess of early spring. She possesses rejuvenating apples of which the gods partake. *Idun.*

IFING. A river which divides the giants from the gods. *Ifing.*

IMD. One of Heimdal's nine giant mothers. *Imd.*

IMR. A son of the giant Vafthrudner. *Im.*

INGUNAR-FREYR. One of the names of Frey. *Ingun's Frey.*

INNSTEINN. The father of Ottar Heimske; the favorite of Freyja. *Instein.*

IVALDI. A dwarf. His sons construct the ship Skidbladner. *Ivald.*

J

JAFNHAR [Equally high]. A name of Odin.

JALKR. A name of Odin (Jack the Giant-killer?). *Jalk.*

JARNSAXA [Iron-chopper]. One of Heimdal's nine giant mothers. *Jarnsaxa.*

JARNVIDR [Iron-wood]. A wood east of Midgard, peopled by giantesses called Jarnvids. This wood had iron leaves. *Jarnvid.*

JARNVIDIUR. The giantesses in the Iron-wood. *Jarnvids.*

JORD. Wife of Odin and mother of Thor. Earth.

JOTUNN. A giant. The giants were the earliest created beings. The gods question them in regard to Balder.

Thor frequently contends with them. Famous giants are: Ymer, Hymer, Hrungner, Orvandel, Gymer, Skrymer, Vafthrudner and Thjasse. *Giant.*

JOTUNHEIMAR (plural). The Utgaard; the home of the giants in the outermost parts of the earth. *Jotunheim.*

K

KERLAUGAR (plural). Two rivers which Thor every day must cross. *Kerlaug.*

KORMT. Another river which Thor every day must pass. *Kormt.*

KVASIR. The hostage given by the vans to the asas. His blood, when slain, was the poetical mead kept by Suttung. *Kvaser.*

L

LAEDINGR. One of the fetters with which the Fenris-wolf was bound. *Laeding.*

LAERADR. A tree near Valhal. *Laerad.*

LANDVIDI [A mountain range overgrown with trees]. Vidar's abode. The primeval forests. *Landvide.*

LAUFEY [Leafy island]. Loke's mother. *Laufey.*

LEIFTHRASIR, LIF. } The two persons preserved in Hodmimer's grove during Surt's conflagration in Ragnarok; the last beings in the old and the first in the new world. *Lif* and *Lifthraser.*

LETTFETI [Light-foot]. One of the horses of the gods. *Lightfoot.*

LITR. A dwarf that Thor kicked into Balder's funeral pile. *Liter.*

LODDFAFNIR. A protege of Odin. *Lodfafner.*

LODURR [To flame]. One of the three gods (Odin, Hæner and Loder) who create Ask and Embla, the first man and woman. He is identical with Loke. *Loder.*

LOKI [To end, finish; Loke is the end and consummation of divinity]. The evil giant-god of the Norse mythology. He steers the ship Naglfar in Ragnarok. He borrows Freyja's feather-garb and accompanies Thor to the giant Thrym, who has stolen Thor's hammer. He is the father of Sleipner; also of the Midgard serpent, of the Fenris-wolf and of Hel. He causes Balder's death, abuses the gods in Æger's feast, but is captured in Fraanangerforce and is bound by the gods. *Loke.*

LOPTR [The aerial]. Another name of Loke. *Lopter.*

M

MAGNI [*megin,* strength]. A son of Thor. *Magne.*

MANI [Eng. *moon*]. Brother of Sol (the sun, feminine), and both were children of the giant Mundilfare. *Moon* or *Maane.*

MARDOLL or MARTHOLL. One of the names of Freyja. *Mardallar gratr* (the tears of Mardal), gold. *Mardal.*

MANAGARMR [Moon-swallower]. A wolf of Loke's offspring. He devours the moon. *Maanegarm* or *Moongarm.*

MANNHEIMAR (plural) [Homes of man]. Our earth. *Manheim.*

MEILI. A son of Odin. *Meile.*

MIDGARDR. [In Cumberland, England, are three farms: *High-garth, Middle-garth, Low-garth.*] The mid-yard, middle-town, that is, the earth, is a mythological word common to all the ancient Teutonic languages. The Icelandic Edda alone has preserved the true mythical bearing of this old Teutonic word. The earth (Midgard), the abode of men, is situated in the middle of the universe, bordered by mountains and surrounded by the great sea; on the other side of this sea is the Utgard (out-yard), the abode of the giants; the Midgard is defended by the yard or burgh Asgard (the burgh of the gods) lying in the middle (the heaven being conceived as rising above the earth). Thus the earth and mankind are represented as a stronghold besieged by the powers of evil from without, defended by the gods from above and from within. *Midgard.*

MIDGARDSORMR [The serpent of Midgaard]. The world-serpent hidden in the ocean, whose coils gird around the whole Midgard. Thor once fishes for him, and gets him on his hook. In Ragnarok Thor slays him, but falls himself poisoned by his breath. *Midgard-serpent.*

MIMAMEIDR. A mythic tree; probably the same as Ygdrasil. It derives its name from Mimer, and means Mimer's tree. *Mimameider.*

MIMIR. The name of the wise giant keeper of the holy well Mimis-brunnr, the burn of Mimer, the well of wisdom, at which Odin pawned his eye for wisdom; a myth which is explained as symbolical of the heavenly vault with its single eye, the sun, setting in the sea.

MJOLNIR. Thor's formidable hammer. After Ragnarok, it is possessed by his sons Mode and Magne. *Mjolner.*

MISTILTEINN [Eng. *mistletoe*]. The mistletoe or mistletwig, the fatal twig by which Balder, the white sun-god, was slain. After the death of Balder, Ragnarok set in. Balder's death was also symbolical of the victory of darkness over light, which comes every year at midwinter. The mistletoe in English households at Christmas time is no doubt a relic of a rite lost in the remotest heathendom, for the fight of light and darkness at midwinter was a foreshadowing of the final overthrow in Ragnarok. The legend and the word are common to all Teutonic peoples of all ages. *Mistletoe.*

MODI [Courage]. A son of Thor. *Mode.*

MODSOGNIR. The dwarf highest in degree or rank. *Modsogner.*

MOINN. A serpent under Ygdrasil. *Moin.*

MUNDILFARI. Father of the sun and moon. *Mundilfare.*

MUNINN [Memory]. One of Odin's ravens. *Munin.*

MUSPELL. The name of an abode of fire. It is populated by a host of fiends, who are to appear at Ragnarok and destroy the world by fire. *Muspel.*

MUSPELLSHEIMR. The abode of Muspel. This interesting word (*Muspell*) was not confined to the Norse mythology, but appears twice in the old Saxon poem Heliand. In these instances *muspel* stands for the *day of judgment, the last day,* and answers to Ragnarok of the Norse mythology.

MOKKURKALFI [A dense cloud]. A clay giant in the myth of Thor and Hrungner. *Mokkerkalfe.*

N

NAGLFAR [Nail-ship]. A mythical ship made of nail-parings. It apears in Ragnarok. *Naglfar. Nailship.*

NAL [Needle]. Mother of Loke. *Naal.*

NANNA. Daughter of Nep (bud); mother of Forsete and wife of Balder. She dies of grief at the death of Balder. *Nanna*.

NARI or NARFI. Son of Loke. Loke was bound by the intestines of Nare. *Nare* or *Narfe*.

NASTROND [The shore of corpses]. A place of punishment for the wicked after Ragnarok. *Naastrand*.

NIDAFJOLL. The Nida-mountains toward the north, where there is after Ragnarok a golden hall for the race of Sindre (the dwarfs). *Nidafell*.

NIDHOGGR. A serpent of the nether world, that tears the carcases of the dead. He also lacerates Ygdrasil. *Nidhug*.

NIFLHEIMR. The world of fog or mist; the nethermost of the rime worlds. The place of punishment (Hades). It was visited by Odin when he went to inquire after the fate of Balder. *Niflheim*.

NJORDR. A van, vanagod. He was husband of Skade, and father of Frey and Freyja. He dwells in Noatun. *Njord*.

NOATUN [Place of ships]. Njord's dwelling; Njord being a divinity of the water or sea. *Noatun*.

NORDRI [North]. A dwarf presiding over the northern regions. *Nordre* or *North*.

NOTT. Night; daughter of Norve. *Night*.

NORN; plural NORNIR. The weird sisters; the three heavenly norns Urd, Verdande, and Skuld (Past, Present, and Future); they dwelt at the fountain of Urd, and ruled the fate of the world. Three norns were also present at the birth of very man and cast the horoscope of his life. *Norn*.

O

ODINN [Anglo-Sax. *Wodan*]. Son of Bor and Bestla. He is the chief of the gods. With Vile and Ve he parcels out Ymer. With Hœner and Loder he creates Ask and Embla. He is the fountain-head of wisdom, the founder of culture, writing and poetry, the progenitor of kings, the lord of battle and victory. He has two ravens, two wolves and a spear. His throne is Hlidskjalf, whence he looks out over all the worlds. In Ragnarok he is devoured by the Fenris-wolf. *Odin.*

ODR. Freyja's husband. *Oder.*

ODROERIR [The spirit-mover]. One of the vessels in which the blood of Kvaser, that is, the poetic mead, was kept. The inspiring nectar. *Odroerer.*

OFNIR. A serpent under Ygdrasil. *Ofner.*

OKOLNIR. After Ragnarok the giants have a hall (ale-*hall*) called Brimer, at Okolner.

OKU-THORR. So called from the Finnish thunder-god Ukko. *Akethor.*

OSKI [Wish]. A name of Odin. *Oske. Wish.*

OTR [OTTER]. A son of Hreidmar; in the form of an otter killed by Loke. *Oter.*

OTTARR or OTTARR HEIMSKI [Stupid]. A son of Instein, a protege of Freyja. He has a contest with Angantyr. Hyndla gives him a cup of remembrance. *Ottar.*

R

RAGNAROK [Sentence, judgment, from *rekja*, is the whole development from creation to dissolution, and would, in this word, denote the dissolution, doomsday, of the gods; or it may be from *rokr* (*reykkr*, smoke), twilight, and then the word means the twilight of the gods]. The last day; the dissolution of the gods and the world. *Ragnarok.*

RAN [Rob]. The goddess of the sea; wife of Æger. *Ran.*

RATATOSKR. A squirrel that runs up and down the branches of Ygdrasil. *Ratatosk.*

RATI. An auger used by Odin in obtaining the poetic mead. *Rate.*

REGINN. Son of Hreidmar; brother of Fafner and Otter. *Regin.*

RINDR. A personification of the hard frozen earth. Mother of Vale. The loves of Odin and Rind resemble those of Zeus and Europa in Greek legends. *Rind.*

ROSKVA. The name of the maiden follower of Thor. She symbolizes the ripe fields of harvest. *Roskva.*

S

SAEHRIMNIR [Rime-producer]. The name of the boar on which the gods and heroes in Valhal constantly feed. *Saehrimner.*

SAGA [History]. The goddess of history. She dwells in Sokvabek.

SESSRUMNIR. Freyja's large-seated palace. *Sesrumner.*

SIDHOTTR [Long-hood]. One of Odin's names, from his traveling in disguise with a large hat on his head hanging down over one side of his face to conceal his missing eye. *Sidhat.*

SIDSKEGGR [Long-beard]. One of Brage's names. It is also a name of Odin in the lay of Grimner. *Sidskeg.*

SIF. The wife of Thor and mother of Uller. The word denotes affinity. Sif, the golden-haired goddess, wife of Thor, betokens mother earth with her bright green grass. She was the goddess of the sanctity of the family and wedlock, and hence her name. *Sif.*

SIGFADIR [Father of victory]. A name of Odin. *Sigfather.*

SIGYN. Loke's wife. She holds a basin to prevent the serpent's venom from dropping into Loke's face. *Sigyn.*

SILFRINTOPPR. One of the horses of the gods. *Silvertop.*

SINDRI. One of the most famous dwarfs. *Sindre.*

SINIR [Sinew]. One of the horses of the gods. *Siner.*

SJOFN. One of the goddesses. She delights in turning men's hearts to love. *Sjofn.*

SKADI [*scathe,* harm, damage]. A giantess; daughter of Thjasse and the wife of Njord. She dwells in Thrymheim, and hangs a venom serpent over Loke's face. *Skade.*

SKEIDBRIMIR [Race-runner]. One of the horses of the gods. *Skeidbrimer.*

SKIDBLADNIR. The name of the famous ship of the god Frey that could move alike on land or sea and could be made small or great at will. *Skidbladner.*

SKINFAXI [Shining-mane]. The horse of Day. *Skinfax.*

SKIRNIR [The bright one]. Frey's messenger. *Skirner.*

SKRYMIR. The name of a giant; also the name assumed by Utgard-Loke. *Skrymer.*

SKULD [Shall]. The norn of the future. *Skuld.*

SKOGUL. A valkyrie. *Skogul.*

SLEIPNIR [The slipper]. The name of Odin's eight-footed steed. He is begotten by Loke with Svadilfare. *Sleipner.*

SNOTRA [Neat]. The name of one of the goddesses. *Snotra.*

SOKKMIMIR [Mimer of the deep]. A giant slain by Odin. *Sokmimer.*

SOKKVABEKKR. A mansion where Odin and Saga quaff from golden beakers. *Sokvabek.*

SOL [Sun]. Daughter of Mundilfare. She drives the horses that draw the car of the sun.

SONR. One of the vessels containing the poetic mead. *Son.*

SUDRI [South]. A dwarf who presides over the south region. *Sudre. South.*

SURTR. A fire-giant in Ragnarok who contends with the gods on the plain of Vigrid and guards Muspelheim. *Surt.*

SUTTUNGR. The giant possessor of the poetic mead. *Suttung.*

SVADILFARI. A horse; the sire of Sleipner. *Svadilfare.*

SVAFNIR. A serpent under Ygdrasil. *Svafner.*

SVALINN [Cooler]. The shield placed before the sun. *Svalin.*

SVASUDR [Delightful]. The name of a giant; the father of the sun. *Svasud.*

SYN. A minor goddess.

T

TYR. Properly the generic name of the highest divinity, and remains in many compounds. In mythology he is the one-armed god of war. The Fenris-wolf bit one hand off him. He goes with Thor to Hymer to borrow a kettle for Æger. He is son of Odin by a giantess. *Tyr.*

THJALFI. The name of the servant and follower of Thor. The word properly means a delver, digger. The names Thjalfe and Roskva indicate that Thor was the friend of the farmers and the god of agriculture. *Thjalfe.*

Thjazi [Thjassi]. A giant; the father of Njord's wife, Skade. His dwelling was Thrymheim; he was slain by Thor. *Thjasse.*

Thorr. The English *Thursday* is a later form, in which the phonetic rule of the Scandinavian tongue has been followed. The god of thunder, keeper of the hammer, the ever-fighting slayer of trolls and destroyer of evil spirits, the friend of mankind, the defender of the earth, the heavens and the gods; for without Thor and his hammer the earth would become the helpless prey of the giants. He was the consecrator, the hammer being the cross or holy sign of the ancient heathen. Thor was the son of Odin and Fjorgyn (mother earth); he was blunt, hot-tempered, without fraud or guile, of few words but of ready stroke—such was Thor, the favorite deity of our forefathers. The finest legends of the Younger Edda and the best lays of the Elder Edda refer to Thor. His hall is Bilskirner. He slays Thjasse, Thrym, Hrungner, and other giants. In Ragnarok he slays the Midgard-serpent, but falls after retreating nine paces, poisoned by the serpent's breath. *Thor.*

Thridi [Third]. A name of Odin in Gylfaginning. *Thride.*

Thrudgelmir. The giant father of Bergelmer. *Thrudgelmer.*

Thrudheimr or Thrudvangr. } Thor's abode. *Thrudheim; Thrudvang.*

Thrudr. The name of a goddess; the daughter of Thor and Sif. *Thrud.*

Thrymheimr. Thjasse's and Skade's dwelling. *Thrymheim.*

Thrymr. The giant who stole Thor's hammer and demanded Freyja as a reward for its return. *Thrym.*

THOKK. The name of a giantess (supposed to have been Loke in disguise) in the myth of Balder. *Thok.*

U

ULFRUN. One of Heimdal's nine giant mothers. *Ulfrun.*

ULLR. The son of Sif and stepson of Thor. His father is not named. He dwells in Ydaler. *Uller.*

URDARBRUNNR. The fountain of the norn Urd. The Urdar-fountain. The weird spring.

URDR [Eng. *weird*]. One of the three norns. The norn of the past. *Urd.*

UTGARDAR [The out-yard]. The abode of the giant Utgard-Loke. *Utgard.*

UTGARDA-LOKI. The giant of Utgard visited by Thor. He calls himself Skrymer. *Utgard-Loke.*

V

VAFTHRUDNIR. A giant visited by Odin. They try each other in questions and answers. The giant is defeated and forfeits his life. *Vafthrudner.*

VALASKJALF. One of Odin's dwellings. *Valaskjalf.*

VALFODR [Father of the slain]. A name of Odin. *Valfather.*

VALGRIND. A gate of Valhal. *Valgrind.*

VALHOLL [The hall of the slain]. The hall to which Odin invited those slain in battle. *Valhal.*

VALKYRJA [The chooser of the slain]. A troop of goddesses, handmaidens of Odin. They serve in Valhal, and are sent on Odin's errands. *Valkyrie.*

VALI. Is a brother of Balder, who slays Hoder when only one night old. He rules with Vidar after Ragnarok. *Vale.*

VALI. A son of Loke. *Vale.*

VALTAMR. A fictitious name of Odin's father. *Valtam.*

VE. A brother of Odin (Odin, Vile and Ve). *Ve.*

VEGTAMR. A name assumed by Odin. *Vegtam.*

VANAHEIMAR. The abode of the vans. *Vanaheim.*

VANR; plural VANIR. Those deities whose abode was in Vanaheim, in contradistinction to the asas, who dwell in Asgard: Njord, Frey and Freyja. The vans waged war with the asas, but were afterwards, by virtue of a treaty, combined and made one with them. The vans were deities of the sea. *Van.*

VEORR [Defender]. A name of Thor. *Veor.*

VERDANDI [To become]. The norn of the present.

VESTRI. The dwarf presiding over the west region. *Vestre. West.*

VIDARR. Son of Odin and the giantess Grid. He dwells in Landvide. He slays the Fenris-wolf in Ragnarok. Rules with Vale after Ragnarok. *Vidar.*

VIGRIDR [A battle]. The field of battle where the gods and the sons of Surt meet in Ragnarok. *Vigrid.*

VILI. Brother of Odin and Ve. These three sons of Bor and Bestla construct the world out of Ymer's body. *Vile.*

VIMUR. A river that Thor crosses. *Vimer.*

VINDSVALR. The father of winter. *Vindsval.*

VINDHEIMR. The place that the sons of Balder and Hoder are to inhabit after Ragnarok. *Vindheim. Windhome.*

VIN-GOLF [The mansion of bliss] The palace of the asynjes. *Vingolf.*

VINGTHORR. A name of Thor. *Vingthor.*

VOR. The goddess of betrothals and marriages. *Vor.*

Y

YDALIR. Uller's dwelling. *Ydaler.*

YGGR. A name of Odin. *Ygg.*

YGGDRASILL [The bearer of Ygg (Odin)]. The world-embracing ash tree. The whole world is symbolized by this tree. *Ygdrasil.*

YMIR. The huge giant in the cosmogony, out of whose body Odin, Vile and Ve created the world. The progenitor of the giants. He was formed out of frost and fire in Ginungagap. *Ymer.*

INDEX

OF

PERSONS AND PLACES.

TEUTONIC MYTHOLOGY.

A

Achilles, 44, 192.
Achivians, 62.
Adalbert, 320.
Adam, 86, 132, 319, 238.
Adam of Bremen, 714.
Adriatic, 62.
Aeduans, 66.
Aegir, 43, 136, 235, 422, 575, 697, 813, 822, 967.
Aeneas, 44, 66, 81, 730.
African, 6.
Agelmund, 858.
Aggo, 104, 861, 893, 953, 1008.
Agni, 587, 605, 886.
Agrippa, 76, 86.
Ahriman, 817.
Ahura, 8.
Ahuramazda, 127, 381, 450.
Ai, 140.
Ajo, 100, 861, 992.
Alamannians, 53, 119, 708.
Alarik, 25.
Alba-Longa, 66.
Aldonus, 101.
Aldrian, 981, 991.
Alexander, 50, 55.
Alf, 167.
Alfather, 376, 220, 340.
Alfheim, 696, 865, 947.

Alfhild, 168.
Alfrandull, 1002.
Alfsol, 168.
Alps, 62.
Almveig, 1000.
Alvalde, 174, 584, 898, 953, 992.
Alveig, 173, 257, 263, 273.
Alveig-Signe, 793, 902.
Alvis, 437.
Alvism, 365, 376.
Alvismal, 436, 445.
Alvitr, 898.
Amala, 293.
Amalgort, 293.
Amalian, 147, 285, 293, 980.
Amazons, 168.
Ambri, 100.
Amelolt, 293.
Amelungs, 147, 293.
America, 940.
Amlethus, 317, 843.
Amlodi, 843, 568.
Amma, 140.
Ammianus, 58.
Amsvartner, 564.
Anarr, 157.
Anchises, 54, 112.
Andlanger, 706.
Andvare, a dwarf, 300, 977.
Angerboda, 226, 275, 558, 707, 809.
Angeyja, 597.

INDEX

INDEX

WS - #0038 - 170321 - C0 - 229/152/21 - PB - 9781330284865